26.04

D0615345

CORPORATE CATALYST

CORPORATE CATALYST

A Chronicle of the (Mis)Management of Canadian Business from a Veteran Insider

by
Tony Griffiths

John Wiley & Sons Canada, Ltd.

Wiley publishes in a variety of print and electronic formats and by print-on-demand. Some material included with standard print versions of this book may not be included in e-books or in print-on-demand. If this book refers to media such as a CD or DVD that is not included in the version you purchased, you may download this material at http://booksupport.wiley.com. For more information about Wiley products, visit www.wiley.com.

Library and Archives Canada Cataloguing in Publication Data

Griffiths, Anthony, 1930-
     Corporate catalyst : a chronicle of the (mis)management of Canadian business from a veteran insider / Anthony Griffiths.

Includes index.
Issued also in electronic formats.
ISBN 978-1-118-15286-7

     1. Griffiths, Tony, 1930–.   2. Chief executive officers—Canada—Biography.
     3. Businessmen—Canada—Biography.   4. Corporate governance—Canada.
     5. Industrial management—Canada.   I. Title.

HC112.5.G75A3 2012   338.092   C2011-908047-8

ePDF: 978-1-118-15956-9; Mobi: 978-1-118-15953-8; ePub: 978-1-118-15955-2

Production Credits

Cover design: Ian Koo
Typesetting: Thomson Digital
Cover image: Lorella Zanetti
Printer: Friesens
Editorial Credits

Executive editor: Don Loney
Managing editor: Alison Maclean
Production editor: Jeremy Hanson-Finger

John Wiley & Sons Canada, Ltd.

6045 Freemont Blvd.
Mississauga, Ontario
L5R 4J3

Printed in Canada
1 2 3 4 5 FP 16 15 14 13 12

ENVIRONMENTAL BENEFITS STATEMENT

John Wiley & Sons - Canada saved the following resources by printing the pages of this book on chlorine free paper made with 100% post-consumer waste.

TREES	WATER	ENERGY	SOLID WASTE	GREENHOUSE GASES
81	37,165	33	2,356	8,241
FULLY GROWN	GALLONS	MILLION BTUs	POUNDS	POUNDS

Environmental impact estimates were made using the Environmental Paper Network Paper Calculator. For more information visit www.papercalculator.org.

For Albert Gnat, who read my original manuscript in 1995 and encouraged me to publish it.

I first got to know Albert in 1973, when he picked up the Canadian Cablesystems file from Bud Estey and I succeeded Bud as CEO. I soon realized that Albert had an encyclopedic memory for detail and the ability to quickly synthesize issues. He had the unique capacity to solve a problem while reading about it. At the same time, he was the consummate "deal junkie" with the caveat that he wanted to do every deal he came across. It was through deals that I got to know Alan Horn, who with me controlled Albert's insatiable appetite.

Albert always put the interests of his friends and clients first, and with me, I knew he was looking out for my welfare, personally and legally. He was a colleague, business partner, and, above all, a true friend. While we had many differences over business matters, there was never a time where we did not remain close. At his 65th birthday party, a few months prior to his premature death, he introduced me as his mentor—for me the ultimate honour. He left a huge void in my life and hardly a day goes by that I do not miss his sage advice and counsel.

Contents

Acknowledgements

First, my thanks to Arnold Gosewich, my literary agent, who introduced me to Wiley and assisted in developing the marketing program with help from Don Bastien. Special appreciation to Don Loney, executive editor at John Wiley & Sons Canada for his patience and good advice. Also to Jane Withey, who was invaluable in editing the manuscript—always with a wonderful sense of humour. I owe an enormous debt to my colleagues and friends, including legal mentors, who assisted in ensuring the text was accurate and authentic. These include those who read the original manuscript: Peter Beattie, Howard Beck, Stevie Cameron, Bill Cox, Paul Davis, Paul Fink, Albert Gnat, Eric Goldstrand, Denise Goulimis, Ron Graham, Paul Griffiths, Alan Horn, Ken Jesudian, Jonathan Levin, Michael MacMillan, Anna Porter, Julian Porter, Frank Potter, Barry Reiter, Paul Rivett, Reed Scowen, Prem Watsa, and Jim Westcott. Any remaining mistakes are mine alone.

In addition, relevant specific chapters were reviewed by those who were involved:

Chapters 5 and 6: Lori Waisberg and Peter Stormonth Darling ($+7$)

Chapters 5, 6, and 7: Don Wright and Ted Jarmain

Chapters 5, 6, 7, and 8: Robin Korthals

Chapter 13: Ed Waitzer

Chapter 16: Paul Davis, Garrett Herman, and Jim McGlone

Chapter 17: Jeff Bramlett and Don Plumley, Claude Lameroux ($+18$)

Paul Fink reviewed and contributed to the early drafts of the manuscript in 1994 and added witty and useful comments. Ron Graham encouraged me to publish and provided me with a very helpful second opinion.

Finally, my wife Penny was an invaluable critic and editor and helped to set the tone and balance throughout. She lived with it for 17 years—living it and breathing it and helping me to improve it.

Note to the Reader

While those of you who have scanned some pages of my book might think I have superhuman powers of recall, let me say that I wrote the bulk of this book in the mid-1990s. I postponed publishing it for a variety of reasons. My original plan was to leave something about my career for my family and future generations. My one great regret is that I did not sit down with a tape recorder with my parents, both of whom had fascinating lives as well as intriguing family histories.

I wanted to put on the record my own account of events that I experienced throughout my business career. As time has marched onward, books have naturally appeared written by journalists and business people giving their views of the *history* of which I was a part. In some cases, biographers and autobiographers have taken considerable licence with the facts. Some of this is inadvertent or innocent since, in many instances, the writer would not necessarily be aware of the other side of the issues. In other cases, there have been clear distortions and reinventing of facts to suit the writer's story. This is especially so in certain high-profile biographies, where the winner in a contest wishes to be remembered in a certain way—of course usually very favourably. It has been said that "victors rewrite history."

Forthrightness is the greatest challenge in writing business and personal memoirs. Do I really want to be frank in opening up situations where some of my colleagues and competitors receive variable assessments? Clearly no—but for my story to have substance and meaning, I have to provide the full account. In many cases I have tried to mitigate this problem. In some situations, my task has been made easier by someone else's published memoirs, which provide me with the opportunity to tell my side of the story, as factually as possible.

Much of what I have to say involves *governance*, which garners more attention every day. In troubled companies, governance issues arise quickly and define agendas both within managements and boardrooms. As situations evolve, governance matters become filled with emotion and differences of views surface, usually with great passion. Increasingly we read, "Where was the board of GM, Enron, Nortel, etc.?" This gives the business community a black eye. Of course, bad governance attracts headlines that dominate the media for long periods of time. Good governance suffers from the penalty of being unreported.

My career has largely involved turnaround situations, and if you do something a number of times, you develop expertise by repetition and sheer experience. There are certain patterns and circumstances that arise in transitional situations that I call *value added*. I have evolved a methodology that works for me and I thought sharing it with others might be of benefit. My own sense of value added is through rejuvenating businesses in trouble, saving thousands of jobs throughout the years as well as creating new ones, and building and working with management teams with the resulting great sense of accomplishment. The challenge, not money, has been my primary motivator throughout my career.

Business success is usually a direct result of values that define the culture of an organization. So much depends on the honesty and integrity of the CEO and his or her relationship with the chair and individual directors. The code of conduct should be guided by what is the *right thing* to do for the entire organization—not what benefits the CEO or the senior management. To this end, compensation should be perceived as fair and should reflect an equitable relationship from the CEO down through the ranks. Wherever I have been, I have strived to achieve this—it earns the respect of the employees at large as well as the shareholders.

In summary, my experiences have been *situational*, where I am cast into problems created by others and must evolve a corrective plan and set the tone for the future. These episodes introduced a variety of personalities and forces—some friendly and co-operative, some difficult and complicated, and others, regrettably, that did not respect the trust of a handshake.

When I look back, I am reminded of the verse in "Elegy Written in a Country Churchyard" by Thomas Gray:

> The boast of heraldry, the pomp of power,
> And all that beauty, all that wealth e'er gave,
> Awaits alike the inevitable hour.
> The paths of glory lead but to the grave.

Toronto, 2012

1

From an Old World to a New: 1896–1956

"Avoiding danger is no safer in the long run than outright exposure. Life is either a daring adventure or nothing."

Helen Keller

To set the framework for a book like this, some insight into the development of the character of the writer is perhaps helpful. I was a product of the last days of the British Empire, the end of the Victorian Era, and a refugee child of the Second World War.

My father, David Thomas Griffiths, was the son of a pub operator in Brecon, Wales. Born in 1896, he ran away from home at the age of 15 and joined the Royal Navy. His childhood must have been unhappy because he never talked about it. I do know that he had a sister who did not marry and, as far as I know, my father never returned to Wales.

He had a brilliant and meteoric career in the Royal Navy during the First World War, becoming the youngest lieutenant commander in the Navy. He was a member of the Admiral of the Fleet's staff and served on HMS *Hood* (which was sunk in May 1941 during the Second World War).

He was present for the Battle of Jutland and was sent to investigate the Halifax explosion of 1917. He also served in the British Naval Contingent in 1917 in Russia. He was naval attaché in Washington, D.C. (where he found time to court my mother, an American from Manhattan).

After the war he went to Cambridge University and studied forestry, then in 1922 joined the British Civil Service and chose a posting to Burma (present-day Myanmar), where he stayed for 27 years. My parents married in November 1922 and went directly to Burma.

The Forestry Service in Burma in the pre–Second World War years was idyllic. My father lived like a king, playing polo and touring the teak forests three months of the year on horseback, with elephants in tow carrying supplies and baggage. Hunting was an everyday event. In 1940, at the age of 44, he became the youngest chief conservator of forests in Burma. Reflecting on the 10 years of my childhood spent in Burma, from 1930–1940, I had absolutely no sense that there was a depression anywhere in the world. I felt lucky to be British, living in the empire where the sun never set, with the feeling that the world was my oyster.

My privileged life clashed in my mind with what was really going on in Burma at the time. While I was not yet 10, looking back, my values and sensibilities were greatly influenced by what I learned from the villagers and their children, who were my friends. Through my parents' conversations and facts I would pick up from time to time, I realized that not all was well between the British and the natives. Occasionally newspapers were delivered soaked in blood because *dacoits* (organized robbers and murderers) had raided a train. News about riots and strikes in Rangoon was discussed and there were whisperings of maltreatment of natives by some of the British. And it is undoubtedly true that, with a few notable exceptions, the Brits were arrogant and aloof toward the native Burmese. I was always on the side of my native friends on these issues and remember saying, "When I come back as a grown-up, it will be different; we'll be the same (meaning equal)." Somehow, at a young age, the concept of justice was impressed upon me.

When the war came, my parents sent my brother Paul and me off to school in the United States. My mother, brother, and I boarded a ship in Rangoon in June 1940, went to Calcutta, and then across India by train to Bombay, where we embarked on the USS *Polk* on its way to the States via the Mediterranean. While in Bombay, we heard the news that France had surrendered to Germany. Italy entered the war and the ship was diverted around Africa via Cape Town. We crossed the Atlantic, with the passengers and crew fearful of the German raider *Graf Spee*, finally arriving in New York in August 1940. My mother returned to Rangoon and my parents were lucky to escape to China by car when the Japanese invaded Burma in 1942. Subsequently my father rejoined the British Navy and was assigned to Washington D.C. to assist in purchasing Lend Lease military equipment from the U.S. government. In 1944, he was assigned by the British to a civilian job in San Francisco broadcasting translated Western news in Burmese through Radio Free Britain.

When the Allies were ready to retake Burma, he was seconded to the British Army as a colonel and assigned to the general staff headed by Lord Mountbatten. My father's knowledge of the interior of Burma as a forestry officer was essential in the mapping of the invasion from India. In 1946, the national hero Aung San became prime minister of the newly independent (from Britain) Republic of Burma.

On July 19, 1947 (my 17th birthday), Aung San and a number of members of his government were gunned down during a cabinet meeting by a rival political faction. My father, in an adjacent office, was one of the first on the scene. He stayed on as an adviser to the new government until 1949.

In 1950, my father joined the Food and Agriculture Organization of the United Nations (FAO) in Rome and, from approximately 1952 to 1955, was head of the FAO mission to Mexico to assist that country with reforestation, soil conservation, and agriculture. He loved Mexico and the Mexicans, thrived as a diplomat, and was able to re-establish the kind of life he enjoyed in Burma because of the low cost of living. However, after five years he chose not to renew his contract with FAO because he could not condone the corruption he saw at all levels of government (and society), where everything had a markup or *mordida* (graft). At the age of 58, he and my mother decided to retire to Australia, where my brother had emigrated in 1950.

* * *

My mother, Margaret Frear Tompkins, was a horse fanatic, an incomparable rider in any equestrian event, and the product of strict Victorian standards. She was born in Manhattan in 1896 of well-to-do parents and was educated by tutors. I do not believe she ever formally attended school, although both she and my father were incredibly well-read. My mother's father, Francesco Bianchi Tompkins, was the grandson of Daniel D. Tompkins, a Republican who was governor of New York state from 1807 to 1817, then vice-president of the United States from 1817 to 1825; he was also a founder of the New York Stock Exchange.

In 1900, F.B. Tompkins purchased a mansion in Bermuda called "Mangroville," which was sold by his second wife in 1964 to the Royal Hamilton Amateur Dinghy Club, in whose hands it remains to this day. For much of their youth, my mother and her sister Madeleine lived in Bermuda. Madeleine married Colonel Carpenter, commander of the Bermuda Regiment, and lived in Bermuda until her death in November 1941 at the age of 53.

My mother, though very feminine in appearance and conduct for social occasions, was a very determined and tough lady, dedicating much of her life to animals. Our house in Burma was full of silverware—the cups and trays she won in show jumping at Madison Square Garden and elsewhere. Day-to-day she wore riding clothes; exercised the 14 or so horses we owned in Burma; practised polo; taught us riding; did all the veterinary work on the horses, dogs, cats, and elephants; and ran the household of 14 grooms, 3 house servants, 2 gardeners, a sweeper, and sundry others.

My relationship with my mother was difficult. Our personalities clashed and, all too often, I was at the wrong end of her eight-foot hunting whip, which she exercised with great precision. She was authoritarian and demanding in everyday conduct, table manners, and deportment. We were raised by nannies, and most of our interaction with our parents was at tea time and our dinner time when my mother read to us. Riding on weekends was difficult for me because of constant criticism and invidious comparisons to my brother's greater skill. If nothing else, my mother imbued in me a sense of discipline, high moral standards, and a demand for excellence in all aspects of conduct and performance. Foremost, she was a symbol of authority and I am sure that my mother's treatment of me resulted in my lifelong disdain for authority, particularly where used abusively or unjustly. She was a woman of great courage—absolutely fearless.

My parents were both demanding in terms of basic honesty, fair play, and respect for fellow men. Both were comfortable with all classes of society and my mother would inevitably side with the underdog in any situation. They learned to read and write Burmese, and became conversant in Hindustani. Neither held any prejudice based on race or colour, and eschewed organized religion—my father maintained that religion was the primary cause of wars.

Burma was 85 percent Buddhist in the 1960s, but the missionaries (mainly Baptist) had been active, beginning in the 19th century. They created dissension in support of the British policy of divide and rule, deliberately separating the hill peoples from the Burmese. My brother and I attended the American Baptist Missionary School in Taunggyi, in the Shan State, only two of four day students in a school of twenty-four run by zealous spinster ladies from the United States. We were the only two non-missionary children in the school, which was about two miles from our home.

My brother Paul was born in September 1928, two years before me, and we grew up speaking Burmese exclusively to one another. Paul was very precocious all through school, occasionally skipping grades, while I was a laggard. In retrospect, I believe I had symptoms of dyslexia, as I was tutored privately to learn to read. In addition to being top in his class, Paul was sent by my parents to learn Latin with the resident

Catholic priest. He excelled academically throughout school and university, graduating with a B.A. from Amherst College *cum laude* in 1950. With a classmate, he took a trip around the world landing in Australia, liked it and lives there to this day, having spent most of his career as a stockbroker.

* * *

In September 1940, shortly after my 10th birthday, our mother literally dumped us at McDonogh School, Maryland, as the school year commenced and the Second World War began in earnest. This school satisfied a number of my mother's criteria for us, particularly in terms of discipline. Although historically Episcopalian, it was non-denominational in practice. With its cavalry of about 200 horses, my mother had ensured that our riding would continue. In addition, the school ran summer camps at Lake Champlain in upper New York state, so they could look after us year-round. The Quaker headmaster, Major Louis E. Lamborn, undertook to keep an eye out for "Big Burma" and "Little Burma," as he referred to us. "Doc" Lamborn was a First World War cavalry officer, a most disciplined and austere man, who ran the school with an iron hand along military lines. He believed in and enforced the rigorous moral tenets of its founder, John McDonogh, a wealthy New Orleans merchant, who originally donated the 865 acres outside Baltimore in 1873 as a farm where orphans could work in exchange for an education. Initially, a uniform was adopted to differentiate paying students from working students; later all students wore the same uniform.

Mother told us she had opened a bank account at Pikesville with $22 for each of us for spending money for the year.

I remember thinking this was a fortune at a time when movies cost 11 cents for children under 12. She then returned to Burma to rejoin my father. For the next 32 years, my brother and I had a "guardian" (not legal) who was a brother of a childhood riding friend of my mother's. This was Leonard Newborg, an investment banker at Hallgarten & Co. in New York, who opened his Park Avenue home to us during school holidays, excepting summers. (Leonard died in 1972.) During our time at school, we saw our parents only sporadically.

The military school was run day-to-day by the students and divided into Lower, Middle, and Upper Schools, each with its own cadre of officers. The discipline exercised by student officers on students was brutal. It was supported by the school's system of rigorous academic and military discipline, with a demerit system and awards for academic, administrative, and sporting progress. I was there for nine years, graduating as the top officer (lieutenant colonel) and won awards for most efficient officer and best athlete, and for character and influence. Looking back, I recognize that, at age 10, I was cast out to fend for myself and make my own decisions. While it was lonely and at times stressful, there's no question that the school taught me responsibility and accountability at an early age—it was a microcosm of any organization, business or otherwise, and reflected the good and bad aspects of different leaders, efficiencies of systems, and human relationships.

I left the school in 1949 expecting to pursue a military career (after all, I knew of little else) and fantasized about joining the French Foreign Legion or the British Fleet Air Arm. Instead, I went to Williams College and was there for a year and a half, until in January 1951, under parental pressure, I moved to Australia where my parents thought we could eventually be together as a family. I went to Melbourne to apply to enter the Royal Military College (Duntroon), Australia's equivalent of West Point. On arrival, I faced a variety of obstacles, not the least of which was that Australian institutions would not recognize my credits from Williams College. I decided to take my brother's advice to study to become a chartered accountant.

I began an accounting course at the Melbourne Technical Institute and joined Wm. Buck & Co. as a student. I was assigned to a charming partner, Geoffrey Garrett, who was married and without children. Mr. Garrett was definitely an elitist, greatly absorbed with his clientele and his hobby of growing roses.

One of my major clients was a large manufacturer of bathing suits. While I was adding up pounds, shillings, and pence, I could see through a partition, behind which models changed bathing suits—most distracting. Surprisingly, I decided that I could never become a chartered accountant, and one day at the bathing suit factory summoned up my nerve to tell Mr. Garrett I was resigning. He tried briefly to dissuade me, but saw that my mind was made up. I had abandoned that career after three months, but have a ringing message from my lectures by Mr. Garrett, "Always be alert to fraud." I would live to heed his warnings many times in later life.

When I left accounting, at the urging of a friend I decided to join the training program at the Myer Emporium, Australia's largest department store. After three months of selling bath towels and low-quality radios (this was 1951), I felt totally adrift, not having learned anything, on an endless program to nowhere. I was vitally aware of the value of a university education, but as my credits at Williams College were not recognized in Australia, I began to think increasingly about returning to North America. My parents were opposed, which compounded my sense of isolation.

* * *

Bermudian friends had been educated in Canada and, in the back of my mind, I knew that Williams College and McGill University had reciprocal exchange agreements, provided students had achieved certain academic standards. I wrote to McGill and was accepted based on my transcripts from Williams. I decided to ignore my parents' opposition and left Melbourne by boat in September 1951. I travelled "dormitory class" for six weeks to Perth, Colombo, Bombay, Aden, through the Suez to Palermo, Naples, Genoa, then Gibraltar, Lisbon, Halifax, and New York, from where I took the overnight train to Montreal, arriving in November 1951, two months into the academic year.

I had three wonderful years at McGill. Having "dropped out" of university, I now appreciated the privilege of higher education. I learned to play top-calibre squash as a senior rank-ing member of the McGill team. I was lucky to have joined the Zeta Psi Fraternity at Williams, so that when I arrived at McGill I had a house of ready-made friends. I knew it was a time to enjoy life and I did—assisted by my many convivial and occasionally drunken friends at the fraternity.

In the spring of 1952 I started selling encyclopedias as a summer job—an early exercise in the school of hard knocks. For "training," six or eight of us neophytes were herded into a car and dropped off at Barclay Avenue, a street with a high turnover of residents, where all encyclopedia companies sent their beginners for shaking out. In the first building I entered, the superintendent called the police. Wisely, I spent half the evening hiding in the basement as the police searched the building without success. I lasted about six weeks on the job, and had mediocre success. Apart from the unpredictability of income, it meant that every night was taken up working and I had no social life. It wouldn't do at all.

A graduate at the fraternity house working in the advertising business knew I was looking for something else and asked me if I would consider becoming a "space salesman." It took me a while to understand what he was talking about, because somehow I pictured myself dressed up in a spacesuit walking over the moon, even though this was only 1952. I was disappointed when I understood that the job involved selling *advertising* space. The next thing I knew I was attending an interview for a job with *Liberty* magazine (later *New Liberty*), owned by Jack Kent Cooke, who later became famous as a television billionaire and the owner of the Washington Redskins and Los Angeles Kings. For the final interview, Mr. Cooke sent his general manager, Mr. Prince, from Toronto. Mr. Prince opened the interview with, "Sell me an encyclopedia." (In his book, *The Last Mogul*, Cooke's biographer, Adrian Havill, noted that Cooke had been an encyclopedia salesman during the Depression.[1]) At the end of my pitch, Mr. Prince put me in an office with a photo album, the first page of which had pasted on it a key to a Buick. The following pages explained how I could win this car by achieving certain milestones.

The rest of the album consisted of a wide variety of newspaper clippings about Cooke being charged criminally over an article published by the magazine entitled "Babies for export." According to Havill: "the December 27, 1947 edition . . . charged that a black market existed for Alberta babies, because of the looseness in western Canadian provinces' adoption laws. The Alberta provincial government, learning that the magazine was about to publish the story, requested that [*Liberty*] withhold the offending piece. The Alberta attorney general then changed the main charge to 'conspiracy to publish defamatory libel.'"[2]

In the end, according to Havill, the magazine got "millions of dollars worth of free publicity" as a result of the Alberta lawsuit.

However, I presume it was important to show this background to recruits to *Liberty*, because some large advertisers avoided the magazine on moral grounds, and management didn't want new salesmen to be surprised if they were rejected because of this. The job paid $200 a month and, for the first time in my life, I felt financially comfortable. As this was a full-time job, I began to have trouble balancing my time when lectures started in the fall. Since my boss, the local manager, kept all the good accounts for himself, I had difficulty meeting my targets with the dregs and my assignment to crack those who were reluctant to advertise on moral grounds. I resigned before Christmas.

The following two summers I joined the Canadian Officers Training Corps (COTC) and was posted first to the Citadel in Quebec City and, in the second year, to Camp Meaford on Georgian Bay in Ontario. One of my most lasting memories of the COTC was that army training was child's play compared to the discipline I had experienced at McDonogh. I also learned that the army training method of "doing it by numbers" (e.g., stripping and cleaning a Bren gun) was a useful concept many times in my future business career. It was a simple disciplined system that had to be followed by the lowest common denominator of humanity and greatly mitigated mistakes by "doing it right the first time." This phrase became popular in the 1980s among Western business enterprises practising Total Quality Management. My third lasting memory is that I witnessed first-hand the resentment the French held for the English: the one English platoon among the seven in total was virtually ostracized by the French, who controlled the mess at the Citadel in Quebec City.

In the spring of 1954, as president of my fraternity, I presided at the annual black-tie "Elders' Banquet" and found myself sitting next to Brother Frank Winser, a vice-president of Alcan and a graduate of the Harvard Graduate School of Business Administration. Frank asked what I planned to do when I graduated that year, and when I replied I had no idea, he said why not go to the Harvard Business School. I hadn't considered this, believing I lacked the academic qualifications, let alone the financial wherewithal. In any case, Frank insisted on arranging an interview with two recruiters from the business school, and by the end of the summer, I had been accepted on a financial-aid scholarship that included the school arranging for a job where I would pick up and deliver laundry door to door.

In September 1954 I went off to Harvard for two formative and exceptional years. I did not tell my father, who by now was in Australia, until I had been there for six or eight weeks, because I knew he would object. He wrote me a disapproving letter saying, "If you want to become a professor, own up to it, otherwise stop avoiding work." Later, having made inquiries about the school, he realized I had made a good decision and ever after was contrite about his initial reaction. My ability to enjoy the environs of the school and greater Boston were seriously constrained by my having zero disposable income. Nevertheless, campus was a great place and the school a great leveller of egos with its pressure-cooker atmosphere. I won the school squash tournament one year (my opponent failed to show up) and made a number of lifelong friends. In the summer of 1955, I got a job at Alcan in Montreal, examining the selling costs in the export, commercial research, and domestic sales divisions. This was a lesson in big business bureaucracy and office politics. It was a great experience and helped me to make up my mind not to join a huge company on graduation.

At the end of my first year, I approached my "Control" course professor, Neil Harlan, and told him I was concerned that my limited exposure to accounting was a liability: I did not feel comfortable that, when in business, someone might take the summer off and leave me with the responsibility of keeping the books. Professor Harlan (who later became chairman and CEO of McKesson) looked at me and asked: "Can you read an income statement? Can you read a balance sheet? Do you understand a source and applications of funds statement?" As I answered these in the affirmative, he said, "That's fine; if you get where we expect you to get, you'll be able to hire your own accountants." This made me feel better, though somewhat uncertain about the realism of the advice.

My second memory of professional advice concerned the objections of business school students to undergraduate women grading student papers. These women from elite schools like Radcliffe and Wellesley were given "a précis solution" for papers and graded them accordingly. As the business students included war vets, qualified accountants, engineers, and many with business experience, being graded by these young girls seemed unacceptable to them. A temporary professor, an MIT graduate, summarized the situation aptly saying, "You'll be judged by incompetents all of your life—you might as well get used to it now!" How often I have thought of that over the years.

2

My Next Education, 1956–1960

"So here is a rule to remember in the future, when anything tempts you to feel bitter: not, 'This is a misfortune,' but 'To bear this worthily is good fortune.'"
Marcus Aurelius, Meditations

In the spring of 1956, student job interviews commenced on the Harvard campus; having completed two years of graduate business school, I attended hoping to find an international assignment in sales or marketing. I hadn't planned to go to Canada because I wanted to live in a warmer climate, but by chance, while waiting in a hallway for an interview, I found myself talking to a recruiter from Montreal. He offered me a job, which I accepted on the spot, as his assistant in the recently established new product development department of Canadian Resins and Chemicals Ltd. (CRC), a vinyl plastics (PVC) manufacturer. CRC was 51-percent owned by Union Carbide (an American company) and 49-percent owned by Shawinigan Chemicals (Canadian), a subsidiary of Shawinigan Water and Power, a wartime "shotgun" joint venture utilizing Carbide's technology and Shawinigan Chemicals's raw materials.

When I joined the company in June 1956, I discovered I was working for the person who had been selected through what was known tongue-in-cheek in the company as "the Genius Ad"—an ad that was so broad and demanding in credentials that only a genius could qualify. The purpose of the new product development department was to identify new products and areas for diversification to make the company less dependent on PVC. My initial role was primarily market research, and I worked on a wide variety of projects and potential acquisitions. My boss was determined to do something significant to change the nature of the company, and in his enthusiasm, would often stretch the facts.

After I was at the company about a year, the president confronted me after a board meeting as to whether a particular set of numbers underpinning a report was obtained through my research. I had to admit it was not. This resulted in the departure of my boss and the disbanding of the department, and I became assistant to the president. This was a fortuitous development for me because I became the CEO's right-hand man. Since his entire business experience had been in sales, I was able, at the age of 27, to exercise influence in all business functions, including overall policy, utilizing my newly minted MBA. In the summer of 1958, Shawinigan announced it was buying out Union Carbide and CRC was to become a division of Shawinigan, losing its autonomy. This was a major blow to the management of CRC. Coincidentally, I was being courted by my previous boss (the "Genius"), who was now in charge of diversification at Canadian Curtiss-Wright (CCW).

CCW was the Canadian subsidiary of Curtiss-Wright Corp., then a cash-rich NYSE-listed company that made its money manufacturing aircraft engines during the Second World and Korean wars. The newly appointed American president, Roy T. Hurley, a fanatical maverick billed as a "production genius" when he was at Ford, decided to diversify the company into an endless variety of projects. In October 1958, *Fortune Magazine* published an article entitled "Can shotgun diversification work?" which described Hurley's strategy as firing a shotgun out his office window and going into whatever business a pellet landed on.

My immediate project was Thermopac, a stored-energy furnace that would make use of low-cost, off-peak electric power from utilities like Ontario Hydro. There were many other projects, including urethane foam (Curon), high-speed trains driven by aircraft engines, and air cars (hovercraft vehicles), as well as highly secret research projects conducted on a 88-square-mile site in Pennsylvania near Penn State University. Two major projects—Project X and Project Y—were so secret that, in Canada, only the company president was aware of their nature. Notwithstanding, much of the efforts of Canadian management were devoted to finding facilities large enough to manufacture aircraft and aircraft engines. In my first six months, I researched and wrote a report totally debunking Thermopac, saying the product was untimely, uneconomic, and uncompetitive. My superiors who supported Thermopac reacted violently against my recommendation to stop wasting money on the project and responded by giving it to someone else, and then letting it die.

I was then put on mergers and acquisition work in search of a company to build Projects X and Y, about which I knew nothing except they were big and secret. I finally succeeded in negotiating the purchase of Otaco Industries in Orillia, Ontario. After settling on the general terms and conditions, the two proprietors, Messrs. Brown and Phelps, who by now knew and trusted me, asked what sort of idiots were buying their company at such a high price and for what purpose. When I assured them I did not know, they expressed concern for the welfare of employees, the community, and themselves.

Meanwhile, I was sharing an apartment with two medical students at McGill, one of whom, John Richardson, was to become my brother-in-law. A good friend of John's was named Joe Hanaway from New Jersey. His father was a director, general counsel, and personal confidant of Roy T. Hurley, CEO of Curtiss-Wright in the United States. I saw little of young Hanaway, but one night over a drink at the apartment he asked me what I was doing at CCW. When he discovered that I didn't know what Projects X and Y were, he laughed and advised that one was a vertical lift-off aircraft and the other a revolutionary, all-purpose, free-piston engine called the Wankel. I was excited at "the light going on" for me and confided (stupidly, as it turned out) to my boss the next day. He promptly told his boss, the president, Everitt (Nick) Carter, who called Hurley, and orders came from New York to fire me immediately. This wasn't the last injustice I was to experience in business and it happened before "wrongful dismissal" came into vogue.

Carter was a peculiar character; then aged 43, he was Hurley's white-haired boy. He kept his office in total darkness except for a spotlight directly over his desk and had a brass sign on his credenza saying *Tenga Fe* ("Have Faith" in Spanish). He spoke in a whisper and you could never clearly see him in the darkness of his office. At the time, all of senior management were padding revenue forecasts for various exotic products, while simultaneously looking for jobs, and Carter was the leader in this charade. About the time I left, the company was shaken by the news that Carter was leaving to become CEO of Oak Industries, taking with him his chief sycophant, Ray Pierce.

It took about 20 years, but Carter and Pierce were deemed by the SEC to be unfit to hold positions as officers or directors of any listed company when Carter was accused of paying his secretary/mistress (a decorator) $2 million in fees to redesign Oak's new headquarters in San Diego. Meanwhile, in 1959, not long after my departure, Curtiss-Wright stock jumped from about $25 to $44 a share when Hurley announced that the company had developed a revolutionary free-piston engine. Then a German company, NSU Motorenwerke A.G., announced that Curtiss-Wright had not developed the Wankel engine, but had merely licensed the North American rights for it. Curtiss-Wright stock plunged and Roy Hurley was fired.

* * *

Fortunately, sometime before *I* was fired, I had decided that Curtiss-Wright was not a good place to be. Also, I was about to get married and my fiancée and I were determined that I should find an exciting international assignment. I wrote to a few U.S.-based management consulting firms and received a reply from Bruce A. Payne & Associates in New York, through its Montreal affiliate, Payne-Ross, asking if I would consider going to work at a meat-packing company in Argentina for two years. I passed all the tests administered by Payne-Ross's industrial psychologist, Jim Westcott, who became a lifelong friend, but as I was applying for visas and work permits a revolution erupted and Bruce A. Payne lost the assignment. I then received a call from the managing partner of Payne-Ross, Gerald G. Fisch, who hired me as a "consultant" based in Montreal. In the back of my mind, I decided to take the job for three years, but as events were to unfold, I left after one year to join a client, Consumers Glass Company, later renamed Consumers Packaging (Consumers).

The management consulting business was interesting, exciting, high pressure (to produce results), and a great confidence builder. At the age of 29, I found myself in the offices of major corporations undergoing serious difficulties, with CEOs listening to my advice on how to solve their problems. I realized then how badly many businesses are run and how many executives rise to the top without adequate credentials, often through contacts or sheer force of personality.

My first assignment was with Canada's largest advertising agency of the time, now extinct, called Cockfield Brown. The CEO was a prominent, engaging Montreal businessman, and a fellow member of the Hillside Tennis Club. I found it somewhat uncomfortable to be advising this pillar of society nearly twice my age.

Among other assignments, I undertook a study for the Japan External Trade Association, when Japan was accused of dumping cheap radios on the Canadian market, destroying the Canadian radio manufacturing industry. What I found was an eye-opener: what actually was happening was that the Japanese were producing radios with transistors, replacing vacuum tubes. The new low-price technology was *creating* explosive growth in radio sales. The problem was that Canadian technology had not caught up and domestic producers were being destroyed by this new technology. I believe my work was critical in persuading Canadian authorities to drop dumping charges against the Japanese.

My next major assignment was with a family-controlled company that had deteriorated to the point that it was in the hands of the Bank of Montreal. I was sitting in the offices of Payne-Ross late one evening in 1959 when Gerry Fisch came in and yelled, "Who's here—we've got a new client that's bankrupt and the chairman hasn't got long to live." This was Consumers Glass Company, which was technically bankrupt, although the chairman did not die and in fact lived until 1981. I was the only person in the office that evening and by the week's end, at least half of the consulting organization was assigned to the new client. This was my first senior "turn-around" assignment, and the consultants virtually operated the company for the next eight months, occupying (or shadowing) every senior management position. I became acting manager of marketing, but in the summer of 1960 was transferred to Toronto by Payne-Ross for other projects.

Late in 1993, Gerry called me after a lapse of more than 30 years. This led to a lunch in Toronto when we reminisced about our experiences at Consumers in 1959, and he reminded me how dire the situation really was. He had reported to the chair and controlling shareholder, Brian Heward, that there was drinking, gambling, and smoking going on in the warehouse and recommended that the president be fired. Heward was incredulous, so Gerry took him on a tour to see for himself. When it came to firing the president, Heward said he had no experience with such a task, and wanted Gerry to be present in case the president became violent. When the meeting took place and Heward did the deed, the president broke into tears and thanked Heward profusely for relieving him of a job he never wanted in the first place!

The last Payne-Ross assignment was to recruit a new chief executive officer for Consumers. It was my guess that the firm dragged its feet on this since Payne-Ross was enjoying a consultant's feast while running the company. In any case, in the summer of 1960, J. Donald Mingay, aged 44, was appointed president of Consumers and immediately set out to torpedo Payne-Ross to save costs, while simultaneously trying to hire several of the consultants. I was one of those he approached to join Consumers as marketing manager—and I leapt at the chance to take on this challenging turnaround at the highest level of management.

3

I Cut My Teeth on Glass, 1960–1968

"Experience is not what happens to you;
it is what you do with what happens to you."
Aldous Huxley

Don Mingay was the eldest of eight children and started selling life insurance before the outbreak of the Second World War, when he joined the army. He left the war as a lieutenant colonel with a distinguished record, including being head of the staff college in Kingston, Ontario. After the war, Don became the leading salesman for life insurance in Canada, as well as a leader in many community and political (federal Liberal) activities. However, his experience operating a business was minimal, and my experience to that point was a good complement to his general leadership and salesman's strengths.

When I joined Consumers, it had revenues of about $12 million and was bleeding cash. It was in the hands of the Bank of Montreal and technically bankrupt.

The common denominator in the business was the mould for making bottles, of which there were probably three thousand types. Multiply this by different packaging, skid size, and delivery requirements, and you can see we were working with a complicated matrix. The industry was dominated by a duopoly, Consumers Glass and Dominion Glass (later renamed Domglas). Dominion was the much larger player, with about 80 percent of the market, and was enjoying watching its arch competitor go to the ropes. In 1959, a third competitor, Iroquois Glass in Quebec, had been founded by Société Générale de Belgique, which upset the cushy world of the duopoly somewhat.

The companies did not compete on price largely because the customer dictated design and other specifications. Since all three companies had the same bottle-making equipment, it was convenient for Owens-Illinois, the American giant in the industry, to set prices. Dominion picked up the price list from distributors in the United States and adjusted its prices for duty and exchange. When Canadian dealers received the adjusted lists, they shared them with Consumers and Iroquois. So while "price fixing," was illegal, "following" wasn't. I recall an amusing illustration of this during my time consulting when I asked Albert Riendeau, vice-president of sales at Consumers, how to price an 8-ounce Pepsi bottle, one of their high-volume items. After trying to find the price himself, he called in various subordinates (experts in pricing), and finally in great frustration picked up the telephone and called his counterpart at Dominion who solved the riddle immediately.

Mingay re-staffed the company with young 30- and 40-year-olds, and we started to attack our competition. Glass-container manufacturing is a high-fixed-cost business. Furnaces run 24 hours a day, seven days a week, at 1700°F. Glass-making is at once a science and an art and, although a mature business in most respects, it is also high-tech. Gobs of molten glass, precisely measured, are clipped at lightning speed from feeders on the furnaces and dropped into precision-measured moulds (at greater than aircraft industry tolerances) to press and blow jars or bottles to precise weights, volumes, and thicknesses.

Dominion made glass in five colours—clear, amber, green, blue, and opal—while Consumers and Iroquois made only clear, amber, and green glass. The colours, the sizes of the bottles, and the draw on the furnaces were among the wide variety of variables affecting efficiency and profitability. The ability to maximize "the pull" on the furnace not only affected output, but also dictated the life of a furnace. When we started, the average life of a $3-million furnace was five years, but with the aid of an alliance and a technical-assistance agreement negotiated by Mingay with Brockway Glass in Pennsylvania, we were soon rebuilding furnaces to last eight years. This yielded tremendous cost savings.

The early days at Consumers Glass were fun because the company had been so badly managed, improvements were easy to make, and their effect on operating profit was quick and measurable. To counteract Dominion's 80-percent share of the market, we developed a strategy focusing on easy-to-make designs of high-volume items for large customers. This enabled us to reduce the number of moulds, minimize job changes, manage the pull on the furnaces more easily, and extend mould and furnace life. Since every production run had a learning curve, the longer the run, the higher the overall utilization of the furnace and efficiency (fewer rejections), and the lower the downtime. We were careful not to cut prices, but had a lot of fun fooling with freight rates, mould amortization, carton purchases, and a variety of other practices. We had the satisfaction of knowing that every time Dominion tried to compete head-to-head with us, it cost them roughly four times as much, since it was four times our size. While reasonably well-financed, Dominion was suffering from management atrophy that had yet to be recognized—there were about eight men, each 60 to 70 years old, heading up Dominion, and whenever I hear someone describe a company as having collectively 200 years of management experience, I think of Dominion Glass.

From a marketing point of view, it became clear to me that, since differentiation on price or product wasn't possible, service and quality were of maximum importance for our customers. Our technical partner, Brockway Glass Company, was an engineering-driven company and, I used to say, no big customer could afford *not* to buy from Brockway. Brockway was the industry leader in quality and production techniques, raising performance levels throughout the United States. Our partnership with Brockway certainly put Consumers well ahead of competition in Canada for the next 25 years. We set out to *systematize* the company, which included computerization of every customer specification sheet, as well as establishing profit centres in distribution management, all the while raising quality standards with the help of Brockway. In the 1960s, Consumers purchased the first IBM 360 in Canada and used it for production scheduling, not financial reporting. By 1966, we were very profitable and had seized the initiative on every front from our competitors. I remembered my army experience of doing things only one way—the right way. "Doing it right the first time" results in zero defects. This lesson in quality was to pay off for me again 20 years later at Mitel.

* * *

I believe in using external consultants only for specific purposes and, having been a consultant, I knew *how* to hire advice. At Consumers, I was struggling to streamline and monitor the warehousing distribution (shipping and receiving), freight cost, and order-processing functions. Apart from order processing, plant managers were responsible for all of these functions, but largely ignored them as they were measured on efficiencies of bottle output in the plant. One day I read an article in *The Harvard Business Review* by John Stolle of Booz Allen Hamilton (BAH) on distribution management and organization in multi-plant manufacturing companies. I telephoned Stolle at his office in Chicago, invited him to make a presentation to our management committee, and told him the $35,000 consultation fee was not something we'd argue about. However, I emphasized that I wanted his team only, not anyone else from BAH, and especially no one from its Canadian subsidiary, as they lacked expertise in this specific area. Stolle made his presentation and we awarded him the job. Then I had a call from the managing partner of BAH Toronto who wanted "to talk about the staffing of the assignment." I called Stolle immediately and told him he'd lost the job. Of course, he'd been pressured by BAH politics, but when he knew I was serious, he agreed to do the assignment my way. BAH did an outstanding job and Consumers benefitted enormously. The lesson learned when hiring any kind of external consultant is to hire the person who has the expertise, not necessarily the consulting firm.

* * *

By now Iroquois was running into quality and production problems, as well as suffering a growing rift between Canadian management and its Belgian masters. Don Mingay monitored the situation carefully and, on the day the Société Générale de Belgique was ready to throw in the towel, was ready with an offer to buy the company. The immediate concern was whether the Canadian government would permit the merger, since Canada had introduced anti-monopoly and undue concentration policies. Our corporate counsel, Jack Geller[1] of Campbell Godfrey & Lewtas (later Fasken & Campbell, now Fasken Martineau), advised us to buy Iroquois, mix our operations quickly, and see if we could escape government scrutiny. This we did, but early one Monday morning, many months later, the receptionist advised me that two gentlemen were waiting in the lobby to see me. By now I was executive vice-president (in today's world, the chief operating officer), and Mingay was away at a meeting at Brockway. Messrs. Decker and Fell from Ottawa, investigating under the Combines Investigation Act, were ushered into my office and announced they had a warrant to investigate the company, without identifying their purpose. This was scary and I called Geller, who calmly said, "I always told you to be a good boy." Decker and Fell sealed every desk and filing cabinet in the building. I learned later that the same thing had happened at Dominion and Iroquois simultaneously. We never heard the results of the investigation, but understood it was triggered by concerns about concentration when we bought Iroquois.

With the purchase of Iroquois, Consumers was now highly profitable: we had expanded our market share and closed down an unpredictable competitor. We now turned our attention to building a plant in western Canada, diversifying into other packaging materials and products, and building a glass-container company in Australia.

Shipping bottles means that you are essentially shipping containers full of air, so they can only be shipped economically for a short distance. This meant, for example, that Winnipeg was a marginal market for Consumers based in Toronto; we were not a national company. In the 1960s, the federal government, through the Department of Regional Economic Expansion (DREE), began to provide incentives to businesses to locate in remote areas of Canada through grants. One designated area was the beautiful Okanagan Valley in British Columbia, where we obtained a $3-million grant to build a $12-million plant. Dominion had plants on both sides of the Rockies: one in Medicine Hat, Alberta, and one in Burnaby, British Columbia. Ours would straddle them neatly and fracture their monopolistic position in the West.

By this time, Consumers's share of the Canadian market had risen from 20 to 40 percent and, more importantly, we had 60 percent of the desirable, high-volume, high-profit portion of the market. An exciting and potentially high-volume new market was developing: non-returnable soft drink bottles. The new market was not without its drawbacks, however, since several U.S. states and the province of Alberta had enacted legislation banning non-returnables because of consumer opposition to litter. The Glass Container Manufacturers Institute fought this legislation, saying that people cause litter, not bottles, cans, or plastics. Eventually, non-returnables and cans were accepted, but not without a major public relations and political battle.

I went to British Columbia and met with senior politicians and bureaucrats, including Einar Gunderson, the chair of BC Hydro and a Socred bagman (Premier W.A.C. Bennett's economic tsar). I also met the minister of trade and commerce, Ralph Loffmark, and others, and received absolute verbal assurances that British Columbia would not ban non-returnable bottles. On the basis of these assurances, we commissioned the building of the plant in Lavington, near Vernon and Kelowna in the Okanagan Valley, but by the time we opened the plant 18 months later, British Columbia had indeed passed legislation banning non-returnables. This was my first real hard lesson in politics.

In due course, we held an opening ceremony for the plant and Mingay, Premier Bennett, Federal Minister of Public Works Arthur Laing, and I sat at a picnic table for lunch before the speeches were made. Mingay said to Bennett, "You gave us an undertaking not to ban non-returnables— now we have a plant with nothing to make in it." "That's too goddamned bad!" was Bennett's reply. End of story. It took a long time to make that plant viable. Amazingly, Mingay was able to contain himself from calling "Wacky" (the premier's nickname) a son-of-a-bitch until the premier was out of earshot. For me, it was a lesson in dealing with politicians, and reminded me of de Gaulle's comment, "Since a politician never believes what he says, he is surprised when others believe him."

* * *

In 1967, we bought a company called Brentwood Containers that made plastic coffee cups and lids with a vacuum-forming process. The company was founded and operated by a young engineering genius named Jim Eyre. Eyre had developed amazing technology, including an automatic feedback of the web (waste) produced in punching out cups and lids, which resulted in 100-percent material utilization. He rented plant space, and the only assets of the business were the machinery and working capital. Unfortunately, only a year or two before, Jim had lost an arm while repairing a press, which caused him great physical pain and depression. His marriage was also on the rocks.

We bought Brentwood on a three-year earn-out, which meant that I had to live with Jim through his emotional trauma. He was a man of utmost integrity and delivered the formula earnings in full. All the time, he kept telling me he was going to leave the country and take his kids with him to save them from his wife, who he said was incapable of caring for them. At first, I thought he was joking, but when I realized he might be serious, I told him that, while I was sorry and concerned, I didn't want to become involved in his personal problems. One day, he disappeared. I was shocked. I believe he resurfaced about 10 years later, having spent the intervening period exiled in Mexico.

* * *

During the earn-out period, we looked at a variety of other acquisitions in the plastics field. We found two companies, Regent Containers and Westek (a breakaway of Regent), that both made plastic cream containers. The companies sold a filling-machine system to dairies and then supplied them with the containers to put the cream in—similar to a company selling both razors and razor blades. Regent Containers was controlled by Edper (the holding company of Edward and Peter Bronfman) and an entrepreneur, while Westek was owned by a volatile entrepreneur, Joe Hemp, in Chicago. The two companies were carrying on a price war almost across the street from one another. My plan was to buy them both and put them together with Brentwood, rationalize all three plants, and raise prices.

Jim Eyre and I toured Regent one day and, as we watched a production line, Jim suddenly grabbed me, went white, and pointed to a woman pushing plastic sheet into a press with no safety guard. Jim walked out saying he would have nothing more to do with the place because he was sure the woman was going to lose her hand. I couldn't mention Regent again to him that day. I thought about it overnight and the next day said to Jim, "Are you worried about your emotional pain or are you really concerned about the woman?" When he said it was the woman he was concerned about, I told him that we had to take control of the company as soon as possible to save her hand. This got him on side and we bought Regent on favourable terms.

At the closing, the lawyer acting for Edper was Trevor Eyton (later president and CEO of Brascan—see chapter 7) and payment was a combination of cash and Consumers stock. Just as we were closing, however, the entrepreneur balked at signing the non-competition agreement. Our lawyer, Jack Geller, advised us to hang tough. We did and eventually closed on our terms. This was my first experience interfacing with an Edper-sponsored company.

I then lay awake at night wondering how to solve the price war with Westek. I tried to talk to Hemp, the owner, about buying the company, but Hemp wanted an unconscionable price. Six weeks later, I got a call from his bank in Chicago saying that Joe Hemp had suddenly died and the bank held his shares as collateral. We went to Chicago and made a reasonable deal with the bank, and put Regent and Westek together under the name of Portion Packaging. We then reaped the benefits of economies of scale and raised prices. In February 1993, Portion Packaging was sold to Winpak Ltd. for $57 million.

* * *

In the early 1960s, my brother Paul started feeding me information about the Australian glass market, which was a virtual monopoly under a very badly managed, sleepy company called Australian Consolidated Industries (ACI). ACI allowed a small operator in Sydney to survive (with less than 2 percent of the market), presumably to permit ACI to maintain the fiction that it was not really a monopoly. This was potentially particularly attractive, but at first I could not persuade Don Mingay to proceed because he thought it was too far away. I told him it wasn't much farther than the Okanagan by the time you flew to Vancouver, rented a car, and drove to the plant at Lavington. I tweaked his pride by suggesting we should let Brockway have a crack at it if Consumers wouldn't. Mingay responded, "Let's do it!" Through my brother we hired Philip Shrapnel, a consultant in Australia, who conducted an industry study utilizing a questionnaire designed by us.

The study was very positive, so we initially tried to buy the little manufacturer in Sydney. They, seeing that we were a large Canadian public company, asked for a ridiculous price for a rundown plant with obsolete equipment, so we decided to build instead. However, we first had to satisfy ourselves about three potential obstacles, which we believed were ACI-spread rumours. These were that:

- ACI held an exclusive agreement with UK-based ICI for soda ash in Australia, a primary ingredient of glass

- ACI had exclusive use of IS equipment in Australia (the main bottle-making machine) with the American manufacturer Emhart Corporation
- ACI controlled all the principal pure silica sand deposits in southeast Australia

One by one we satisfied ourselves that these were all myths and decided to forge ahead with our building. To provide required Australian content, we teamed up with a local group of mining promoters. We built the plant in Penrith, near Sydney; after stumbling because of our own management problems, Glass Containers Ltd. (GCL) became a roaring success. It was a public company, and sometime around 1981, a private group from Melbourne approached Consumers with an offer to buy that was so attractive Consumers could not refuse. Some years later, this group sold GCL to ACI, having struggled to keep GCL profitable, so the company came full circle. In the early 1990s, ACI was taken over by BTR (the UK conglomerate) and huge cost reductions were wrung out of its bloated management infrastructure. When I went to Australia in 1968 to get the project underway, I had lunch with my old accounting boss, Geoff Garrett. It had been 17 years since I had resigned at the bathing suit factory and Mr. Garrett was somewhat shocked that his apprentice was now "managing director" of a major Canadian manufacturing enterprise!

4

Looking Past Glass, 1969–1971

"When you get to a fork in the road, you take it."

Yogi Berra

In January 1969, Don Mingay called me into his office and said he was going to Australia with his wife for two weeks to check out operations and then take four weeks' vacation in Asia, visiting Singapore and Japan. He had always maintained that he would be president for 10 years, then turn the company over to a successor. So, upon his return, he wanted me to replace him as president and CEO, and he would become chair, take an office downtown, and leave the company in my hands. He told me to consider, while he was away, any organizational and other changes I would like to make and to pursue the idea of acquiring a company we had been looking at in the aluminium extrusion business called General Impact Extrusions (GIE). I thanked him and said I would. This came as no surprise to me because Don often alluded to getting out and, since I had been running the company day-to-day anyway as chief operating officer, I was his clear successor.

However, in the six weeks he was away, I undertook a complete personal appraisal, and found that the more I thought about becoming president of Consumers, the less it appealed to me. I was 38 and totally fed up with spending a large part of my business life fighting with bureaucrats and politicians over plans to ban non-returnable bottles. Recycling was becoming a major issue, and the Canadian government, under the newly-elected Prime Minister Pierre Trudeau, was leaning left and not interested in supporting business. I kept a list in my desk drawer of 18 key customers who accounted for roughly 75 percent of our volume, but these traditional glass applications were under threat from cans and plastics. Frankly, I was bored by the bottle business. The controlling shareholder wouldn't offer me share options and, while I was making a good salary, my after-tax income was quickly spent supporting my family of four children under the age of seven and I was unable to build any capital. In the meantime, my friends in the financial business were living well, involved in various industries, earning good salaries, and building equity.

So, when Don returned, I told him my thoughts and said, "The problem is you're 15 years older, but we've both been here 10 years and reached the same conclusion at the same time." Don was shaken because he had counted on me to succeed him and said there was no one else in line.

I maintained my stance as we discussed the situation back and forth over the next few weeks. Finally he realized that I was serious, and asked me to stay for one year while we found a successor. He also promised he would help me find a position in the financial community. In retrospect, our agreement created a real problem because, as much as we both dedicated ourselves to our company roles, we were preoccupied with our personal situations and our focus must have diminished. The company was facing many pressures, with a new plant struggling in British Columbia, a start-up in Australia, and plastics businesses to amalgamate and build. And as mentioned, there was a competitive environment for glass containers in alternate materials, and a new government with a mandate that was going to strangle enterprise.

* * *

In the meantime, we pursued the prospect of acquiring GIE to allow us to diversify into metal technology. GIE was a thinly traded public company controlled by a group of three or four people, one of whom, Donald C. (Ben) Webster, was a personal friend. In fact, I was a small shareholder and board member of Ben's venture capital company Helix Investments, through which Ben held 20 percent of GIE. Neither Ben nor the Helix board knew much about GIE apart from normal public company reporting. It was operated by two other major shareholders, one the chair and the other the president.

As negotiations proceeded, the economic outlook in early 1970 darkened with the release by the Trudeau government of its infamous White Paper on Tax Reform late in 1969.[1] Stock markets declined and Consumers's share price fell from a high of $30 in 1969 to under $20. The management of Consumers began to get cold feet about the GIE transaction. The other side, however, became quite aggressive and creative, offering various alternatives to offset our concerns, including pegging the price of Consumers well above market at $24 per share, for the non-cash portion of the purchase price. I was in a quandary because of my personal deliberations about leaving the company: on one hand, I hoped that GIE would go away as it complicated my agenda, while on the other hand, I felt it would be best for Consumers shareholders to proceed with the transaction in light of the ominous signs for non-returnable glass bottles. On this subject I felt very isolated, because other Consumers management and board members felt I was unduly pessimistic about the future of non-returnables. My intuition was correct but, as usual, I was early by a few years.

The GIE people kept the heat on, and the week of the closing I asked the general manager of GIE to give me a status report. When I did not receive this by closing date as requested, I felt uncomfortable. There were disparate reports trickling in from GIE, showing slower releases against orders, lower backlog, and pricing problems. However, the GIE people continued to express confidence, even optimism, and we closed the transaction on a Monday. When I received the general manager's report the following Friday, I was horrified and immediately called Don Mingay at home to tell him that, as far as I was concerned, we'd been duped.

GIE turned into a horror story; I believed then the acquisition was a write-off and we quickly moved to downsize operations, eventually closing altogether within three years. Then GIE shareholders dumped their stock in Consumers, driving our share price down and breaking verbal assurances that they would hold the stock. GIE became an overwhelming and unpleasant topic at board meetings, a disaster that stained our otherwise excellent 10 years of progress. The lawyers advised us to sue on the basis that we bought the company on *written* warranties and, while various changes may have been communicated verbally before closing, there had been material changes in the business not communicated in writing which, had we known, we would not have closed.

Due to legal manoeuvres, health problems with lawyers and judges, and attempts to settle out of court, the case did not come to trial for seven years. Mingay, R.D. (Bob) Morison, vice-president of finance (who eventually became president), and I were made to look foolish in court. I was particularly targeted as a Harvard Business School graduate, merger and acquisition expert, and executive vice-president ("chief operating officer"). I was also obliquely accused of having a conflict of interest because of my connection with Helix, even though this had been disclosed to all parties long before the transaction.

We thought the other side was going to accuse us of taking over the business and mismanaging it. Not so: they attacked us on the basis that we were smart, sophisticated, qualified people who got all the right information but did not do our homework before the transaction closed. GIE's defence was ancient: *caveat emptor* and no doubt they were partly right. The judge agreed and on a more than $8.5-million lawsuit, awarded Consumers only $400,000 for specific items such as inventory adjustments. So much for our lawyers' arguments about the written warranties we had received. The lesson learned? Rein in the lawyers when they're competing over legal principles. Lawyers will always be ready for a legal challenge, and meanwhile, the client has to pay, whatever the outcome. The second lesson I learned was to take notes of any and all meetings in business deals, a practice I continued throughout my career and that proved helpful in writing these memoirs. I was too trusting and, at trial, the other side produced endless notes—some, I believed, written after the fact. I had taken few notes during negotiations and delegated the due diligence to my financial staff and the lawyers.

One happy event of this soul-destroying episode was that Ben Webster called me a few days before the trial and said he was standing aside and hoped we would continue our friendship. We did, and have had many good times since. When I joined the board of Mitel in 1984, Ben was already there as a major investor. It was through me that he got to know Albert Gnat, who became one of his key advisers.

* * *

By August 1970 we had still not found a successor for the president's post, and I told Don Mingay I was going to talk to a few select people discreetly. Don came up with a couple of helpful suggestions of his own. Eventually Bob Morison, then VP finance, moved into the post in a caretaker role, keeping the company on a relatively even keel for the next few years.

I left the management of Consumers in February 1971 to join Jonlab Investments Limited, with the understanding that, after an introductory period, I would be number two to J.H. (Jake) Moore at Brascan in Canada. Jonlab had effective control of Brascan, through management and by holding the largest block of Brascan shares (8 percent). I remained on the board of directors of Consumers until January 1978.

During the '70s, the board of Consumers was divided between the "good ol' boys" from the Westmount (Montreal) establishment and Cecil Franklin, a farmer who had been a successful miner and was by then an industrialist and the chair of Algonquin Mercantile, which he controlled. Franklin had been a client of Jones Heward, a stockbroker and money manager, and, at Brian Heward's invitation, joined the board of Consumers. He simultaneously purchased a large share position not long after the GIE fiasco when the share price dropped significantly. Periodically, Franklin topped up to his position.

One day in 1977, I arrived late to a Consumers board meeting at the St. James Club in Montreal. I walked into a room charged with tension, the animosity palpable. At a break, I asked the president, Bob Morison, what was going on. Morison snapped, "Didn't you see the *Globe and Mail* this morning?" and showed me the brief clip from the summary section of the previous day's trading reports. A reporter had called Franklin, who acknowledged having bought a relatively significant block of Consumers shares. The reporter asked Franklin if he was intending to go for control, and Franklin gave an ambivalent response: he didn't say he was or wasn't. Clearly Heward saw this as a threat and was furious. Franklin was not a smooth St. James Street (or Bay Street) financier, but rather a no-nonsense, somewhat abrasive businessman. He wasn't happy with the progress of Consumers and felt that management hid behind the skirts of the family patriarch, Brian Heward, who acted the feudal lord.

Heward behaved as if he controlled the company. In fact, through family trusts and accounts managed by Jones Heward & Co. Limited, his brokerage firm, he held about 20 percent of the stock, while another 10-percent block held by the employee pension fund was voted by him. Another 18 percent was held Brockway Glass Company as a result of the partnership formed in 1960 by Don Mingay.

Heward took other tactics and, at one point in 1977, railroaded the board into agreeing to the formation of an executive committee of the board that excluded Franklin. I spoke against the idea (philosophically) as did Franklin, on the basis that it created two classes of directors. Later on, Franklin was added to the committee as the other directors realized they had created an unhealthy situation with a major shareholder. However, this wasn't the last time I would witness a clique controlling and manipulating the board of a public company.

After that meeting, I shared a taxi to the airport with Franklin and we flew back to Toronto together. I didn't know Franklin well, but asked him, "Why do you put up with that nonsense? Why don't you get in or out?" He replied that he would prefer to gain control and do something constructive with the company, but didn't have enough resources to do so. I said, "I'll find you a partner if you like and put together a plan." Franklin said, "Great! Let's get on with it."

Before I moved on this idea, I left the board. Brian Heward had asked me to go, as I was clearly not spiritually part of the Heward block. Small irritants divided me from the inner sanctum—one day Morison called to say "the chairman" had asked him to call me because Heward wanted to buy more Consumers stock for the employee pension fund. I replied, "Why would you buy Consumers at a P/E of 20 and no dividend, when you can buy Brockway at a P/E of 10 and a yield of 5½ percent?" Of course, this was not the desired response as Heward was clearly trying to add to his control position. It was typical of Heward to avoid an unpleasant task by sending Morison to make the call, knowing full well that I would disagree with the proposal.

* * *

I brought in Albert Gnat, a friend and a lawyer, and together we developed a plan for Franklin, which was to bid $18 per share (the stock was then trading at about $12). There were enough redundant assets in the company that the premium would not have been a stretch. I recommended a wealthy Canadian real estate operator as a financial partner and, on February 22, 1978, made introductions. The two accepted the plan I put forward, agreed to go fifty-fifty in funding and shook hands. I was to be an adviser and participant. Before he left, I gave Franklin some advice, "You must not discuss this with anyone, especially Brockway, who will pick up the telephone and call Heward. And, you must prepare the tender offer and approach Heward directly, but be prepared to publicly announce the tender offer immediately. You know he will oppose it."

Franklin agreed and then weeks passed by. One Friday in May, just as I was leaving with my wife for a two-week vacation in Britain, I received a call from Franklin inviting me for an update. At lunch, Franklin apologized for not having kept me abreast of events, but said he had decided not to partner with my candidate, as he had been persuaded by his adviser at Triarch Corporation to partner with Brascan. He said that my role was assured, even though he knew of my difficult relationship with Jake Moore, the chair of Brascan. He then told me that he and his Triarch adviser had travelled to Pittsburgh to meet Brockway management, where they had a very constructive meeting. I interrupted his last sentence and said, "You're dead." He assured me Brockway would remain neutral and not breach its assurance of confidentiality. I reiterated," You're dead—absolutely finished."

I went on my holiday, and when I returned, Bay Street was abuzz with the news of Franklin's aborted takeover bid.

As predicted, Brockway had alerted the Montreal group on the Consumers board to the bid, giving them time to prepare their defences, threatening lawsuits and alleging insider trading, Franklin being chair of the audit committee. In the crisis, Franklin ran for cover, and sold his 10-percent position to Brascan.

* * *

To finish the story, Brascan was taken over by Edper in 1979. Edper was treated as an undesirable shareholder by the management of Consumers in concert with the Montreal group on the board. Edper built its stake to 25.5 percent, and then sold it to Enfield Corporation, formed in April 1984 by Michael Blair, a former vice-president of engineering with Canadian General Electric. Enfield was funded 50 percent by Pagurian Corporation controlled by Christopher Ondaatje, 25 percent by Ben Webster, and 25 percent (mainly founder shares) by Blair.

By 1985, Enfield bought 19 percent of Consumers Packaging and in 1986 brought Brascan's 26 percent of Consumers and later the Brockway holding, giving Enfield 59 percent of Consumers. By 1988, Blair had an unhappy falling out with Ondaatje over a disputed transaction. In May 1989, Enfield caused Consumers Packaging to acquire its arch-competitor, Domglas, creating a virtual monopoly for glass containers in Canada.

In 1985 and 1986, I periodically had lunch with Michael Blair, CEO of Enfield, to discuss a variety of subjects. Inevitably, Consumers would come up in the conversation and Blair would tell me how unwelcome the Montreal group on the board and Consumers management had made him feel. He told me that the management of Consumers had called a board meeting when they knew Blair was supposed to be in Japan, intending to have their friendly directors pass some significant matters relating to management compensation and pensions. Someone tipped Blair off and he flew back from Japan on the weekend and, on the Monday, he persuaded the board to fire Morison and several other members of management.

Unfortunately, Consumers overpaid for Dominion, and the timing for the transaction was completely atrocious: it coincided with the advent of free trade, meaning lower tariffs as well as unfavourable exchange rates. In addition, glass container customers generally ensured that they had two suppliers to assure quality, service, and constant supply; by creating a monopoly in Canada, customers had to find alternative suppliers, so the transaction effectively opened the door to the Canadian market for American companies. Finally, the merger was apparently very badly managed and the company became chaotic. The stock fell from $26 per share in 1989 to a low of 40 cents in 1992. By that time it was a "walking bankruptcy" (once again!), this time with the Bank of Nova Scotia keeping it alive, while Burns Fry tried to find an equity investor. At $26, the market capitalization had been $676 million; at 40 cents, it dropped to $10.4 million.

* * *

In May 1993, over a chance social lunch, Rob Franklin, Cecil's son, then chair of Placer Dome,[2] told me that Ted Kernaghan, of Thomson Kernaghan & Company, had been analyzing Consumers Packaging and felt there may be an opportunity to put a group together to rescue the company. This led to a meeting of the three of us on May 19, 1993, with Jim Bacon, president and CEO of Consumers. I didn't realize I knew Jim until I saw him—we had worked together at Canadian Resins and Chemicals Ltd. in Montreal in 1957–58, where he had been a salesman. Jim had risen to the presidency of Consumers through the plastics division.

After a lengthy discussion, we came to the conclusion the company was headed for bankruptcy unless a substantial equity infusion was made. We decided it was not for us.

On August 31, 1993, control (57.7 percent) of Consumers was sold to Glenshaw (G&G Investments Inc.), a U.S. company, for $9.7 million, or 65 cents per share.

* * *

Going back to my personal story, in August 1970, I called Bill Wilder, then chair and CEO of Wood Gundy, the investment bank, and invited him to lunch. I was happy to find that Bill was not surprised at my decision to leave Consumers. He asked me what I'd like to do, and I replied that ideally I'd like to be CEO of a widely diversified company with strong financial resources. Immediately Bill said, "What about Brascan?" I replied that sounded like it had potential. Consumers had recently sent a team of technical experts to Brazil to assess an investment in a glass container operation that Brascan would buy, with funds locked in Brazil and which Consumers would operate for a fee while holding a minority interest. Also, I knew Jake Moore, the president of Brascan who was also chair of John Labatt Limited, the beer, food, and wine conglomerate, in which Brascan held a 24 percent interest. Labatt was a major customer of mine at Consumers and I had met Moore at industry and customer functions.

In 1964, U.S.-based Joseph Schlitz Brewing Company was headed by an ex-Canadian Breweries executive, Jim Blyth. Schlitz made a successful tender offer to buy Labatt for $39 million, but the U.S. Department of Justice upset the bid when it placed an anti-trust restraining order on the transaction because Labatt owned a brewery in the United States, which the anti-trust panel said would constitute restraint of trade. As a consequence, Labatt was on the lookout for a "white knight" to step in and keep the company Canadian.

Enter Tony Griffin of Triarch Corporation, a small Toronto merchant bank, spawned in 1953 by Sir Siegmund Warburg, founder of S.G. Warburg & Co. in London. Griffin and the management of Labatt (together with Brascan and loans from CIBC) created Jonlab Investments Ltd. to buy the Labatt block of shares back from Schlitz. Subsequently, Moore became president of Brascan, and early in 1970, an 8-percent block of Brascan was purchased from International Utilities, funded by the sale of Jonlab's holding in Labatt to Brascan. The result was that Jonlab ended up with 8 percent of Brascan, the vast electric utility in Brazil, which in turn owned 24 percent of Labatt, and 40 percent of Jonlab, as well as cash and other investments. Clearly there was a lot of scope for deal-making and, according to Wilder, Moore needed someone to help him at the top, as well as a successor. Wilder approached Moore on my behalf and Moore agreed I was an ideal candidate for the position. At the end of the lunch with Wilder, I asked a key and prophetic question, "I hear you, but does Moore *really* want someone?" Bill assured me that he did.

We agreed I would start in February 1971, as executive vice-president of Jonlab (strictly a holding company), and have an office in Brascan. When I arrived at Brascan it quickly became apparent that Moore was a consummate microman-ager, making key decisions for Labatt and other subsidiaries, as well as for Brascan. Coincident with my arrival, Jonlab bought Triarch for an exorbitant price, Moore's idea being to use it as a nucleus for building an international merchant bank, British-style.

5

From Candy Mergers to Cable Mergers, 1971–1974

"When you get to be President, there are all those
things, the honours, the twenty-one gun salutes, all
those things you have to remember it isn't for you.
It's for the Presidency, and you've got to keep
yourself separate from that in your mind."

Harry S. Truman

Within the first two or three weeks of starting work, I went
to Jake Moore and asked him why he wanted me around, as I
seemed to have no real role in the company. After some discussion he suggested I go to Brazil to meet the head of Brascan's
operations there, Antonio Gallotti, with the idea that if Gallotti
liked me, Moore would make me executive vice-president of
Brascan and give me appropriate responsibilities. However,
the next day, having consulted with his wife, Moore said he'd
changed his mind and I now had two options: I could move
to Triarch as president, or I would have to go to Brascan and
"earn my position." I wasn't comfortable with these choices
and told him I'd made a mistake and would resign.

I called Don Mingay for lunch and he tried to persuade me
to return to Consumers Glass as president. I said I couldn't
go back. Don cautioned me: "You can't go around declining
presidencies every day." I thought about it overnight then went

back to Moore and suggested that I move to Triarch, spend one year expanding the company or securing a merger partner in order to give the company critical mass, and recruit a successor for Tony Griffin (the founder and incumbent CEO). After this, I would leave and Moore and I would part friends. He agreed and I went to Triarch as chairman of the executive committee and also became president and CEO of Jonlab, the top holding company.

As I became more deeply involved in Triarch's business, I found that I got along extremely well with Tony Griffin. Because of the similarity of our names, we have been forever confused, sometimes in amusing circumstances. On one occasion, Griffin and I were each meeting guests whom we did not know personally at the Toronto Club. The receptionist announced that my guest had arrived. On meeting a stuffy Englishman about 20 years older than the American I thought I was meeting, I led him upstairs to the second-floor dining room and ordered drinks. After some polite but stilted conversation, I finally said, to his astonishment, "I know what's happened; you're here to meet Tony *Griffin*. I'm Tony *Griffiths*." I led the man, still looking very puzzled, back downstairs and found my guest had arrived. Griffin called me the following day, roaring with laughter saying, "Thanks. I dined out on that story last night." Not only did Tony Griffin and I become close personal friends, but at times Tony also acted as the buffer between Jake Moore and me. Tony introduced me around the London banks, including Warburg, Kleinwort Benson, Hill Samuel, Schroders, Hambros, Samuel Montagu, and Baring Brothers. I remember writing my father that there was a veil of mystery around the "merchant bankers" and in many ways they were more form than substance. I said in my letter, "It's a bit like the blind leading the blind." Forty years later, as

I write this book, not much has changed—investment bankers continue to dazzle with their smoke and mirrors—although they have been generally hugely profitable.

About the time I agreed to join Triarch, I received a call from Pat Rourke, an executive search consultant from Montreal. Pat had joined Payne-Ross as Jim Westcott's understudy at about the time I started with Consumers Glass. Pat met me in Toronto and said he had the ideal job for me: president of Standard Brands Canada in Montreal. Pat asked if I would meet the chair of the company, Gaetan Morrissette, who was coming to Toronto. Standard Brands had been a customer of mine at Consumers, which is how Morrissette knew of me. I told Pat I didn't think it would work because I had a fine home in Toronto, was building a country house at my farm at Creemore near Georgian Bay, and preferred not to move back to Montreal. In addition, I felt I had to honour my obligation to Moore and Wilder, whom I had kept abreast of my tribulations at Jonlab, even though I had begun to realize I could not work with Moore. At Rourke's insistence, I agreed to meet Morrissette for breakfast in his suite the next morning at the Royal York Hotel. Morrissette encouraged me to pursue the job by meeting with the Standard Brands people in the United States who would make the decision, but discussions stopped when I suggested the corporate (executive) office be moved to Toronto from Montreal.

About two months later, after a big blow-up with Moore, I picked up the phone and asked Rourke if the Standard Brands job was still open. Rourke checked, called me back, and told me if I flew to Montreal, I could meet Morrissette and a senior vice-president, Les Applegate from New York, at the St. Denis Club for dinner. I immediately went to Montreal and, when I met Morrissette, he asked me what had changed my mind.

I told him I couldn't work with Moore. At the end of dinner, he and Applegate said, "We've got one problem: we've offered the job to someone else and, if he accepts, we feel honour bound to let him have it." That person was F. Ross Johnson, who was also someone I knew personally. Ross accepted the job. (He would become famous in the late 1980s in the RJR Nabisco takeover activities recounted in the book *Barbarians at the Gate*.[1])

* * *

In March 1972, Ross came to see me at Triarch and asked for my view of a suggestion to merge Standard Brands's two chocolate companies—Moirs in Halifax and Lowney in Montreal—with Labatt's Laura Secord. Moirs had an obsolete plant and too much business to be accommodated by Lowney. Laura Secord[2] had a brand-new plant, which was working well below capacity and could easily accommodate the requirements of both Moirs *and* Lowney. Ross said he didn't care who controlled the merged entity—that should depend on the ultimate revenue and profit configuration of the company. Ross was always in favour of "monopolies that made lots of money" and had been investigated under the Combines Investigation Act while at three different companies: Canadian General Electric, Eaton's, and General Steel Wares (GSW). When we compared notes , Ross told me that in the last of his three inquisitions led by Dr. Henry, Henry had asked how Ross's salesmen knew the prices of his competitors' product. In a typical Ross Johnson response—seizing the offensive—he replied, "If I ever catch one of my salesmen not knowing his competitors' prices, he's fired."

I said we should examine his proposal and he agreed to send me Standard's numbers. When I put them together with Laura Secord's figures the scenario appeared to hold water, except that Standard would be the dominant company by virtue of its greater revenues, profits, and other criteria. It worked out that Labatt could sell Laura Secord to Standard and *more than recover* the inflated price it had originally paid for the company. As Labatt was well underwater on the Laura Secord purchase based on the original purchase price and subsequent investments in the company, the deal would have been a tremendous coup for Labatt shareholders.

I took the plan to Moore who initially liked it, but when told who the prospective purchaser was, replied, "There's no goddamned way I'll sell to the Americans." I went home and thought about it, and went in to see Moore the next day. With considerable trepidation I said, "We all know Laura's a 'dog' and that 'we' overpaid for it; let's lay it off on those goddamned Americans."

Unfortunately, Moore was offended by this comment and the project was killed. I now had the problem of explaining this to Johnson. I told him the truth, at which he roared with laughter. Johnson then stole Laura Secord's young general manager, Peter Rogers, who became a key player at Standard Brands and Nabisco in the United States over the next 10 to 15 years, running Planters Nut and Curtiss Candy.

* * *

During my early years with Jonlab/Brascan, Moore asked me to evaluate a proposed Brascan investment in the Sukunka Coal Mine Project in northern British Columbia. For at least a year, a Brascan vice-president had been studying a major investment in this underground coal mining project. I met with him in his office, where he was surrounded by volumes of blue binders, most of which were reports from a variety of consultants. It quickly became evident to me that not only had Sukunka taken on a life of its own within Brascan but it was also the man's raison d'être. Without it, he was out of a job. However, he also knew that he didn't have Moore's confidence, a fact that Moore admitted. I suggested to Moore that he should let the vice-president go with appropriate severance. Moore agreed, but predictably did not follow up—his method of dealing with these situations being to ignore them and hope they would go away, which, of course, was cowardly and mean, causing stress and uncertainty for those involved.

Through an international coal dealer, Moore had connected with a small Australian company called Austen & Butta, who he had decided was going to operate Sukunka. Because of my Australian experience, I was sent to evaluate Austen & Butta. After two weeks, I decided that the company was too small for the undertaking, being essentially a one-man operation (Dick Austen). Moreover, Austen & Butta were strip miners, while Sukunka was an underground project. In addition, Dick Austen expressed his misgivings about the point man for the project, knowing of his position vis-à-vis Moore. I again recommended that Moore level with his vice-president.

I also met with a former consultant to the project, Dr. David Robertson, a geologist, who said he thought it would be a disaster because of the uneven geology in the ore body. When Robertson submitted his report to the vice-president, he was removed from the project. I asked

Robertson if he was willing to tell Moore his views if I arranged a meeting. Robertson agreed and met with Moore, who ignored his advice.

In the end, I recommended to Moore that he find a large, competent North American mining partner to take on the project. However, Moore also ignored *my* advice, and Brascan bought a minority holding in Austen & Butta. The vice-president was moved to Vancouver to coordinate building the infrastructure for the mine.

A year or so later, it became evident that Sukunka was a disaster and Brascan was forced to write it off.[3] In his book *The Canadian Establishment: Volume Two: The Acquisitors*, Peter C. Newman said of Brascan: "It was this kind of ineptitude that gradually established an undercurrent of dissatisfaction with Moore's management style. 'Brascan's record of earnings has been one of the worst in North America over the past five years,' Andy Sarlos (Canadian financier and Bay Street power broker) told the *Toronto Star*."[4]

* * *

While this was happening, I became heavily involved in a company called Toronto & London Investments Limited (T&L), a publicly traded, closed-end investment fund, managed by Elliott & Page, a 100-percent-owned investment advisory subsidiary of Triarch. Various companies held stakes in T&L, including Triarch, 9 percent; S.G. Warburg, 12 percent; Samuel Montagu & Co., 8 percent; and various closed-end funds controlled by Sir Denys Lowson, 17 percent. Tony Griffin was chair; I was on the board representing Triarch and Jonlab; and Peter Stormonth Darling represented S.G. Warburg.

The main public investors were the "little old widows of Kent," as Warburg referred to them.

Peter had done a stint at Triarch with Tony Griffin before returning to S. G. Warburg in London. While Tony and Peter were the glue between Triarch and Warburg, I was the interface with Jonlab. Privately we shared our worries about the uncertain relationship with Moore regarding Triarch/T&L versus Jonlab/Brascan—Moore was always a loose cannon, waiting to use T&L for Brascan purposes.

Warburg maintained that it controlled the investment policy of T&L by virtue of having sponsored it for many years. T&L was a conservative, unexciting fund and the Jonlab people wanted to turn it into a high-growth vehicle, concentrating on 8 to 10 stocks, rather than the 30 to 40 it was then holding. Jake Moore saw it as a possible place to park some Brascan stock, as well as holdings in other potential acquisitions for Jonlab. However, to change the portfolio mix so radically would jeopardize the dividend, which Warburg adamantly opposed. I suggested to Moore that we canvass Lowson's views, since he was the largest single shareholder but was not represented on the board. Warburg was opposed to letting Lowson on the board because they felt his business methods were controversial. Lowson had been Lord Mayor of London during Coronation Year (1953) and had made a wide variety of international investments through a complicated network of closed-end trusts (most with cross-ownerships). He also owned three well-known restaurants in London, one of which was the fashionable Le Caprice.

In October 1972, Tony Griffin and I met with Lowson in London and he immediately endorsed the idea of transforming T&L into a growth portfolio, even if it meant dropping the dividend. Lowson insisted upon board representation and, eventually, Lowson's Canadian lawyer, Doug Berlis of Aird & Berlis, joined the board of T&L.

In May 1973, I received a very fancy invitation from Sir Denys Lowson to attend a dinner at the Plaisterers' Hall at which Premier David Barrett of British Columbia (a socialist) was the speaker. This was a major event with champagne and caviar flowing, chamber music and orchestras, toastmaster, and guests that included bankers, labour leaders, etc. I was seated at the head table and that night Lowson was the toast of London.

I had agreed to meet Peter Darling the next day for a drink at 6:00 p.m. at the Berkeley Hotel. I got back to the hotel about 4:00 p.m. and decided to take a walk in Knightsbridge. At the first newspaper kiosk I passed, I saw the headline: "LOWSON INDICTED!" The accompanying article described a transaction where Lowson bought a company in his closed-end investment trusts, with the knowledge that another company was prepared to pay a multiple of his purchase price, allowing him to flip the investment for a big profit. The shareholders who sold to Lowson were now suing him for not disclosing that he had a buyer on the other side. There was a subsequent investigation, which humiliated Lowson. He died a few years later with his reputation in tatters.

* * *

About six months later I learned from Doug Berlis that Sir Denys and his son Ian were coming to Canada for a visit and that Sir Denys would like to see me. I suggested to Jake Moore that we should hold a small dinner for Sir Denys as, in light of his circumstances, he might want to sell his 17-percent holding in T&L. Moore was horrified at the suggestion and declined. Finally Eddie Goodman helped me convince Moore, who would only agree to entertain Lowson out of the public eye. I arranged a dinner in a private dining room at Toronto's upscale La Scala restaurant, which was attended by the two Lowsons, Berlis, Moore, Goodman, Norman E. (Peter) Hardy, and me. Several weeks later my telephone rang and Berlis advised that Jonlab could buy Lowson's T&L holding at market price, which we did, giving us a commanding 26 percent of the stock. We then met with Warburg and, in the interests of ongoing relations, agreed to co-operate in the sale of T&L. It was bought by Slater Walker of Canada, which then changed its name to an acronym, Talcorp.

* * *

In 1972, Eddie Goodman persuaded the Jonlab board that we should invest in the cable television business, which had the earmarks of high-growth potential. At the time, there were three alternatives for entry into the business:

- Rogers Cable, controlled by E.S. (Ted) Rogers, which was financed by high-interest debt
- Cablecasting, a small company holding properties with high subscriber-growth potential controlled by two Harvard Business School entrepreneurs, David Graham and Jim Meekison
- Canadian Cablesystems, a public company comprising the communications operations spun off from Famous Players, a theatre and real estate company. In the reorganization of assets, Cablesystems retained 49 percent ownership in Famous Players with Gulf & Western Industries (G&W) holding the balance through Paramount, a G&W subsidiary at that time.

Cablesystems held the second-largest shareholding in Bushnell Communications (CJOH television) in Ottawa, which in turn held cable investments, as well as holdings in BCTV, and four major CATV franchises: Metro Cable in residential central Toronto, Grand River (Kitchener & Waterloo), part of Hamilton, and all of Cornwall. The company had two professional managers (in marketing and finance) and the president was Willard Z. (Bud) Estey, who also ran one of Toronto's largest law practices, Robertson, Lane, Perrett, Frankish & Estey, and was involved in political strategy with Pierre Trudeau, John Turner, and others.

My life would become intertwined with each of these three cable TV companies over the next 12 years. A quick appraisal of the three alternatives led Jonlab to Cablesystems. Rogers and Cablecasting were both controlled and run by entrepreneurs who would not be easy to live with. One of Jonlab's key objectives was to provide liquidity to its shareholders by becoming a publicly traded company, and Cablesystems could provide a suitable vehicle for this. Cablesystems offered the prospect of allowing Jonlab to exercise effective control of the company, with the possibility of a merger through a reverse takeover.

The promoters of a Jonlab investment in Cablesystems were Bob Wisener and Larry Brenzel of Wisener & Partners, a Toronto stock brokerage. A dinner was arranged at the Albany Club in Toronto in three adjacent rooms, one each for Jonlab, Cablesystems, and Wisener, to see if a deal could be negotiated. After considerable coming and going, Jake Moore asked for a straw vote of the Jonlab directors on the proposition that

Jonlab acquire 12 percent of Cablesystems, the largest single ownership block giving effective control of the company, at a stipulated price.

When it came to my turn to speak as a director, I spoke against the purchase saying that the price at 20 times earnings was too expensive and the company had thin, weak management with little technical expertise. At the time, Metro Cable had serious equipment and operational problems and would have to rebuild or face losing its licence—we had no idea what the cost of this work would be. There were complicating factors from Cablesystems's stake in Famous Players: half of Cablesystems's earnings were from Famous Players, which was controlled by a "madman" (according to Estey) in New York, Charles Bluhdorn, founder and controlling shareholder and chair of G&W. Finally, my information was that the president, Estey, would not be an easy man to influence. In my view, all of these factors made the possibility of a reverse takeover remote.

When the final vote was taken, however, I was the lone opposer and Jonlab forged ahead. I joined the board of Cablesystems together with John Cronyn (another Jonlab director) to represent Jonlab.

* * *

During the next year, all the problems I had foreseen became real, and Jonlab soon found itself as a minority shareholder with two of thirteen or so board seats. Bud Estey had little confidence in his two managers and often overruled their decisions. In addition, Bud seemed to be increasingly busy with his burgeoning law practice and Moore began pressing me to get certain things done at Cablesystems. As a director, however, I had no operational authority. At Christmas time in 1972, I met Moore at Labatt headquarters in London, Ontario, about a Brascan matter, and he expressed his exasperation at Cablesystems's apparently slow progress. When I told him I didn't think there was anything we could do as long as Bud Estey was in charge, Moore paused reflectively and to my surprise said, "Maybe he'll die."

Then, one day in January 1973, I had an urgent call from Bud Estey. I went to Bud's office across the street and he told me in greatest confidence that he was going to be appointed to the Ontario Court of Appeal (he was eventually appointed to the Supreme Court of Canada in 1977). He felt that I was the logical person to succeed him as president of Cablesystems. I thanked him for his confidence in me, and agreed on the spot to take the job, partly to build further distance between myself and Jake Moore. I thought Moore would be delighted to send me off to a "subsidiary," out of his hair. Our relationship chafed continually and he was becoming increasingly uncivil toward me. While Jake Moore was my boss, he was also my nemesis.

When I relayed my decision to become CEO of Cablesystems to the Jonlab directors, they deliberated about letting me go. They didn't know it, but my mind was made up. I argued that they'd always wanted to control Cablesystems, and now was their chance by getting their man in there. A compromise was reached whereby I would become president and CEO of Cablesystems and continue in my role as president and CEO of the holding company Jonlab. My salary and related costs would be shared between the companies. This dual role of CEO of two companies while also a director on both boards would complicate my life in the near future.

* * *

Just prior to taking the Cablesystems position, I had pursued with Estey the idea of Cablesystems buying Jonlab, on the premise that the takeover would give Jonlab shareholders marketability and liquidity, and Estey could be the chair of the combined entity. Much to my surprise he agreed, and both sides had worked diligently toward finalizing the terms and conditions of the deal. The project moved quickly to the point of pricing and taking the pulse of the Canadian Radio-television and Telecommunications Commission (CRTC) toward the transaction. It turned out that the CRTC was enthusiastic about the merger because it would have provided Cablesystems with ballast and taken it off the vulnerability list as a takeover target (with no one shareholder having effective control of the company, Cablesystems was an attractive target for other players and the CRTC was looking for stability in the market). The draft prospectus was printed and final pricing was being negotiated when suddenly Moore called a break-fast meeting of the Jonlab directors and announced Brascan was not proceeding. He had been advised by his Brascan legal counsel, Alex McIntosh of Blake, Cassels & Graydon, that if the issue of foreign ownership in Cablesystems (through the Brascan holding) was questioned at the CRTC hearings, this might prompt the Brazilian government to question Canadian ownership of a Brazilian enterprise.

I thought this a bit far-fetched and said so, pointing out that when the merger of Cablesystems and Jonlab occurred, the Brascan holding in the combined company would be approximately 16 percent, well under the 20 percent that was permitted under the Canadian Broadcasting Act. Moore threw a tantrum saying, "That's the trouble with you—you don't understand these things." I soon learned that with Moore, Alex McIntosh's advice went unchallenged.

I left the breakfast and flew to Ottawa to attend my first board meeting of Bushnell Communications, where I had succeeded Bud Estey as the representative of Cablesystems. I arrived at a meeting where the atmosphere could have been cut with a knife. Bushnell was the target of a takeover bid by Western Broadcasting Corp. (WIC), under the leadership of its controlling shareholder Frank Griffiths; Bushnell was headed by Stuart Griffiths (neither of whom was related to me or to each other). This also happened to be the day of the Bushnell annual general meeting, and a proxy fight was anticipated on the floor.

At the AGM that afternoon, John Holmes, head of the Ownership Section of the CRTC, approached me and said, "I guess we'll be seeing a lot more of each other." When we agreed he was referring to the proposed Jonlab/Cablesystems merger, I said, "Forget it. That died this morning at break-fast." When I explained the Moore/McIntosh rationale, Holmes said, "That isn't a problem; why don't you talk to the chair [of the CRTC], Pierre Juneau?"

Like a good soldier I went back to Toronto and commu-nicated this to Eddie Goodman, Jonlab's legal adviser and director, and this led to Goodman, McIntosh (representing Brascan), Albert Gnat (representing Cablesystems as Estey's successor as legal counsel), and myself travelling to Ottawa for a private meeting with Juneau. When McIntosh expressed his concerns on Brascan's behalf, Juneau told him not to worry. He said, "If an intervention should arise at the hearing that may in anyway make you [Brascan] uncomfortable, we can withdraw your application without explanation." We all went back to Toronto, Goodman, Gnat, and I feeling confident. However, in a day or two, Moore told Goodman he was not prepared to proceed and the deal died. I felt disappointed, but also realized that the merger would have put me back directly under Moore's thumb.

This whole episode was a lost opportunity. The deal would have given the Jonlab shareholders everything they wanted. Many of those involved in the transaction (including me) believed that the real reason behind McIntosh's concern was his potential loss of influence over Brascan—with the power shifting to the Cablesystems/Jonlab shareholder axis and into Goodman's orbit. Moore lost his opportunity to guarantee control of the empire through Jonlab, as we shall see as the saga continues.

* * *

In mid-1973, while I settled into the CEO role at Cablesystems, I was also still CEO of Jonlab. Wearing my Jonlab hat, I continued searching for a strong partner to merge with Triarch to give it breadth and critical mass. Through a business acquaintance, Matthew Gaasanbeek, I came across Commerce Capital Corporation (CCC) run by Jack Whitely. With my fellow directors interested, I negotiated a deal with Whitely to merge Triarch with CCC, in which Jonlab would wind up with 20 percent plus of CCC, have board representation, be able to "equity account" the earnings, and become the largest single shareholder, *without putting up any cash*! The combination of Triarch with CCC would accomplish all my objectives when I made the commitment to Moore in 1971 to build or merge Triarch into a viable enterprise.

However, at this point my relationship with Moore had become untenable. Basically he was tired of listening to advice he didn't want to hear. On my part, I was not prepared to acquiesce in business transactions I did not think made sense and for which I would wind up being responsible as management.

My unhappy relationship with Jake Moore was not unique. In their book *The Brass Ring*, authors Patricia Best and Ann Shortell give what I believe is a reasonably balanced description of his management style:

> Jake Moore was not well liked. He was a large man physically, and within the company he played the part he looked—a bullying capitalist. Moore relished the trappings of office. In 1978, he was the country's third-highest-paid executive. He had constructed a disproportionately large head-office staff. He particularly wanted young MBAs to be available at a moment's notice to do an analysis of anything that struck his fancy. That sort of meddling and second-guessing of their work drove executives at some of the subsidiaries crazy.[5]

The management of Jonlab (myself as CEO) and Triarch were becoming concerned about Jonlab's debt levels, but Moore's view was quite the opposite. Since his key directors were cronies, they went along with him, rarely expressing objections. Board meetings were relaxed and cheery without him, but dour and humourless when he was present. Norman (Peter) Hardy was Moore's chief lieutenant. We crowned him "the organ grinder's monkey" since he was very obsequious in the presence of Moore.

Moore had also put a new director, an ex-Labatt manager, on the Jonlab board. This was Joseph William Carson, a yes-man of Moore's, who began expressing more than normal interest (for a director) in the affairs of Jonlab.

Early in 1974, as I was about to conclude the agreement between CCC and Triarch, I suddenly discovered that, *without advising me*, Moore had unilaterally sent Hardy to make a different deal with Whitely. The new transaction provided that Jonlab would purchase 33 percent of CCC *for $3.3 million* cash. This was an unnecessary expenditure of cash at a point when Jonlab was already over-leveraged.

When Carson came to my office the day after the completion of the CCC transaction, I asked him directly what was going on. When he gave me the usual oblique non-answer, I lost my temper. He confessed that Moore had hired him to look up my skirts. I told Carson that they were all a bunch of devious cowards. This led to an informal board meeting of Jonlab in June 1974, which I did not attend. It was later reported to me that all directors spoke highly of me, and apparently Moore "acknowledged my talents" but said he could not work with me.

It was decided that I would go to Cablesystems full time, which suited me, though I was regretfully still within the Brascan orbit. Peter Hardy succeeded me as president (and chair) of Jonlab. Soon after consummating the merger of Triarch with CCC, there was a major falling-out between Whitely and the Jonlab directors (particularly Hardy, Carson, and Moore), at which point, Jonlab determined to rid itself of the CCC investment.

6

Cable Wars Go Public, 1973–1977

"The fault, dear Brutus, is not in our stars,
but in ourselves. . ."
Shakespeare, Julius Caesar

I became president of Cablesystems in February 1973, and quickly set about putting in proper budgets, management reporting systems, and controls, all of which were lacking. The earliest cable TV systems, from the 1950s, were typically built by individuals who today might be considered to have limited qualifications for the task—master antenna installers, and radio and TV technicians, for example. There were very few graduate engineers in the fledgling industry, and the fact is, they too were new to the game. It was not until the 1970s that the first fully qualified radio frequency engineer was employed (by Cablesystems) and that's when the engineering side of cable TV systems truly began to professionalize. Famous Players owned interests in numerous cable TV systems across Canada in the early years. Its modus operandi was to rely on local partners, even where it had a controlling interest.

One of these systems was run by the Jarmain family from London, Ontario.

The Jarmains had assembled six cable TV systems in Ontario, covering two-thirds of London and the towns of Brantford, Newmarket, Kingston, Oshawa, and Chatham (which they owned as a 50-percent partnership). They had the technical discipline and engineering talent that Cablesystems lacked. The Jarmains had planned a public offering of shares in 1970 but that was pulled because of an adverse ruling from the CRTC. I approached Ted Jarmain, suggesting they merge with Cablesystems, with Ted coming in to run the cable operations. We would pay them half cash and half shares, and they would become the second-largest shareholder in Cablesystems, holding 8 percent, after Jonlab's 13 percent (later raised to 26 percent). Since the Jarmain and Labatt groups were both based in London, they knew each other and felt comfortable as shareholders with goals in common. As part of the deal, Jonlab gave a verbal commitment that it would not unilaterally sell its shares without including the Jarmains in the deal, in order to maintain effective control of the company. (Later, to my dismay and embarrassment, this understanding was not honoured.)

Soon after the transaction was completed in January 1974, Ted Jarmain became president (COO) and I became chair (CEO). Now holding 10 cable systems, we set out to standardize operations and reporting systems. In late 1973, anticipating the transaction, we inherited Cableshare (founded by the Jarmains), a computer utility for all of our systems, in a joint venture with Terry Pocock.[1] In addition, we created Cablesystems Engineering to explore leading-edge technical applications and ensure standardization of equipment throughout our systems. Our vision was to become the leader in cable TV across all aspects of the business.

* * *

In 1974, the stock market fell precipitously to new lows. At the same time, Jonlab was becoming highly leveraged. This put Jonlab under pressure with the Canadian Imperial Bank of Commerce, where Moore was on the executive committee, because the company's asset base consisted of shares in its underlying companies.

Out of the blue, on February 8, 1974, a week after we concluded the purchase of the Jarmain companies, Cablesystems stock started to trade heavily at higher prices and it soon became apparent that Ted Rogers was the buyer. He purchased 13 percent of the shares in the company and began making overtures to Jonlab principals, Jake Moore, Goodman, et al., about taking control of Cablesystems in concert with Jonlab. Jonlab and Cablesystems complained to the CRTC and eventually the chair, Pierre Juneau, ordered Rogers to sell his Cablesystems shares. Jonlab bought them for $11 million ($18.30 per share), increasing its position to 26 percent. Together with the Jarmain holdings and management holdings, this amounted to about 35 percent of the company. In the aftermath, I believe the Jonlab people felt their emotions had overtaken their financial common sense.

When news of Rogers's purchases surfaced, Eddie Goodman went ballistic. Goodman, who was legal adviser and confidant to John Bassett, ranted that Rogers had breached his partnership agreement with Bassett at Baton, where the two held broadcasting and cable licences together. According to Goodman, Rogers had unfairly used a recent CRTC decision forcing the separation of cable from broadcasting to his advantage, breaking the spirit of the partnership. Ted Jarmain remembers Goodman taunting his fellow directors, "Are we going to let him do this to us?" and hearing the rejoinder, "Hell no!"[2] The irony is that Rogers may have succeeded had he gone about it more diplomatically, rather than blundering into the game as a raider.

On March 2, 1974, the *Financial Post* ran an article with the headline "Cablesystems: honors go to (Sir) Anthony" and, under a photograph of Rogers and me, ran the caption: "Still standing after the joust." The article began:

> Jousting for control of Canadian Cablesystems Ltd. appears to be over for now. And one of the two knights who fought each other with flails loaded with million-dollar bills now lies in the dust.
>
> Whether he may yet rise and resume the contest remains to be seen. Certainly, Anthony F. Griffiths, forty-three-year-old president of Cablesystems, is the knight left standing, firmly in control of the company.

In reality, I had nothing to do with the "joust," as I was neutralized by being CEO of both Jonlab and Cablesystems. In fact, I was not even in the room when the decision was made. Nevertheless, Rogers must have thought I was the one who stiffed him, when in reality it was Goodman.[3]

* * *

One of the first problems I had to deal with at Cablesystems was irritating, but also had its amusing aspects. In the summer of 1972, Bud Estey, who was a hockey buff, presented the board of Cablesystems with a proposal to invest in the Edmonton Oilers, a team playing in the newly formed World Hockey League (WHL). For $1 million, Cablesystems could buy 23 percent of the Oilers, while the other investors received a carried interest without putting up cash. The key partners in Edmonton were Dr. Charles Allard of Allarco, and his friends Zane Feldman and "Wild Bill" Hunter, who was a hockey addict and promoter of the league and the team. Hunter was slated to be the general manager of the team and the City of Edmonton was committed to building a 30,000-seat arena (replacing the existing 8,000-capacity arena) to be ready for the opening season. Estey put together an optimistic one-page financial model and told the board this was a unique opportunity for which "there was a lineup" and we had 24 hours to make our decision. Bud had an overpowering manner that did not tolerate opposition, and he pressed the board for a decision. The board acquiesced, albeit with some in opposition and considerable discomfort.

As soon as I became president of Cablesystems, I had a call from Charles Allard, whom I had not met, saying *we* had to hold a shareholders' meeting of the Oilers as soon as possible. When I asked why, he said we were out of money. After this sunk in, I said, "We already put up our money." You could have heard a pin drop at the other end. I agreed to go out and meet, but made it clear that Cablesystems was not putting up any more money, at least until our partners put their pro rata share in. Charles soon started paying the bills himself. In the meantime, matters went from bad to worse as losses mounted. Hunter had no controls and we discovered he had 36 players on the roster when we had been told there were 22.

Pictures appeared of the team travelling in a private jet, which turned out to be leased from Allarco. I'm not a hockey fan but knew enough of the history of the game to appreciate the gaffe Hunter made when he signed Jacques Plante, the former star goalie of the Montreal Canadiens, to an expensive three-year contract 10 years after Plante had retired. He played three or four games, "sprained his thumb," and seemed to disappear. After Charles and presumably Zane had put up the pro rata money for the Edmonton shareholders, the cash calls continued and, eventually, we allowed Cablesystems's share to be diluted down to nothing.

The Oilers investment was a good example of getting into something we, a cable company, had no business being in, especially as a minority shareholder in a start-up. It consumed an inordinate amount of management and board time because it was (embarrassingly) high profile. Charles was a wonderful man, who had been a very successful brain surgeon in Edmonton, and used his abundant cash flow to build Allarco into a very successful real estate, broadcasting, and hotel conglomerate. He admitted to having a blind spot in his dealings with Bill Hunter and, as Hunter was a good friend, Charles would not fire him. Because of his loyalty, Charles would rather keep paying the bills than shut down the project. My friend and colleague, Albert Gnat, once observed that Charles had an iron hand in a velvet glove, but in the case of Hunter, Charles was paralyzed.

* * *

One of my responsibilities as CEO was to represent Cablesystems on the Bushnell board. In February 1973,

I attended a board meeting at which feelings were running very high. Stuart Griffiths, the president, and Roy Faibish, the executive vice-president, were threatening to resign. Apparently, Frank Griffiths, the chair of Western Broadcasting (WIC), had indicated weeks before that he would support the board's nominations for directors at the annual general meeting. The previous night, however, he had advised that he was going to vote WIC's 51 percent to elect Bill Hughes, executive vice-president of WIC, to the board of Bushnell.

At the time, WIC was under an order by the CRTC to divest itself of Bushnell shares, which WIC had assembled in a "creeping takeover" without the approval of the CRTC. A CRTC hearing was scheduled, at which WIC intended to formally apply for approval to control Bushnell.

Around 11:00 a.m., Bushnell's external corporate legal counsel, Charlie O'Connor of Gowling Henderson, arrived. After remarking that he felt like he had walked into a funeral, he casually asked if anyone had checked WIC's proxies to see if the corporate seal was on them, without which they were not valid. Remarking that, "trust companies are notoriously sloppy," Charlie went out to check. When he came back half an hour later, he had a big smile on his face—his guess had been correct and WIC wouldn't have enough valid proxies to defeat management. A vote was held on the floor at the annual meeting later in the day and management won.

This was, however, a pyrrhic victory, because when WIC was forced to divest itself of the shares, a series of time-consuming and debilitating (for Bushnell management) hearings ensued over the next year or two, at which various parties sought approval from the CRTC to take control of the company by buying WIC's 51-percent block of shares.

Among the suitors were Robert Campeau, Allan Slaight represented by Trevor Eyton as legal counsel, and Standard Broadcasting, then controlled by Argus Corporation.

Standard eventually won approval and at the first meeting of the new board, Argus management, led by Brigadier General Bruce Matthews, arrived on the Argus jet. At the end of the meeting, General Matthews announced that Standard was going to charge Bushnell a "management fee." The three independent directors—Alvin Hamilton, the long-serving Tory MP and Diefenbaker cabinet minister; Gordon Blair, a lawyer later to become a judge; and I—were stunned. I asked the Argus directors to excuse themselves while we caucused—Matthews looked shocked that we would do this—and, when they left, I said to my colleagues, "I don't know about you, but there's no way I can bring myself to approve this." They both agreed and then insisted I be the spokesman when General Matthews returned. I explained that management fees could only be paid for services rendered, which were not apparent, and furthermore, because of Bushnell's relatively high profile with the CRTC, Argus should rethink the issue and raise it in six months or a year, if they still felt strongly about it. Matthews reluctantly agreed to this suggestion. Eventually Standard bought up 100 percent of Bushnell and, despite their asking me to stay, I decided to resign from the board.

* * *

By early 1975, we had a superb and aggressive management team at Cablesystems and, by most standards, were the industry leader. In the second week of May 1975, I attended the launch of the communications satellite Anik II at Cape Canaveral (now

Kennedy) in Florida and ran into Ben Torchinsky, the founder and CEO of Agra Industries. Agra had an investment in cable television through a subsidiary, Cablenet, with franchises in Oakville and Scarborough, Ontario, and in British Columbia. Over drinks before the launch, Ben approached me with the idea that Cablesystems and Agra form a joint venture to lease transponders on Anik II to deliver signals from the satellite to cable subscribers—a unique arrangement at the time. I immediately agreed to a fifty-fifty partnership and we approached David Golden, chair of Telesat,[4] about leasing the transponders. We followed up with Telesat over the next couple of weeks, paid a small fee, and sealed an agreement subject to CRTC approval. The fifty-fifty company we created was called CableSat. This was regarded as a coup within the industry when we announced it at the cable TV convention in Vancouver the third week in May, and aroused the envy and anger of others who viewed themselves as cable pioneers, including Ted Rogers and Geoff Conway, founder and CEO of another CATV group called CUC.

In June 1977, the senior management of Cablesystems travelled to Syracuse, N.Y., to apply for the city's cable franchise in competition with major U.S. operators. We won this contest, and Cablesystems became the first Canadian operator with a major franchise in the United States.

* * *

In late 1976, when Harry Boyle had succeeded Pierre Juneau as chair of the CRTC, Rogers purchased 21 percent of Premier Cablevision based in Vancouver. Premier was the largest (by subscriber count) cable television operator in Canada. Founded by Syd Welsh, a plumber, and some of his friends, the company was now experiencing dissension among the owners due to the death of one of the founders and liquidity requirements of some of the partners.

When I learned that Rogers had purchased 21 percent of Premier, I knew that Syd Welsh, the chair and controlling shareholder, would not be happy. I called Syd and suggested we meet to discuss a deal between Cablesystems and Premier to ward off takeovers. With Syd's encouragement, I telephoned Harry Boyle, chair of the CRTC, who indicated that the rules on cable concentration were changing and the CRTC was not going to disallow Rogers's purchase of Premier's shares. I then asked, "Then you won't object to Canadian Cablesystems getting together with Premier?" Harry said, "The field is open; we'll look at each case on its merits."

Syd Welsh's first preference was to do a deal with his friend Frank Griffiths of WIC, so we at Cablesystems waited on the sidelines to see what would transpire. Rumour had it that the CRTC would not permit WIC's attempt to buy 32 percent of Premier at $10.50 a share cash plus a share option for reasons to do with voting rights in a proposed merger of the two companies. On January 31, 1977, Rogers agreed to sell his shares in Premier to Western (WIC) for $10.30 per share.

We at Cablesystems geared up for a tender offer and, as soon as WIC's bid was turned down by the CRTC on July 29, 1977, we bid $10.50 a share for any Canadian-held Premier shares, up to 51 percent of the outstanding shares.

Meanwhile, we were also negotiating to acquire a cable franchise in the United States. The last week in July the CRTC approved Cablesystems's purchase of Community Antenna Television Ltd., which serviced half of the city of Calgary. We were on a roll.

On August 11, 1977, a telegram came addressed to: Mr. Tony Griffiths, Chairman, Cdn. Cablesystems Metro Ltd., that said:

DELIGHTED TO HEAR OF YOUR CLOSING IN CALGARY THRILLED TO HEAR OF YOUR SUCCESS IN SYRACUSE CONGRATULATIONS BUT PLEASE STAY AWAY FROM THE HAT TRICK BEST REGARDS
TED AND PHIL

This was Rogers and his sidekick Phil Lind referring to our bid for Premier.

On August 26, we raised our offer to $12 per share. CBS held 18 percent of Premier and did not want to sell at this price. We had many discussions with CBS and they finally agreed to co-operate with us, but wanted to stay out of the public (read: political) limelight. We also knew we were vulnerable because Brascan was getting itchy to sell its Cablesystems holdings. On Friday, September 2, 1977, Rogers bought Brascan's 26-percent holding of Cablesystems. (More on this story in a later chapter.)

As to Premier, Syd Welsh continued to defer to the advice of his friend Frank Griffiths, who persuaded Syd to take yet another approach to combining Premier and Western.

In 1975, an announcement in the *Globe and Mail* of the sale of Jonlab to Brascan caught me by surprise! To put this into context, the federal government had struck the Royal Commission on Corporate Concentration, known as the Bryce

Commission, to investigate corporate concentration, self-dealing, and the like. As reported:

> Brascan had paid an inordinate premium for the 60 percent of Jonlab it did not already own ($8 per share as compared with the $5 valuation by the Bryce Commission), that is, for the shares owned by Moore, Hardy, Goodman, Cronyn, Carson and others of the original Labatt LBO group. For several years, Jonlab, Labatt's and Brascan, had bought and sold each other's stock. . . . But in addition to the price tag of $13 million, Brascan had to assume a $30 million debt when Jonlab's bank, the Commerce, cashed in some preferred shares it held in the company. Brascan's legal officer resigned over the purchase.[5]

* * *

When I became president of Canadian Cablesystems in February 1973, I succeeded Bud Estey as a director of Famous Players Limited representing Cablesystems's 49-percent holding in Famous. Gulf & Western Industries (G&W) controlled Famous through Paramount. My first directors meeting was a few weeks later in Toronto and I was grateful to be invited to the Famous offices early, to be introduced to Don Gaston, executive vice-president. He was spokesman for Charles Bluhdorn when Bluhdorn was not there. Although Bluhdorn was chair of Famous, he rarely attended board meetings. Bluhdorn was the founder of G&W, the high-flying conglomerate of the 1960s, and was a flamboyant, mercurial, highly intelligent financial wheeler-dealer.

On my arrival at Famous, I received a surprise when Gaston told me his reason for asking to see me before the meeting was to advise me of a special agenda item: to hire The Richards Group, a company managed by a "shell home" builder on Long Island named Richard Wasserman. The Richards Group was owned 50-percent by Richard Wasserman and 50-percent by G&W. The proposal was to approve a consulting arrangement for The Richards Group (i.e., Wasserman) to advise Famous on real estate matters, for which Richards would receive a fee of $10,000 per month, a fee for selling any properties, a share of the profits on selling properties, and a few other things. I knew from Estey's reports to the Cablesystems board that Famous was experiencing management difficulties in its real estate arm, but coincident with my joining the board, had hired a supposedly hotshot real estate operator to head the real estate division.

I immediately told Gaston that I thought G&W had a conflict of interest; we didn't need residential real estate advice in a commercial operation as we had just hired an expert at considerable cost and, most importantly, the deal was unfair to the shareholders of Cablesystems who were going to be paying for 75 percent of The Richards Group fees, since 50 percent of Richards was owned by G&W. Gaston decided then to introduce me to Dick Wasserman, who was waiting outside. Wasserman came in and tried to persuade me of the benefits of his experience. I stood my ground then, and again later at the board meeting, where the item was deferred to the next meeting.

Early the next week, I received a call from Charles Bluhdorn introducing himself and asking me if I would mind going to New York to have lunch with him. "Charlie," as everyone called him, spoke with a thick Austrian accent and was one of the most direct and decisive people I've ever met.

Before accepting his invitation, I advised my Cablesystems directors that if Bluhdorn became abusive or shouted at me, as Estey had described was his manner on many occasions, I would ask him to calm down and, if he didn't, I would get up and leave. The board agreed to this strategy and, with some considerable trepidation anticipating the ogre I was about to meet, I went to New York on Monday, April 30, 1973. After being kept waiting for half an hour, I was led into Charlie's surprisingly modest office. Over the next 90 minutes we struck up a rapport, discussing a wide variety of subjects, including Robert Vesco's embezzlement from International Controls Corporation (Charlie had had dealings with him), the time Charlie commanded his jet to be flown out of Nagoya against Japanese airport regulations, and how the Shah banned Paramount in Iran because Charlie had ignored his directive not to raise theatre prices and withdrew *The Godfather* from the screens. Then Charlie moved us to a small dining room adjacent to his office.

He quickly turned to the subject at hand and began discussing The Richards Group. I cut him off and told him of the request I'd made to my directors regarding his possible behaviour and told him I was surprised to have been in his office so long and he hadn't even shouted at me once! He found this quite amusing. I then told him G&W had a conflict with respect to Cablesystems and The Richards Group and that he had placed me in a difficult and unacceptable position and I was "not going to let the shareholders of Cablesystems get fucked by G&W and The Richards Group." Charlie laughed, agreed I was right, and said, "Forget The Richards Group;

I want to work with you." Later I told my Cablesystems board that I had "passed my Wasserman test."

I suggested we find a competent commercial real estate developer, split Famous into two companies (theatres and real estate), and joint venture the real estate entity with a capable developer. Charlie seemed to like this idea and we discussed Canadian developers. I had in mind Western Realty, operated by Sam Belzberg, whom I had met when he tried to hire me in the summer of 1972. Charlie agreed that I should explore this idea with Belzberg and then asked me all about Jonlab, Brascan, and Jake Moore. At the end of that conversation, Charlie turned very serious and said, "I want you to come and work for Gulf & Western. You'll be our man in Canada." I was taken aback and flattered, but frankly didn't altogether believe his overture—when Charlie wanted to turn on the charm and be persuasive, he had no equal. I declined, saying that I had taken on a number of commitments to the board of Cablesystems, Jonlab, and to Jake Moore. Charlie then called Don Gaston into his office and in meticulous detail recounted our four-hour discussion, including quoting my profanity with respect to The Richards Group. A month or two later, to help Charlie save face, I agreed to paying $10,000 per month to The Richards Group, provided Cablesystems paid only its proportionate share, i.e., $2,500 per month.

I left New York feeling elated that I had accomplished so much so quickly. However, this turned out to be illusory, as there was very little follow up by G&W who, with 50.1 percent, were in absolute control of Famous. I opened discussions with Belzberg until one day he pulled out suddenly, saying he couldn't explain why. About two months later the news came out that he had sold his controlling position in Western Realty at a premium.

It became increasingly clear that G&W had no intention of following through on joint venturing Famous Players Realty, although the company was split for operational purposes into two entities: theatres and realty. I sat on the board and watched in frustration its inept management until, one day, a bomb hit the real estate company. Contrary to the board's instructions, the realty management proceeded with a major development in Montreal, ignoring board conditions of having financing in place, a signed agreement with the contractor, and a signed lead tenant. A hole was already dug in the ground and the project was now in orbit with no controls in place, and the labour situation was tight and volatile because the entire construction industry was building the city for the Olympics.

This, together with a few other improprieties, led to the wholesale dismissal of realty management and G&W unilaterally sent a "workout expert" from its organization. This man was probably the most objectionable individual I ever encountered in business and he quickly became known in Famous as "Dracula" or "The Pig." He was a totally brainwashed G&W man, with no regard for the board, the other shareholder (Cablesystems), or anyone else. At one point I had to confront Bluhdorn with a threat to sue G&W for "oppression of minority shareholders' rights." This got Bluhdorn's attention.

In response, he hired Senator John Aird, a respected lawyer with Aird & Berlis, to represent G&W on the board of Famous. (Aird's partner, Doug Berlis, was the man who joined the board of Toronto & London Investments, representing Sir Denys Lowson.) Aird was a senator and later became chancellor of the University of Toronto and finally the lieutenant-governor of Ontario. He was also on a variety of large company boards including INCO, Consumers Gas, and the Molson Companies, and was vice-chair of Power Corporation. The rocky relationship continued with G&W and eventually Cablesystems was again brought to the point of suing G&W. As a courtesy, I went to Aird and told him what was coming. When he understood our grievances, Aird said, "I agree with you. Let me have one more attempt to get Bluhdorn to co-operate and, if he doesn't, I'll resign." Aird got Bluhdorn to behave and things went along quite smoothly. Out of all this, John Aird and I became good friends.

* * *

While it may appear that my relationship with Charlie was fractured, strangely we got along very well, especially one-on-one. It was quoted that Charlie once chased me around a boardroom in a pique of anger, but that is absolute nonsense.[6] I had the feeling he was a bit like a kid trying out how much he could get away with and, when confronted, he'd back off.

On one occasion Charlie told me the story of how he started G&W. He and a fellow commodity trader had made substantial gains in sugar and coffee futures. They decided to buy control of an industrial company and searched *Barron's* and other periodicals for undervalued cash-rich targets. They identified a company manufacturing automobile bumpers in Michigan and quietly accumulated stock. Soon they had control. Charlie told me, "I flew out to Grand Rapids and saw the president. I said, 'I'm Charles Bluhdorn and I own 51 percent of the company.' I then told him I didn't care about bumpers—I was interested in redeploying the cash. The president then took me down to the plant floor and pointed to a long line of brand-new machines. He then said to me,

'There's your cash!'" This was particularly amazing in light of G&W corporate brochures, which described the careful planning behind the evolution of G&W. When I asked Don Gaston about the content of these brochures, he laughed and said they were the creations of G&W's PR department.

* * *

The October day in 1974 when the news hit that the Franklin National Bank collapsed, I happened to be at the G&W building at Columbus Circle in New York City talking with Don Gaston, when Roy Abbott, then VP finance of G&W's subsidiary Associates Finance, came out of Charlie's office. In great excitement he approached Gaston and said, "What'd ya say we put up half a million to help Michele (Sindona) for old times' sake? Charlie is onside." Don said, "Okay by me." In 1972, Sindona had gained control of Franklin National under circumstances that led him to be charged with fraud. In 1980, he was convicted of fraud and perjury, then was extradited to Italy, where he died of cyanide poisoning in 1986, two years after being sentenced to life imprisonment for conspiracy to murder.[7] According to *Vanity Fair* magazine, March 2000, during the filming of *The Godfather,* "Charlie Bluhdorn was even doing business with a shadowy Sicilian named Michele Sindona, a money-launderer and advisor to the Gambino and other Mob families as well as the Vatican Bank. In 1970, the year *The Godfather* began production at Paramount, Bluhdorn made a deal with Sindona that resulted in the mobster's construction and real-estate companies owning a major share of the Paramount lot."

* * *

By now it was 1977 and things were progressing most satisfactorily at Cablesystems. However, despite repeated denials by
Brascan (now that it had absorbed Jonlab) that their 26-percent
block in Cablesystems was for sale, there were persistent
rumours on the street and in the industry that Brascan was
trying to sell. With this potential risk, we basically had three
unattractive alternatives: acquisition by or merger with an
established cable industry player; acquisition by or merger
with a non-industry player; or take our chances on the CRTC
(and on Jonlab honouring its commitment).

About this time, I called Charles Allard and suggested
Allarco take control of Canadian Cablesystems. However,
Charles was devastated by the recent death of his wife and said
he could not focus on such a matter at that point in his life.

Suddenly, on Friday, September 2, 1977, Rogers bought
Brascan's 26 percent of Cablesystems and we were launched
into a lengthy, acrimonious public takeover fight for the next
year and a half. I believe this was the first major adversarial
corporate battle in Canada and, Cablesystems being a regulated
company, the struggle became very public.

* * *

During the mid-1970s, one of the people who entered my life
was Conrad Black. He was 32 years old and looking for things
to do, while quietly building Sterling Newspapers with his
partners David Radler and Peter White. While this was going
on, Conrad approached me with the idea of rolling Sterling
into Cablesystems in exchange for shares. This idea appealed
to me and we set about conducting due diligence on Sterling.
While we at Cablesystems had no serious disagreement with

the valuations of Sterling, we came to the conclusion that the newspapers were too tightly and efficiently operated by Radler, that there was little room, if any, for improvement and, if something went wrong, we had a big downside and no expertise in the business. Moreover, despite Conrad's assurances to the contrary, I was worried that as soon as Radler got $2 million in his pocket he would want to leave and do something else. Conrad also suggested he put a group together headed by Bud McDougald, chair of Argus Corporation, to quietly buy up blocks of Cablesystems shares. McDougald didn't really like the cable industry and nothing came of this idea.

In searching for white knights, Robin Korthals,[8] who was at the time executive vice-president (later president) of the Toronto-Dominion Bank, suggested I contact Israel (Izzy) Asper of CanWest Capital in Winnipeg. Asper and his sidekick Gerald Schwartz had just started CanWest with the Toronto-Dominion as banker and an investor, and was setting up to do management buyouts, venture capital transactions, and merchant banking. Canwest quickly started due diligence, but in the end found the circumstances too risky and got cold feet. Asper and Schwartz had intense discussions with Ted Jarmain. As these were entirely shareholder related, I was not privy to them. I was aware that the Jarmains, understandably, wanted to maintain the balance in control, which they had in the eyes of the CRTC when Jonlab owned 26 percent and was passive. Ted Jarmain recalls that discussions foundered on agreement details regarding sharing control and financial issues and Izzy called me to say that he was not proceeding. Having gotten to know Izzy Asper, I decided I should introduce him to Conrad Black—two consummate mega-deal junkies. To this end I arranged a dinner for the three of us at La Scala in Toronto. They hit it off famously and continued their relationship, culminating in Asper's buyout of the *National Post* in two stages in 2000 and 2001.

* * *

Meanwhile, Rogers also tried to buy half the Royal Trust block of 15 percent of Cablesystems, thereby increasing his position to 32 percent and simultaneously breaking up the last major block of shares. About this time I had a visit from John Graham, Ted Rogers's stepfather. Graham was reaching out to tell me that the Rogers group wanted us to co-operate with them. I listened calmly, then asked him if they had tried to buy the Royal Trust block of Cablesystems. Graham firmly denied this.

What John Graham didn't know was that, after he left the Royal Trust offices in Montreal a day or so before to return to Toronto, Roger Otley of Royal Trust telephoned me to tell me Graham had approached them about buying their Cablesystems block. When I told Graham this, he went apoplectic. I had caught him out. It was not a good beginning to our relationship. This event had a profound effect on my attitude going forward, since both Rogers and Graham had proferred John Graham as the elder statesman, Rogers's mentor/stepfather/ally and negotiator—the mediator and trustable bridge between Rogers and us (me) at Cablesystems. But, "Rogers backed out of his deal with Royal Trust, opting to buy Jonlab's share block."[9]

In the meantime, I had had a call from Jim Connacher of Gordon Capital, who had been monitoring the Jonlab/Brascan/Cablesystems situation for a long time. Connacher invited me to lunch at Le Mascaron restaurant and we talked about everything under the sun, including our respective philosophies and objectives in life. At the end of the lunch, Connacher allowed that he was just a broker. "I'm just a whore," he said. During lunch he asked me about the situation at Cablesystems with Rogers now holding the 26 percent. I told him management and the Jarmains were looking for a friendly partner and where the major remaining blocks of stock were held: 15 percent at the Royal Trust, 5 percent at the Montreal Trust, some at Guardian Capital, etc.

He called me a few times over the next few days saying he had an interested party, but for reasons of confidentiality, would not tell me who it was. Then one day, large blocks of Cablesystems started to trade through Gordon Securities and at lunchtime, when a major block changed hands, I telephoned Connacher and asked, "What the hell is going on?" He said it was his client buying, whose identity he could not reveal. I asked whether the client was a friend or enemy of management, to which the reply was, after a pause, "neutral." I asked, "Jim, are you as big a whore as I think you may be?" and he replied, "Perhaps I am."

7

Oral Assurances, 1977–1979

"The stupid neither forgive nor forget; the naive forgive
and forget; the wise forgive but do not forget."
Thomas Szasz, Forbes, *July 19, 2010*

When I arrived home on September 27, 1977, around
6:00 p.m., the telephone was ringing. A very officious
voice at the other end of the line said, "Tony, this is Trevor
Eyton. I'm calling from an airport to tell you that today
my client, Edper Investments, bought 350,000 shares of
Canadian Cablesystems; we may buy more. I'd like to get
together with you when I get back to Toronto." I asked
Eyton whether he had had any discussions with Ted Rogers,
which he denied. For clarity, I rephrased my question: "Do
you have any understanding or arrangements with Rogers?"
Again, his answer was, "No." I didn't believe him.

Over the next few days Edper accumulated 25 percent of
Cablesystems in the market, including a 5-percent block held
by Montreal Trust and shares held in various client accounts
at Guardian Capital. Clearly I had been duped by Connacher
and had naively helped to seal my own fate by giving him
information. Edper and Rogers announced that between them

they held 51 percent of the common stock of Cablesystems, but were not seeking control of the company. However, they had "oral assurances" that they would each nominate three directors (out of a total of fifteen) and support their election to the board of Cablesystems.

Meanwhile, in the boardroom at Cablesystems, we were under siege. We couldn't believe that Edper would put up such a huge sum of money without some sort of agreement with Rogers. We had retained Robert J. Wright, Q.C., of Lang Michener Cranston Farquharson & Wright, as outside counsel to the board.[1] When Wright and I met with Eyton, Wright confronted him with the accusation that he must have a deal with Rogers, but Eyton resolutely denied any such agreement. However, we were so sure of our suspicions that we sent a delegation of the board with written submissions of complaint to the Ontario Securities Commission (OSC) and the CRTC. In turn, Edper and Rogers wrote to both regulatory bodies denying they had any agreement.

Meanwhile, I received a call from Eyton saying that the Edper people wanted to meet with the management of Cablesystems to discuss their request for board representation. I invited them to an 11:00 a.m. meeting in our boardroom, followed by lunch at Metro Cable's modern studio in the north end of Toronto.

At this point, we at Cablesystems believed that Rogers operated an over-leveraged, second-rate company with distinctly third-rate management. In our view, Rogers was very much a one-man show, surrounded by sycophants, and was operating in mediocre facilities. Cablesystems, on the other hand, had state-of-the-art facilities and equipment and was a well-managed, dynamic public corporation.

At the appointed hour, a contingent led by Jack Cockwell and Peter Bronfman of the Edper Group arrived. I had issued firm instructions that, even though we were somewhat suspicious of their motives, we were going to greet them with the same courtesy and provide the same information that we would to any other shareholder. We held preliminary discussions in the boardroom, after which we were anxious to show them a modern, professional studio.

As we got into the cars for the half-hour ride to Metro Cable, I asked Peter Bronfman to ride with me. As soon as we were alone, I told him bluntly that we were upset at the way Edper had acquired their shareholding for two reasons: their seemingly underhanded methods of assembling their stockholding, which in our view was unacceptable; and their links, even if informal, with Rogers, who had a clear conflict in the CATV business.

Peter quickly became both defensive and apologetic, saying, "You know, that's too bad. I wish I'd known that," all the while defending Eyton and Cockwell, saying, "Jack's a star." After lunch at Metro Cable I grabbed Peter again and insisted on driving him to the airport. When he got out of my car, still defensive and apologizing, he used an expression I had not heard before: "Let's hope the lemons turn into lemonade."

The Edper share acquisitions led the CRTC to convene a hearing to review the situation. By now Pierre Juneau had retired and Harry Boyle was chair, and my old colleague, Roy Faibish, had left Bushnell and was a commissioner. The Rogers/Edper approach to the commission was that they had no plans to control Cablesystems, but merely wanted representation on the board. The fact that Rogers was a competitor in the industry (even though individual franchises were exclusive) was completely omitted from their application.

Under the CRTC rules, no new information was allowed to be submitted two weeks prior to the hearing, in order to give commission staff time to organize the submissions and inter-ventions, and generally prepare for the hearing. Nevertheless, in the two-week window before the hearing, Rogers and Edper not only tabled their written agreement, but also the written memorandum that led to their agreement, which had been negotiated before Edper bought any Cablesystems shares in the market. Among other things, this agreement stipulated that Edper and Rogers would each have three representatives on a board of fifteen members and would support each other in attaining these seats; Edper and Rogers gave each other a right of first refusal on their holdings; and they had a buy-sell (shotgun) agreement.

So much for "oral assurances."

We were to learn during the hearing and afterward that, while Edper and Rogers were telling the regulatory bodies that they had only "oral assurances" and "gentlemen's agree-ments" between them, it was clear that they had been locked in concert by September 26, 1977, before Edper had even started purchasing Cablesystems shares. Furthermore, Edper continued to buy shares even after Fortier, a vice-chair of the CRTC, had requested that Edper take no further steps to acquire shares in Cablesystems during the period.

Edper and Rogers maintained the public position that they did not want to control Cablesystems, but only wanted board representation. We, however, were not fooled by this creeping takeover approach. Indeed, our suspicions were confirmed later in a book written with Rogers's tacit co-operation, which stated: "Eyton called Rogers. . .to tell him Edper *planned to go after CCL* [Cablesystems]."[2] (Italics are mine.) And after Rogers eventually gained control in 1979, I was given a memorandum by Larry Brenzel, a stockbroker and friend of Eddie Goodman and the Jonlab group, in which Brenzel listed 52 meetings or telephone conversations in the period from January 13, 1975, to September 29, 1977, where he tried to sell control of Cablesystems on behalf of Jonlab/Brascan for a commission. Six or seven of these meetings were with Edper or Rogers to discuss taking control of Cablesystems. At the meetings late in September, Brenzel noted he was demanding the payment of commission from Jonlab for the sale of Cablesystems to Rogers. Brenzel was very bitter, having never received a commission from Jonlab, despite threatening legal action.

* * *

Although Rogers and Edper repeatedly denied wanting control of the company, we decided to test them by putting together a management buyout plan to purchase outstanding shares of Cablesystems through a newly formed company. Rogers and Edper would each be offered a 24-percent interest in the new entity, with proportionate representation on the Cablesystems board—precisely what they had demanded under "oral assurances." This elicited a visit from Jack Cockwell and others, where Jack read us the riot act on shareholder rights and treated us to a lecture on the subject. In a heated moment, I nudged Albert Gnat who was sitting on my right and said, "Remember the man with the iron hand in the velvet glove?" (referring to Charles Allard). I continued, pointing under the table at Cockwell, "There's the man with an iron hand in an *iron* glove."

From my point of view, the intervention of Edper into Cablesystems was a short period—six months—of my life. It made me wonder why Edper brought such antagonism to the table. In their heyday, it was their style. Moreover, because of their shotgun link with Rogers, their involvement undoubtedly added a level of toxicity to Cablesystems's dealings with Rogers.

* * *

While Rogers and Edper were pressing for board representation, their relationships with the board and management of Cablesystems were becoming publicly more acrimonious. Out of the blue, I received a call from Adam Zimmerman, president of Noranda Forest Products, a subsidiary of Noranda Mines Ltd., offering to mediate between Cablesystems and the Bronfmans. I served on the board of Branksome Hall, a girls' private school, with Adam. He said, "I know Peter Bronfman very well and, for some reason, he views me as an uncle or elderly adviser. I've been watching what's going on and if I can help by bringing you together with Peter for a meeting, I'd be happy to do so." I told Adam I'd like to think about it overnight and get back to him. I called him on that Friday and said I'd like to take up his suggestion, and we agreed to meet at 8:00 a.m. Monday at his office. I told Adam I would immediately deliver some internal memoranda and correspondence so that he would have the flavour of the situation before we met.

When I walked into his office on Monday morning, Adam said, "No wonder you're so mad. If half of this is true, it's awful." I replied, "It's all true and I have only included what I can legally substantiate, because we may all end up in court some day." Nothing came of this because, as the reader will see, events quickly overtook the situation. First, however, it's ironic to see what happened to Adam about two years later.

* * *

In October 1979, Brascan (now controlled by Edper) bought 7.9 million shares of Noranda from Hollinger (now under the control of Conrad Black) and then started buying more stock. The Bronfmans, having acquired control of Brascan earlier in the year (dethroning Jake Moore), were now targeting Noranda. My telephone rang and it was Adam Zimmerman wanting to pick my brain. We met for lunch at the 54th Floor Restaurant at the Toronto-Dominion Centre. I was so busy telling Adam what he was in for with his friends the Bronfmans that I swallowed a fish bone and had to excuse myself to visit a nearby health clinic to have it dislodged. The Edper/Brascan versus Noranda affair was long and acrimonious, but in the end Brascan triumphed, overpaying enormously for the already over-leveraged mining conglomerate.

Actions similar to those that happened in the Cablesystems and Brascan takeovers by Edper followed.[3] To fend off Edper, Noranda developed the Zinor scheme. The Zinor scheme, approved November 16, 1979, by Noranda's board, was complicated, providing that various subsidiaries of Noranda would buy the parent company's treasury shares, continually diluting Brascan. The Ontario Securities Commission immediately launched an investigation.

Later, when Brascan obtained control of Noranda, I was saddened to see that both Zimmerman and Powis, the president and CEO of Noranda, rolled over and worked for their conquerors, seduced by offers to be chair of Noranda Forest and Noranda respectively. Within two years, both Zimmerman and Powis were terminated.

* * *

But I've gotten ahead of my story.

In the midst of our deliberations, on April 5, 1978, eight months after Rogers bought the Brascan 26-percent block, Edper pulled the trigger in their shotgun agreement with Rogers, apparently thinking Rogers would not have the resources to buy them out. However, Rogers met Edper's price and filed an application with the CRTC to take control of Cablesystems. At the same time, the CRTC was faced with the threat that, if they didn't approve Rogers, by the terms of their agreement, Edper could then apply for control. Then, if Edper were turned down, Rogers might apply again or Rogers *and* Edper might put their shares in Cablesystems up for sale, creating a new hearing on control. Clearly this created a nightmare for the CRTC, which by now was a leaderless body—chair Harry Boyle's retirement having been announced. When the new chair was appointed many months later, he turned out to be singularly passive and ineffective.

The week of Edper's purchase also coincided with a change of the chair at the OSC. The new chair, James Baillie, was from the firm of Tory, Tory, DesLauriers & Binnington (now Torys), who were corporate lawyers for Rogers and Edper. John Tory Sr.[4] was the trustee and confidant of Ted Rogers and family and Trevor Eyton was a partner there. Rogers articled at Torys before going into business full time. A wonderful example of synchronicity for the events at hand. (John H. Tory became CEO of Rogers Cable from 1999 to 2003.)

During the period leading up to the hearings, acrimonious letters were exchanged between Rogers/Edper and Cablesystems. Rogers was prone to taking conversations and quoting them out of context, copying his correspondence to the CRTC. It became so insidious and unpleasant that I recommended to the board of Cablesystems, who agreed, that I turn over all correspondence from Rogers to our counsel, Bob Wright of Lang Michener, for formal response in order to depersonalize the situation.

A chance conversation with an old high school debating opponent of Rogers's, Peter Harris, put Rogers's methodology in perspective for me. Harris told me that he and Ted Rogers were once on opposite debating teams; Rogers was the last speaker and "wowed" everyone with his presentation of facts. When Harris approached Rogers after the debate and asked, "Ted, where did you get all those facts?" Rogers's reply was, "I made them up."[5]

* * *

In July 1978, I persuaded the board of Cablesystems that we might save ourselves from the adversarial takeover by acquiring the 35-percent block of Western Broadcasting shares owned by Torstar Limited. Previously, Torstar had attempted to take control of Western and a bitter fight had ensued between Torstar and Western's chair and CEO, Frank Griffiths. Our plan was to acquire the block and then reorganize Western's share capital into voting and non-voting shares. If I could persuade Western to acquiesce in Cablesystems buying the Torstar block of Western, we would agree to issue an equivalent amount of Cablesystems stock to Western. Since Western already owned

21 percent of Premier, this step would link Western and Premier together with Cablesystems. On September 27, 1978, I pressed Frank Griffiths to proceed and he replied he did "not want to have anything to do with Rogers, but if Rogers is denied by the CRTC, he did not have any concerns" about our scheme. I suggested as an alternative, Western and Cablesystems exchange shareholdings of 20 to 25 percent. Frank again stated that he would not proceed while Rogers was in the picture.

The CRTC hearing of Rogers's application to take control of Cablesystems was publicly televised. Each side hired a battery of lawyers and experts, and lobbied politically. There were many interventions by various groups interested in the broadcasting and cable industry.

I had kept Royal Trust, who still held a 15-percent block of Cablesystems shares, abreast of the reasons that the board opposed Rogers taking control. I visited John Scholes, president, and Roger Otley, vice-president investments, one morning in Montreal and, on the way back to Toronto, answered Bob Foster's telephone message as I waited for a plane in Montreal. Foster was an investment banker with Dominion Securities, whom we had retained to monitor our actions in the investor community and ensure we kept the high road both in practice and in perception.[6] Foster said, "I've been watching the battle and, unless you get more shareholder support, it may begin to look as though management is protecting its ass. Knowing you, you don't want that to happen." I realized this was good advice and when I got back to my office in Toronto that same day, I called Roger Otley and said, "You people say you don't want Rogers to get control of Cablesystems; if you don't do something, I'm going to go over to Rogers right now and congratulate him and hand him the keys." Otley replied, "What do we have to do?" and I answered, "File an intervention against

Rogers." Royal Trust joined the fray and the battle continued. Later, in 1983, when Edper took control of Royal Trust through Trilon, I called Otley and offered my condolences; we laughed about being raped and pillaged by the Edper barbarians.

* * *

One amusing contact maintained throughout the hearing by both sides was someone we in Cablesystems management called "Deep Throat." Deep Throat was a member of the CRTC who had declared his friendship with both parties and recused himself from the panel. I would call him late at night at his home in Ottawa and listen as he critiqued our strategy against Rogers and offered advice, guarded though it was. We suspected (assumed) that the same conversations were being held with Rogers. After the CRTC decision, our suspicions were proved true when Deep Throat was quickly hired by Rogers and posted to London, England, to monitor the embryonic cable TV industry in Britain. Right or wrong, the appointment had the stench of a payoff.

Deep Throat was in fact Roy Faibish, my ex-colleague from Bushnell. Later, when Rogers suffered a financial squeeze, he jettisoned Faibish, who was then hired by David Graham of Cablecasting. David lived in London and, although his cable operations were in Canada and the United States, he had aspirations to acquire franchises in the UK. To finish this story, David got into financial difficulties and Faibish went to work for British Telecom as their resident CATV expert, then operated as an independent consultant in cable TV and telecommunications worldwide. He passed away in London in March 2001.

* * *

The hearing lasted more than a week and I found it debilitating. My intuition was telling me that momentum was building against us and information began to leak from the CRTC that the Jarmains and management should have resolved the ownership issue. This point was summarized succinctly when Ted Jarmain and I flew to Phoenix in December 1978, seeking to buy or partner with the local cable franchise holder Bruce Merrill. As our meeting opened Merrill said, "I've watched you build Cablesystems with great admiration. You've done everything right. . . except one thing. You didn't look after the ownership matter." That said it all.

During this period Rogers and his people were lobbying on all fronts, particularly at the CRTC and the Department of Communications in Ottawa. At one point, John Christodoulou, my partner from Triarch days, came to see me; he had been approached by Bruce Walters of Pitfield & Company on behalf of Rogers, to find out what Rogers could do to get me to support him. I laughed and immediately responded, "Tell Rogers I have a Swiss bank account and I'll keep winking my left eye. When there's enough money in the account, I'll wink my right eye." John said, "I can't tell him that." I replied, "Tell him—let's have some fun."

Also in this period, Chris Ondaatje, who was associated in business with Rogers's father-in-law Lord Martonmere, invited me to have lunch, and said Rogers wanted to know what he could do to get me on side. I told him that Rogers had created such bad feelings and difficulties for the board of Cablesystems and all its constituencies that he had alienated everyone.

There were other interventions at the CRTC hearing—specifically from Ed Jarmain, who defended Cablesystems, speaking as a cable pioneer and major shareholder. He said

Cablesystems was "regarded as a 'superbly run' company with decentralized style of management and engineering expertise that was far superior to Rogers Cable."[7] Jarmain "painted Rogers as an amateur who would jeopardize the effectiveness of his tight-knit team if the CRTC permitted the takeover." Ed went on: "Cablesystems' management has the quality seldom found, even among engineers." Rogers replied, upset and hurt by the remarks, "I admire and revere Mr. Jarmain . . . I don't have the same knowledge in engineering, but I do have the same commitment."[8] As the reader has seen, senior Cablesystems personnel came to dominate the combined company management after the takeover.

Regardless of Rogers's true feelings and reaction to Ed Jarmain's presentation to the CRTC, Rogers was walking a thin line with Ed Jarmain and his son Ted. "The growing enmity between the two sides was such that Phil Lind's[9] close friend, Colin Watson, a CCL [Cablesystems] vice-president who was running Metro Cable, angrily remarked, 'Rogers is treating this whole thing as if it were a takeover of Acme Screw and Gear.' Lind would later caution his friend to lie low. He didn't want any bad blood to fester between him and Rogers if they emerged the victor, especially since Rogers hoped to keep the management team intact. Lind walked a delicate line between the two camps, caught between his friendship with Watson and his loyalty to Rogers."[10]

* * *

The CRTC decision was delivered on January 8, 1979, approving the Rogers bid for control. I immediately received a call from Don Angus, a Cablesystems director, who said he had been sent to see me by the Rogers's board. Rogers wanted me to stay as CEO. I told Angus, "There is no chemistry and there is only room for one CEO and it wouldn't be me."

Rogers then called me and came to our boardroom. I congratulated him and wished him luck. Tony Gooch, Cablesystems's CFO, resigned immediately. Ted Jarmain announced immediately that he, too, would resign, but stayed for a few months to provide some continuity. Much to everyone's surprise, the majority of Cablesystems's management stayed with Rogers, which was critical to Rogers's later success. Over time, these managers evolved from feeling disdain toward Rogers, to being skeptical of his abilities, to eventually being converted to admiration for him. I take my hat off to him for retaining them and winning their respect.

* * *

As soon as Rogers gained control of Cablesystems, Bluhdorn called a meeting of the Famous board; afterward, Charlie asked to see me privately in his office. He was very sympathetic, and said, "You're down now, but don't worry, you'll be up again." He then became very serious and said, "What am I going to do about Mr. Rogers?" I replied, "Charlie, you should buy him out; don't delay." I told him Rogers would do everything to make life difficult for G&W in Canada. Charlie asked what price I'd recommend and I said, "Start by offering book value, but get him out." In fact, in 1981, Rogers made a deal to sell back the Famous Players shareholding to Bluhdorn at a bargain price.

In 1983, I was in New York for a weekend visiting my daughter. On Sunday, she came over to my hotel for breakfast and brought the *New York Times*. The headline read "Charles Bluhdorn dead." I was stunned and saddened—he died of a heart attack at age 56. Later I wondered what he would have done when Paramount, the successor of G&W, was the subject of a takeover bid in 1993–94——Charlie had always been the raider.

* * *

In January 1979, I said my tearful goodbyes at Cablesystems, and Lang Michener kindly offered me a spare office until I found something else to do. This was a depressing and lonely period; for all their kindness, I did not have much in common with the lawyers who were busy with their clients' affairs. I sat alone in an office surrounded by boxes of files and papers. After about two months, I received a contrite call from Albert Gnat asking would I mind if he did some work for Rogers? My response was that I wouldn't mind at all——he should go for it. By the time of his death, Albert was one of Rogers's closest advisers.

I joined the board of Home Oil, looked at a variety of investments, and was invited to apply for several CEO positions. However, I also found during this period that a number of opportunities mysteriously evaporated. On digging for clues I soon realized that Jake Moore was quietly carrying on, as Conrad Black was to put it, "a vendetta" against me in various boardrooms. At one point I went to see John Aird because I felt I should seek legal recourse. When I told Aird my problem, he said, "Don't pay attention to it," signalling with his thumb and index finger that Moore had a small mind. Aird added that Moore's actions "will reflect badly on him, not you."

One of the most gratifying episodes occurred earlier, in November 1977. I had a call from Peter Darling who said Sir Siegmund Warburg was in Toronto and would like to see me.

The next morning, I went to Sir Siegmund's suite at the Royal York Hotel and had a nice conversation. He wanted to know what I was doing and made his usual joke about Peter Hardy. Siegmund had instinctively disliked Peter Hardy on first meeting him in New York City over the dispute between Warburg's and Jonlab over Toronto and London investments. He thought Hardy a bit of a dandy and very much Moore's gofer. He then asked in his German accent, "And how iss our friend Mr. Mooore?" I said he was around, but I really didn't know. Sir Siegmund said, "What a strange man; I liked him at first but then, why does he have people like you around him. You know, his problem was he didn't know how to listen." Coming from Sir Siegmund, I found this most comforting.

* * *

Shortly prior to the CRTC decision granting Rogers control of Cablesystems, I received a telephone call from Syd Welsh, asking if I would consider becoming president and CEO of Premier. I told Syd that in principle I was interested, but I wanted to wait until after the CRTC decision on Cablesystems. As I thought about Syd's proposition, I decided I didn't want another professional manager's job—I wanted to have my own company. With the help of Albert Gnat, I put together a proposal to buy Premier for $60 million, of which $2 million was equity and $58 million funded by loans from the Bank of Montreal, Penfund, and others. In February 1979, Albert and I met with Syd at the Carlyle Hotel in New York, where Syd and his pal Frank Griffiths were attending the Canada-Russia hockey series. Syd was ambivalent and Frank had his own agenda with Premier. Syd was rightly concerned about being strung along while the CRTC deliberated on change of control for Premier for probably a year, with no assurance of the deal being approved.

I therefore addressed the idea of buying Premier *without* CRTC approval. Peter Beattie of McCarthy & McCarthy (later McCarthy Tétrault) came up with an ingenious solution: make the bid for $59.8 million and the $200,000 would not be paid until the CRTC approved. The existing board, plus our representatives, would stay in place so that *technically* control would not have changed. As the bank was nervous, I had to find a financial partner to bear the risk in the remote event that the CRTC did not grant approval. I first went to Les Shaw of ShawCor who, in the end, thought the deal was too risky. I then went to Sam Belzberg, who agreed in principle. He asked what the split should be and I suggested fifty-fifty. Sam responded 85 percent to Belzberg and the balance to us, or he wouldn't do the deal. "The guy with the gold makes the rules." Reluctantly I agreed and called Syd Welsh.

I told Syd I had a partner and was ready to do a deal without CRTC approval. Syd came right over to my hotel room at the Four Seasons in Vancouver. I explained the transaction and we agreed he would remain as chair with a retainer equivalent to his then compensation. The meeting was short and we shook hands as he left my room. Before I closed the door he came back in and said, "I'd like two or three days—Frank [Griffiths] is away and I'd like to talk with him when he returns." What could I say? My stomach seized with apprehension.

Syd listened to Frank, who had his own agenda to merge Premier and WIC and advised Syd not to sell to us. Eventually Premier went into play. A number of bidders appeared, but Rogers outbid everyone with a price 66 percent higher than my offer. To ensure success, Rogers acceded to paying non-refundable deposits to Premier in case the CRTC turned him down. In one year, Rogers had become the dominant player in the CATV industry in Canada.

* * *

Late in 1978, Brascan sold its main Brazilian subsidiary, Light-Servicos de Electricidade, for $447 million. I made a private bet with my friends, including Tony Griffin, who agreed with me, that Moore would be so insensitive to his shareholders' dismay over his poor management performance that he would harbour all this cash, making Brascan a plum takeover target. Because he had lost shareholder support, I said, if he were smart, Moore would pay out at least half of the funds as a special dividend, which would earn some respect from his shareholders and reduce the attractiveness of Brascan as a target. As I predicted, he decided to find a way to spend all of this money.

Early in 1979, Edper formed a joint investment subsidiary with the Patino family, the tin kings of Bolivia, which purchased over one million shares of Brascan. As Newman records in *The Acquisitors*:[11]

Trevor Eyton, the Edper lawyer, arranged a secret rendez-vous with Jake Moore. Accompanied by Bruce Lockwood, a lawyer from Blake, Cassels & Graydon, Moore arrived at the designated suite of the Royal York Hotel at 1:00 p.m. on April 5, his step heavy with reputation, a bankable man taking time out to dismiss these unwanted intruders. Eyton promptly outlined Edper's intention of making a 51-percent takeover bid, accompanied by pledges to co-operate with Brascan's existing directors and management. Moore responded with the verbal equivalent of a shrug, pointing out that partial offers weren't fair to shareholders. The following day at the Brascan board meeting, both his offer of Woolworth's and the Bronfman bid for Brascan went public.

What ensued between Edper and Brascan was extremely acrimonious. Newman quotes Andrew Sarlos, a participant and ally of Edper in the bid for Brascan:[12]

"Brascan management," noted Sarlos, who became chief spokesman for the informal coalition of anti-Moore share-holders, "has tossed aside the Edper bid and made an offer to Woolworth's in its own interest to protect its own jobs and power. Normally, shareholders are permitted to vote on such matters."

In the heat of the battle, on one occasion, I found myself talking with Bill Wilder and Hal Jackman at a recess of a Home Oil board meeting in Calgary, when Wilder said, "Poor Jake, he's being taken through the wringer. Among other issues, he's upset that Edper's partial offer isn't fair to all shareholders." I interrupted, "Where was all his high morality when he sold 26 percent of Cablesystems to Rogers?" Jackman commented dryly, "Yeah, Bill, live by the sword and die by the sword." Later in the year Wilder, who was a director of Noranda, would experience the Edper tactics first-hand.

By the end of May, Moore surrendered and, through the office of Eddie Goodman, negotiated from Brascan a $250,000 severance plus a pension of $100,000 per annum for his life-time, indexed to the consumer price index, transferable to his wife for her lifetime should he predecease her. In June 1979, coincidentally the same day that his appointment as president of Brascan was announced, I invited Trevor Eyton as well as Jack Cockwell to lunch; we were now sociable again and I had a suggestion for them about their investment in Consumers Glass. I asked Trevor, "Why did you pay Moore after he had referred to the Bronfmans [Edper] as crooks, thieves, and liars?" Eyton said, "Well, now he has to be a good boy and say nice things about us." I told Eyton I thought the payment was both unnecessary and unconscionable.

* * *

After the bitter takeover of Brascan by Edper in 1979, the Hees-Edper group was on a roll. Ten years later the group owned or controlled an estimated 150 companies with assets of about $120 billion. But in 1993, the real estate collapse humbled Jack Cockwell and Trevor Eyton. With the mercy of Edper's bankers, management was allowed to remain in place—perhaps because of the complex corporate structure. By 1997, the group was renamed Edper Brascan and in 2000, Brascan Corporation. To his credit, Jack Cockwell, the reputed pugilist, rose up after the count of eight, to reorganize and simplify the corporate structure and re-staff the management. In 2002, Bruce Flatt, CEO of Brookfield Properties, succeeded Cockwell as CEO of Brascan. In 2005, the group changed its name again, to Brookfield Asset Management, and like the rise of the phoenix, restored the group to its former stature.

Trevor Eyton completed his term as a member of the Canadian Senate at age 75, is an officer of the Order of Canada and Queen's Counsel for Ontario, and holds a list of accolades too lengthy to list here. His honours are a testimony to his high standing in the community.

8

Trolling for Takeovers, 1975–1978

"God is love, but get it in writing."
Gypsy Rose Lee

In the early 1970s it dawned on me that I had become a professional manager, skilled at earning wealth for others but not amassing equity for myself. By this point, Albert Gnat had succeeded Bud Estey in his law practice, and we had become good friends, linked by our responsibilities at Cablesystems, where he was legal counsel and I was a director. Another colleague from Triarch, John Christodoulou, had also just returned to Toronto from Bermuda, where he had lived for a few years. The three of us established an informal relationship looking for investment opportunities.

By 1975, the stock market had not yet recovered from the crash of 1974. Companies were being sold at low price-earnings ratios or at discounts to book value, and "going private" was becoming popular. Institutional investors were accepting low prices to realize their investments in small and medium-sized companies. Christodoulou suggested that we start looking for leveraged buyout opportunities for our books, using the target company's own cash flow to finance the purchase, a method of acquisition that became increasingly common. His first suggestion in the fall of 1976 was a nursing home company called Extendicare, which was controlled (30 percent) by the Ivey family (AllPak) from London, Ontario. With John's consent, I brought Albert Gnat and his tax partner from Lang Michener, Arnold Englander, on board.

We were on a steep learning curve, and our first mistake was not approaching AllPak with a view to tying up its 30-percent block. Instead we approached Harold Livergant, the president of Extendicare, and told him what we wanted to do, emphasizing we wanted management's involvement; we did not want to manage the company—we wanted to buy it and build it. After the third meeting with Livergant, I told John and Albert, "We're dead. We told him how to do it and now he doesn't need us." I was right, but Livergant did not follow through; he merely leveraged his own position by borrowing from the bank. Years later, after Crownx had taken over Extendicare, I read in *Canadian Business* magazine that Livergant's main regret in life was that he had never owned his own company. In 1976, we had offered him that chance and, through greed, he missed it, and so did we.

* * *

An amusing episode occurred in October 1976. This was a time when "Arab money" was allegedly easily available. I had heard that Ross McGregor, a cable TV operator and erstwhile manager of Cablecasting, had teamed up with a 32-year-old investment promoter, who, operating under the company name of Harvard Investments, claimed to have access to long-term, low-interest Arab money through his relationship with a sheikh. At the time, this was appealing to me because we could have used access to these kinds of funds in structuring the Extendicare buyout. Apparently, the management of two cable companies, Premier and CableWest, had just negotiated loans through Harvard Investments.

Albert Gnat and I met McGregor and the operator for lunch and at the end of lunch McGregor asked me what I thought of the idea. I replied, "I hope you know what you're doing. Have you met the sheikh?" McGregor confided, "It's Sheikh Yamani[1] and I'm going to meet him when he's in Vancouver next week." The "deal" required applicants to fill out a loan request form, make a deposit of 10 percent against costs and for assurance of completion, and Harvard would secure the money from the sheikh in England. I said we would not put up a deposit, but would have our bank hold a guarantee in trust to be released when we received the loan. To cut a long story short, the operator was conducting a scam and at least two cable operators lost deposits in the order of $200,000 to $250,000 each.

* * *

Our group's next investment opportunity arose when one of Albert's clients, Conn Chem, announced it was accepting an offer from Jannock Corporation, the brick and steel tube company. Brothers Gordon and Jim Lang had inherited Conn Chem from their father, and Gordon had bought out Jim's share of the company when the latter wanted to retire to farming. In 1976, Conn Chem had revenues of about $60 million and pre-tax profits of $11 million, operating in custom packaging and consumer aerosol spray products. Now, Gordon had decided to sell the company to Jannock. The stock had been trading at the $4 to $6 per share level before the 1974 crash, and had risen to $6 to $7 when Jannock offered $12 to the controlling multiple voting shareholder (Lang) and $10 to the ordinary common shareholders.

The takeover circular had been printed, but a day or two before it was released, a lead headline in the *Toronto Star* said that there was evidence from Sweden that fluorocarbons (used in aerosols) were destroying the ozone layer. The directors of Jannock panicked and told Lang they were deferring the bid until they were satisfied that the alleged environmental problem would not affect the company. Lang was furious and told Jannock to proceed or Lang would not deal with them—ever.

I happened to be travelling with Albert and he showed me the latest Conn Chem annual report. On reviewing it, I told Albert that Lang should be buying, not selling. Albert arranged a luncheon meeting for me with Lang and I persuaded him to consider a leveraged buyout, in which he would maintain his position of 35 percent, Dow Chemical (a supplier and existing shareholder) would continue to hold 20 percent, and three key managers would receive 5 percent each, with the balance of the shares for employees and financing. In return for arranging the legal and financial requirements of the takeover bid, our group would get 20 percent. Albert had also advised Lang that as we had recently been cut out of the Extendicare deal, we hoped that Lang would protect our participation. Lang liked the idea I presented and said he would discuss it with Ed Dobson, executive vice-president of

Conn Chem. Albert warned me that the meeting would be difficult as Dobson was unpredictable and tricky.

A week or so later I received a call from Lang inviting me to a meeting with Dobson at his office. The meeting lasted about three hours and was completely frustrating because Dobson was adamantly opposed to our idea, saying that it was too risky, there would be too much debt, and that money was not his (Dobson's) driving interest. When I left it was dark and snowing and I called Albert and said we should forget it.

About two months later, I received a call from Lang who said, "Remember the transaction you proposed? I've decided we're going to do it, only we'll give you guys 10 percent, I'll take 49 percent, Dobson and two key people will each have 5 percent," and Dow and some employees would hold the balance. I was somewhat surprised and asked Gordon, "How did you persuade your friend Dobson to agree?" He replied, "I took him to meet our accountant, Wayne McLeod, who told him he was crazy if he didn't do the deal."

In the course of the transaction, McLeod was hired as president and became part-owner as well. In taking the company private, Lang was able to create two classes of shares: a small number of Class A shares with voting rights and Class B non-voting shares, thereby locking up control indefinitely. The transaction also allowed him to estate plan. We took the company private at $10 per share for a total cost of $22 million.

In April 1980, Conn Chem went public again, listing under the name CCL Limited with a share price of $6, establishing a market value of $43 million. The share price climbed to a peak of $21.25 in 1986, making a market capitalization of $342 million. In 1992, CCL had revenues of $709 million and shareholder equity worth $303 million. Gordon Lang remained chair and the controlling shareholder until his death in 2001 and Wayne McLeod was CEO from 1984 to early 1988, and chair and CEO until 1999. For a number of years, Gordon Lang and I had an annual lunch, and every year he said, "I can't tell you how much I appreciate what you did for me. That deal changed my life. I don't know what I would have done with myself if I'd sold out." Ironically, sometime later I saw a cover story in *Canadian Business* magazine entitled "Corporate buyouts." The lead story was an interview with Ed Dobson, describing how he took Conn Chem private.

CCL progressed well over the ensuing years. At year-end 2010, the company had revenues of $1.2 billion, net earnings of $71.1 million, and shareholders' equity of $789 million. Gordon Lang's son Donald is now the executive chairman.

* * *

One Saturday in 1978, I was reading *The Globe and Mail* at home and noticed a comment that trading in the stock of Nachurs Limited, a manufacturer of liquid fertilizer, was causing analysts to speculate that a takeover could be in the making. In times past, I used to read the Nachurs annual report for their entertainment value. In those days, it was run by a man named McCormick, who wrote like a snake-oil salesman. For a long time the company had been highly leveraged.

Out of curiosity, at the office on Monday, I pulled out the Nachurs *Financial Post* card (the predecessor to the Internet) and quickly saw that the large debt had been paid off and the company was generating enormous cash flow. On further study, I discovered that the largest block of shares was about 3 percent held by management, and the president was a man named Wally Evans based in London, Ontario. I called Arthur Mingay, president of London-based Canada Trust (and brother of Don Mingay, my old boss at Consumers), and asked if he knew Evans. I felt sure that Evans was not aware that he was sitting on a fabulous leveraged buyout opportunity and, if he didn't do something quickly, the company would be taken out from under him.

On Mingay's recommendation, Evans telephoned me and explained that he was aware that the company was a takeover target and he and his board had examined methods of maintaining control, but because of tax complications and the fact that 98 percent of the business was based in the United States, it was not feasible to take it private. This didn't make sense to me and, with Evans's permission, I met with Jack Petch of Osler Harcourt, legal counsel to and director of Nachurs. Evans had explained that he had tried to interest some people in the London area (Alan Taylor, Jake Moore!) "to buy 35 percent," but that option hadn't been pursued.

I then asked Evans if he had ever thought of buying 100 percent of the company. Evans responded, "Where would you ever get the money to do that?" When I told him that I had $31 million arranged with the Bank of Montreal, he agreed that I could speak with Petch again to obtain his opinion. On contacting Petch, he concurred that at 100 percent the deal could be done. Petch asked me to provide resumés for the members of my group (Albert Gnat, John Christodoulou, Arnie Englander, and myself) and a letter from the bank confirming they would finance the takeover in time for a Nachurs board meeting the following week.

We did this, but heard nothing after the meeting, and when I called Evans, I was given the somewhat unconvincing answer that they had looked at our proposal but had decided to pursue other alternatives. I noted that one of the directors of Nachurs was Don Foyston, a partner of A.E. Ames, investment dealers, so I called Peter Harris, president of Ames, and invited him to lunch. I told Peter the background to the story and he volunteered to find out what happened. I said, "Before you do, I'll *tell you* what happened: they were uncomfortable undertaking this with four individuals they've never heard of." Peter reported back a day or two later, saying my thoughts were essentially correct. I then put to him that I presumed, if we could come up with a corporate partner, like a Triarch or Roymark, we could proceed, and Peter agreed.

This occurred just as CanWest had decided not to pursue control of Canadian Cablesystems, so I called Izzy Asper in Winnipeg and explained the Nachurs opportunity. He told me to call his partner Gerry Schwartz in Toronto. Schwartz immediately saw the merits of the proposal, and we proceeded on the basis that CanWest would take over the deal and allow the four of us to participate for 10 percent of the shares for originating and structuring the deal, and arranging financing, which Schwartz said he would obtain from CanWest's bankers, the Toronto-Dominion Bank. We also assisted CanWest with its due diligence. At one point Schwartz almost withdrew from the transaction when the Toronto-Dominion declined to finance it. However, I encouraged him to use the funds we had previously arranged with the Bank of Montreal, after which the bid was made and completed. I attended the closing dinner with the management of Nachurs, the bankers, and CanWest people.

My partners were upset with me because ultimately CanWest did not allow us 10 percent of the shares, as originally agreed. After the closing, I flew to Winnipeg and met Asper at his home. Since I had initiated the transaction with him, I expected him to protect the verbal agreement for our participation in the ongoing entity. After much difficult negotiation, we finally settled for a consulting fee. There was an added awkwardness because, at the same time, Asper and Schwartz were trying to entice me to join them at CanWest as an equal partner because they had concluded that they needed my operational expertise. While the proposal was intriguing, the timing was inopportune for me.

Nachurs had a much less successful outcome. After CanWest acquired it, apparently they changed the distribution strategy and the company experienced difficulty. Today the company exists under the name Nachurs Alpine, distributing liquid fertilizers.

* * *

In the closing weeks of the Canadian Cablesystems takeover by Rogers, Albert Gnat sent me a package of information about a small zinc and aluminium die-casting business called Jutras Die Casting. This was an estate sale in the hands of National Trust and had been around for about eight months since the death of the owner Mr. Jutras. I gave Albert an immediate response: I didn't like it. The business was too small with revenues of $5 million, was only marginally profitable, and reminded me of the plastics injection moulding business I'd seen at Consumers Glass, which sold "machine time" only. However, Albert was persistent and kept pushing me to do the deal. Reluctantly, I agreed, *provided*: we form a syndicate (I didn't want to own more than 10 percent); we include someone in the group who could help us if it got into trouble; and we decide upon a price at which we were comfortable and put a bid to National Trust with a "three-day fuse." With these terms agreed, I talked to Albert and John Christodoulou, and we formed a group including Tony Griffin, John Addison, John Turner (our future prime minister), and Karl Sanderson, a client of Albert's who ran businesses similar to this one.

At the time of Mr. Jutras's death, there was a 32-year-old general manager in place, Blair Belanger, who was eager to build the company. At the eleventh hour, Tony Griffin called and suggested a sailing friend of his from the UK be included in the deal, since he was looking for small businesses to run. We agreed and made Tony's friend president. We picked a lowball price, bid the trust company and, to our surprise, bought the company.

Six months later we were horrified to learn that instead of attaining annualized budgeted earnings of $400,000, we were on the way to losing $400,000 through mismanagement. The bank threatened to call the loan. I called an emergency meeting of the shareholders at the Granite Club in Toronto at 8:00 a.m. and, when I arrived, received a message that Blair, the general manager, had suffered a severe heart attack the night before and was in surgery. He was not able to return to Jutras. This prompted us to create an executive committee of three consisting of Sanderson, the president, and myself, and we met regularly every week for a year until we turned the company around. I thanked my stars that I had insisted on including Sanderson in the group. However, the chemistry between the syndicate and the president deteriorated to the point that we decided to put the company up for sale, hoping at least to "come out whole" without having to pay money toward bank guarantees. After much unpleasantness amongst the executive committee, Jutras was bought by Meridian Technologies, a company that operated primarily in auto parts, founded and controlled by two partners, one of whom was Tony Griffin's son Scott. About a year later, Tony, who by now was 70, asked me to join the board of Meridian with him. I did and served as chair from 1981 to 1998. (By 1993, Jutras, as a division of Meridian, had revenues of approximately $17 million and pre-tax profits of $370,000.)

Jutras was one "turnaround" that I didn't need in my life. It made me realize as well that the company was too small for my management skills. Companies of that size require hands-on managers like Karl Sanderson, who know how to adjust things on the shop floor at any time of the day.

Under Scott Griffin's leadership, Meridian broadened its activities to include aluminum and then magnesium die-casting. In its last year as a public company, 1997, Meridian earned revenues of $365.8 million, earnings before interest and taxes of $13.3 million, and had shareholder equity equalling $124.3 million.

Meridian Technologies Inc. was bought out by Teksid (a subsidiary of Fiat S.p.A. of Italy) and Norsk Hydro in 1998, at which time, the board and myself as chair left the company. Scott Griffin had left sometime before when he purchased a Meridian subsidiary, which he controls today, and it has been very successful. In December 2006, Meridian was sold to a Swiss company called Estatia AG.

9

Weaving a Recovery,
1979–1982

"Put from you the belief that 'I have been wronged,'
and with it will go the feeling. Reject your sense of injury,
and the injury itself disappears."
Marcus Aurelius, Meditations

When I moved to an office at Lang Michener in January 1979, Don Wright, Bob's brother, introduced me to Leslie Shaw, chair and controlling shareholder of Shaw Industries (now ShawCor). With his brother Jim, who later changed his name to JR Shaw, they controlled Capital Cable TV Limited based in Edmonton, which later became Shaw Cablesystems and is now Shaw Communications. The brothers asked me to undertake consulting work for them and I was eventually invited to join both of their boards.

One day, Les and Jim came to my office at Lang Michener. They had been analyzing Ben Torchinsky's conglomerate Agra Industries, which was a mishmash of engineering companies; consulting, real estate, food, and beverage businesses; medical labs; and a cable TV subsidiary called Cablenet. Because of Agra's poor earnings and lack of management focus, the company's stock was selling at about $5 per share, while the

ᵥas around $10 per share and the breakup value
,ywhere from $12 to $20. I studied the company
ᵣ readily apparent that the cable properties alone
ᵣrth $7 to $8 per share, making the balance of the
buᵣ   ᵣses "free." This was a value investor's dream and took
me back to my studies of Graham and Dodd's *Security Analysis*
at business school.

About this time I received a call from John Clark inviting me over for a cup of coffee. John and his partner Gerry
Connor had worked together in a couple of U.S. brokerage companies, latterly with Canadian subsidiaries, and had
decided to set up their own money management business,
Connor Clark & Company Limited. I had known them from
when they visited Canadian Cablesystems once or twice a
year wearing their analyst hats, asking me about the cable
and theatre businesses, and the state of the company generally. When I visited their office on Bay Street, it comprised a
small reception area, a room with a trading desk where they
spent the majority of their time, and a spare office where they
could meet privately with clients; their only staff was a girl
Friday, Cheryl Johnson.

Over the phone, John told me that Connor Clark owned
an 11-percent position in Premier Cablevision (Syd Welsh's
company) on behalf of their clients and he was wondering
what he should advise his clients to do in view of the fact
that Premier was about to merge with Western Broadcasting
(WIC, run by Frank Griffiths, see chapter 6), leaving public shareholders holding non-voting shares. I immediately
responded that he should consider filing an intervention at
the CRTC against the merger on behalf of his clients. John
replied he did not know what an "intervention" was, and when

we investigated we found that, in any case, the time limit for filing interventions was due to expire in two days. I told him I would see what I could do to help, scrambled around and found Peter Grant at McCarthy & McCarthy (later McCarthy Tétrault) who was willing to do the work. We filed an opposition intervention on behalf of Connor Clark and its clients, which was pivotal in upsetting the proposed merger.

Over coffee, John suggested that I move to Connor Clark and use a spare office. I could participate on my public investment recommendations through commissions "in and out," and we would split participations on financings of private companies. I agreed readily, with one proviso: I wasn't sure I wanted to manage money for a living and if a really interesting management opportunity came along, I wanted to be free to jump in. John and Gerry agreed and after about a year, I was invited to buy into the firm. In my first weeks at Connor Clark, I recommended we accumulate Extendicare stock, and eventually our clients did very well on that investment.

The Shaws became clients of Connor Clark and we started to buy shares in Agra on the "offer." Pretty soon the Shaws had bought their limit, and I believe that at one time clients of Connor Clark (including the Shaws) owned 23 percent of Agra. Jim Shaw and I decided that it would be of mutual interest to Shaw Cablesystems and Cablenet to merge. Both companies would benefit from increased critical mass and Torchinsky's holdings in cable TV would reflect the considerably higher market valuations enjoyed by cable companies, which were currently lost in Agra's diverse businesses. Torchinsky could participate in the future growth of the cable TV industry through his shareholding in Shaw Cablesystems and would have a seat on the Shaw Cablesystem's board.

The two sides agreed to retain me to value the two entities using accepted methods. The fit turned out to be excellent, both in terms of numbers and geographic coverage. Finally, the question arose as to who would run the company, and Ben said I would have to convince his partner, Will Manolson, who was head of both Cablenet and Agra's medical lab company, that Jim Shaw should run the combined cable companies. After two meetings, Manolson wouldn't agree, perhaps because he would be losing much of his empire and the merger fell apart. Meanwhile, of course, Connor Clark's clients still owned 23 percent of Agra.

* * *

In April 1982, Grant Devine became premier of Saskatchewan, and in good Tory style, announced that governments don't belong in business. Saskatchewan put its investments in private enterprises up for sale, one of which was a 10-percent holding in Agra. This holding dated back to the early 1970s when the government of Saskatchewan had injected funds into the Saskatoon-based company to save it from bankruptcy. The Shaws liked their investment in Agra and decided to try to buy the government's holding.

Coincidentally, an acquaintance of mine, Earl Curley from Ottawa, who was a psychic I had met through a university friend, called me and I mentioned that I wished I had a contact in the new government of Saskatchewan. (I used to talk to Earl from time to time for fun, but not for business!) To my amazement, Earl said he knew Grant Devine, whose upset election victory Earl had predicted on a television show on meeting Devine a few days before the election. I took up Earl's offer to arrange a meeting, and an hour later he called me back to say, "*We* have a private dinner meeting with Devine next week in Regina." As much as I liked Earl, I was concerned about having a psychic at my side over dinner with the premier, and instructed Earl under no circumstances to discuss business. I was not going to embarrass Devine by being specific about Agra, but wanted to know more about his policy and the government's procedure for divesting itself of investments.

Premier Devine, his executive assistant John McKenzie, Earl, and I had dinner in a private dining room at a hotel in Regina on November 17, 1982. At 8:00 p.m., after dinner, the premier thanked me and went home to spend some time with his children. Earl took me across the street to another hotel where he had arranged for some RCMP officers to meet us for a drink. These officers had been trained by Earl to utilize their innate psychic powers to solve crimes and identify missing persons—all very fascinating for me.

A couple of days later when I was back in my office in Toronto, I received a telephone message from the 214 area code. I dialled the number without checking the location, and the voice at the other end said, "I'm so-and-so from *The Globe and Mail*; I understand you had dinner with the premier of Saskatchewan on Tuesday night." I was stunned. I allowed that I had indeed had dinner with Premier Devine, but wasn't prepared to talk about it, since the conversation had been strictly private. The reporter pressed me but I did not give him any information. I immediately called Earl and assailed him for his indiscretion. He denied leaking details of the meeting to the press, but I told him Devine, his assistant, and I were unlikely sources, which only left Earl. I sensed from his voice that he was guilty and rang off; the damage was done. The next day, *The Globe and Mail* carried the following (in part):

Devine has close encounter with psychic

From the Winnipeg Bureau

REGINA – Saskatchewan Premier Grant Devine had supper last month with business consultant Earl Curley, who is also a psychic.

The encounter made Mr. Devine the laughing stock of Regina—comic relief from the cold winter that has gripped the Prairie capital.

One newspaper cartoon had him resorting to a crystal ball and consulting a pointed-hat wizard trying to sell him the Brooklyn Bridge. Mr. Devine was compared in the Legislature to Prime Minister Mackenzie King, and Opposition Leader Allan Blakeney had a field day with it at the Premier's expense.

It started innocently enough when Mr. Devine agreed to have supper on Nov. 17 with Mr. Curley, who is from Ottawa, and Toronto businessman Anthony F. Griffiths, of Harding Carpets Ltd., at L'Habitant restaurant in Regina.

They wanted to talk to Mr. Devine about possible investments in Saskatchewan. Mr. Devine agreed and brought along his executive assistant, John McKenzie, who later told reporters about the meeting.

Somehow the story that came out was that Mr. Devine was consulting a psychic about the province's economic future. The supper was the topic of items by Wayne Mantyka of CKCK-TV and *Leader-Post* columnist Dale Eisler. And then Mr. Blakeney got into the act.

In the Legislature on Nov. 24, Mr. Blakeney said he had heard that Mr. Devine has been dissatisfied with the advice he's been getting from his Cabinet and caucus, and had "apparently been seeking counsel from one Earl Curley, Psychic and sometime adviser to Pierre Trudeau and Ronald Reagan."

Mr. Blakeney mockingly inquired as to the "nature of the advice" the Premier had received.

"Someone told me you were going to ask that question," Mr. Devine replied amid guffaws.

Mr. Devine said that he did meet a businessman and that Mr. Curley was indeed along, but that the meeting had nothing to do with forecasting the future for Saskatchewan.

Quipped one MLA: "The last one who consulted psychics was around for 30 years."

Clearly, Devine must have been embarrassed; nevertheless, when I met him a year or so later, he was very friendly.

Shortly afterward, the government put all their investments in the private sector up for sale and Ben Torchinsky and his friends exercised their right of first refusal to buy back the Agra shares. Agra then split the shares into voting and non-voting classes and sealed Torchinsky's control over the company. By that time, Connor Clark and its clients had made a satisfactory profit and sold out of the stock.

Since about 1972, I had been on the board of directors of Harding Carpets Limited. Harding had once been a high-growth darling of the stock market, and about the time I joined the board, a long-time employee, an accountant, was appointed president. For a while, momentum carried the company, but then it began to lose market share and became less profitable. The chair, C. Malim Harding, had taken over the company from his father, but devoted his attention to other corporate directorships and the University of Toronto where he was chancellor. The board became restive and finally convinced Malim that we should find a marketing person, preferably with carpet industry experience, to become CEO.

We brought in a new president and charged him with turning the company around. The board left him alone for most of the year to get on with the task, but the company kept sliding. Bank covenants were breached and the budget for the ensuing year projected further losses. The board became uncomfortable with the lack of speed in change and the fact that no clear strategy had been proposed: Harding Carpets was clearly heading for bankruptcy.

A board member, Ralph Barford,[1] fingered me to take a more active role in managing the company, appointing me vice-chair. The president had told us things were bad in the industry and that no one was making any money. I pulled out about eight or ten public carpet company reports and, in about two hours, determined that, in fact, some companies were quite profitable. As I studied the ratios, I soon came to the conclusion that Harding was not competitive at the manufacturing level. I hired a carpet industry consultant who quickly zeroed in on the problems.

It was apparent that there were too many companies in Canada with too much capacity and that Harding might not be able to change sufficiently in time to survive. I began looking for a merger partner and entered into discussions and later negotiations with the Canadian subsidiary of a large U.S. textile company whose carpet operations in Canada were also losing money. Together we identified about $8 million of savings that would be achieved by merging, and forecast that the merged company would become profitable. However, as I delved further into the situation and took account of severance costs, union problems, brand overlaps, and management issues, I began to get cold feet. I called the merger off on the basis that two losers couldn't make a winner in this industry.

By now I had become president and CEO of Harding, and decided to telephone Bram Garber, the chair and CEO and a major shareholder of Harding's main competitor, Peerless Carpet Corporation. Peerless was one of the high-growth strong competitors, and was profitable and paying a dividend. Oddly, Peerless was selling at a relatively lower price in the market than Harding, which was losing money.

Garber somewhat reluctantly agreed to meet with me. He brought with him from Montreal his right-hand man, George Fisher, and the three of us met in Garber's suite at the Hyatt Hotel in Toronto. I told him that Harding and Peerless fit like a glove except that Harding was losing money. I postulated that by combining market share, raw material buying power, the utilization of factories, and closing and selling off redundant offices and warehouses, the two companies together should yield savings of at least $8 million a year. I told Garber he could run it, change its name, and have full control of the company or whatever he wanted. Garber was a little surprised at my confident prediction of $8 million in savings as I wasn't a carpet man and he was a lifelong authority—but I could not reveal that I'd just been through a merger study with one of his competitors. While I had his interest piqued, he was also somewhat leery.

I suggested we choose an independent consultant to undertake a study and we agreed on the well-respected textile consultants, Kurt Salmon Associates (KSA) of Atlanta, Georgia. Garber was still sceptical. Finally, I put a challenge to him that he couldn't refuse: I said, "Let's hire KSA, and if the savings are $8 million or less, Harding will pay for the entire study. If savings are more than $8 million, we'll split the fees." Garber agreed and we proceeded.

An aside: When I became president of Harding, I ran into Ray Wolfe, a fellow director of Confederation Life and chair of the Oshawa Group, who said, "I see that you just became president of Harding. What do you know about the carpet business?" I replied, "Nothing, Ray; that's the best thing going for me." He reflected and said, "Maybe you're right."

Over my career, I have operated in perhaps a dozen different industries and find that there is a real benefit to being an outsider, coming in with a fresh view, distanced from the usually vicious daily competition of the business with its myopia and distrust of competitors. I have on occasion been criticized for my lack of knowledge of a specific industry, but my response has always been that I usually end up in companies that are in serious trouble that were taken there in every case by the mismanagement of "experts" from within the industry!

* * *

When the KSA study was completed, Garber and I met with the consultants in Montreal. The report said there was the potential for savings of at least $15 million. We were all now very excited.

In June 1981, I retained Albert Gnat for his skills in structuring financial transactions, and together we set about pursuing the merger. Peerless was then trading at about $5 to $6 per share, paying a dividend, and had a book value of $10 to $12. A family in the greater New York area controlled about 34 percent of the Peerless stock and, while they attended our negotiation sessions, they appeared to be guided by their lawyers. We offered them $7 to $7.50 per share in cash, the full current market value, plus $7 in paper, totalling $14.50—generous, we felt, given the thin trading at $5.50 only weeks before. They, however, kept trying to ratchet up the price to the $15 area and demanding more cash. We dropped the discussions in exasperation and decided to search out a financial partner to take the family out. We spoke to 10 or 15 potential investors, all of whom declined to invest in the carpet business.

The timing was now approaching 1982, interest rates began to rise precipitously and, one day, orders at Harding evaporated. Carpets are largely discretionary items and consumers were postponing purchases and/or not buying. The financial situation eroded rapidly and, despite radical cost-cutting, the bank covenants had already been breached.

I had been approached in November 1981 by a Malaysian Chinese businessman, Dato H.H. Loy. He was interested in immigrating to Canada, and had purchased a carpet dealership owned and operated by a former Harding employee, Jim Laing. Loy wanted to buy Harding and roll his dealership into it. The carpet industry and the financial community knew by now that Harding was in financial difficulty. Over lunch,

I told Loy he had to speak with Malim Harding, the chair and controlling shareholder, and offer to inject "real money" into the company. He proposed and I agreed that $3 million was required immediately to satisfy the banks and further backup should be available if required. As to procedure, I suggested he draft a formal letter of intent addressed to the board of directors. To my amazement, before the afternoon was over, the letter was delivered. Meanwhile I checked with Loy's two banks, which confirmed that Loy had substantial resources.

The resulting plan was that Loy would inject $1.5 million immediately and the balance on or before December 3, 1982. While this may seem a relatively small amount of money for voting control, the fact was that no other investor had been found to put new money in and, technically, the company was in bankruptcy. Moreover, at the time, $3 million represented one-third of total market capitalization and the transaction was to be completed at book value ($3.65 per share), an 88-percent premium over market price. Loy had ambitions in Canada beyond Harding, which included real estate and financial services. On several occasions he told me he wanted me to be his man in Canada and chair of the company. I was anxious to help him rescue Harding from disaster and we agreed to commence a search for a new CEO to succeed me.

In the meantime, the economy and the carpet business went into free fall. Pressures mounted and Loy, who was travelling every four to five weeks between Malaysia and Canada, left his lawyer, K.K. Chong, behind to complete negotiations and conclude the transaction. During the six- or eight-week period it took to put together the transaction, business got worse. I told Loy the complete facts as I did not want to find myself accused later of not providing full disclosure. In fact, I told Loy I thought he was crazy. Chong was opposed to the deal—as was Loy's accountant, Eric Slavens of Laventhol & Horwath—and said so. But Loy, an eternal optimist, told us that by 1985 the economy would be booming and the real estate in Harding, some of which was redundant, would be tremendously valuable. In hindsight, I suppose Loy was right about future real estate values, but the full brunt of the recession was yet to come. Loy was a classic one-man-show/entrepreneur, paying lip service to his advisers, Harding management, and the board. To my horror, before closing I discovered from sources outside the board that he had unilaterally hired a CEO. A quick check of references suggested there were better candidates, but the man had already been hired.

Three months before the final tranche was due from Loy, I became convinced the company could not survive without substantial additional funding beyond that which was due. Meanwhile, Loy himself was spending more time in Malaysia, where his financial and real estate holdings were under growing pressure as the recession deepened around the world. The new president had not taken certain actions sanctioned by the board and the last time I met with Loy, he agreed with me that the president was a disaster. I told Loy to fire him right away. Loy said he was too busy, so I volunteered. Loy said he would do it when he came back from Malaysia in six weeks, but he never returned.

I convinced the board, against the strong objections of Chong, who now held a management position in the company, that we should seek insolvency advice. I felt that the financial situation would become so serious that Loy would not complete the transaction, which turned out to be the case. On behalf of the board, I retained Ron McKinley of the Clarkson Gordon (now Ernst & Young) insolvency department. By the time the banks called the loan and sent in their monitors (receivers), McKinley had done his homework and was on top of the situation. Over a period of weeks, he was able to orchestrate a soft, non-public, bankruptcy by working with the banks, creditors, debenture holders, and suppliers to negotiate a debt compromise. Fortunately, the Ontario Development Corporation kicked in some money as well. In my view, it was the decision to hire McKinley that saved the company before its loans were officially called.

As the recession abated, the industry began to improve and again, through McKinley's efforts, new equity was injected by a pool of pension funds. In December 1982, Loy and Chong resigned as directors of Harding amid a lawsuit over the share purchase agreement. Harding threatened legal action against Loy when Loy failed to deliver the second tranche of cash. Loy, meanwhile, alleged that the warranties given in the agreement had been breached. In the final outcome, Loy had placed his shares in trust to be voted by the board for a period of time. In the fallout of the Loy debacle, a pension-funded private equity group took over Harding Carpets and injected equity into the enterprise. At the same time, the Canadian economy improved and so did Harding. As I recollect, the values improved to the point that everyone agreed to drop all legal action.

* * *

In late 1996, I was advising Joe Pacione of TacFast Systems on how to commercialize his novel new carpet tile system.

Joe had given an exclusive distribution licence for Canada to Peerless Carpet Corporation a couple of years previously and was disappointed in Peerless's lack of performance in commercializing TacFast. As it happened, Peerless had started to deteriorate financially, losing $25 million on sales of $268 million in 1995, and $12 million on sales of $226 million in 1996.

Coincidentally, I was talking to Eric Sprott of Sprott Securities.[2] When I mentioned Peerless, Eric said he felt Peerless's management had misled him in a financing he had arranged two years previously. I then introduced Eric to Joe and together, with me as the catalyst, we decided to take over Peerless. Eric quickly determined that more than 50 percent of Peerless's shares were held by a few institutions, most of which were known to Sprott. We assembled sufficient proxies for control and approached Bram Garber and the board of Peerless to take control of the company and its management. I believe Garber was relieved that we came to the table because Peerless was on a downward trajectory, and my 15-year relationship with him helped smooth the transition.

In January 1997, Eric and I joined the board, and I recruited two Quebec-based directors: my friend Reed Scowen and Serge Racine, chair of Shermag Inc., a furniture manufacturer. In addition, Peter Gilchrist of Blake, Cassels & Graydon, Pacione's lawyer, joined the board. I became the interim CEO, and as I took up my new assignment, I commenced a search for a permanent CEO. In a few months I was able to recruit Jeffrey Casselman, a carpet expert who was also known favourably to Pacione, and I became chair.

In the meantime, we closed the offices in downtown Montreal and relocated the corporate headquarters to the main factory in Acton Vale, Quebec. In the first year, 1997, net income was $3 million or 23 cents per share on $197 million sales compared with a loss of $6 million (or 97 cents per share) on sales of $226 million the previous year. We thought we were on the way to a major turnaround when, on June 29, 1998, an early morning fire destroyed the bath and floor fashions division factory. Two firefighters were killed fighting the blaze and several employees were injured. This division comprised about 25 percent of the sales of Peerless and was very profitable, providing sufficient profit to subsidize the broadloom operations, which were undergoing wrenching changes. Fortunately the company was fully insured and we were not insolvent. The tragedy was a blow to morale and, of course, resulted in the loss of customers.

We began to search for a merger partner. Fate was on our side and Beaulieu of America came to our rescue. Beaulieu had bought Coronet Canada based in Quebec in 1990 and bought 100 percent of Peerless at $3.10 per share in 1998, a 69-percent premium over book value at year-end in 1997. Despite the horrible tragedy, financially, the shareholders recovered.

10

From Supergun to Handgun, or Down and Out in L.A., 1979–1984

> "This is the classic symptom of folly: refusal to draw conclusions from the evidence, addiction to the counter-productive."
> *Barbara Tuchman,* The March of Folly

In early 1979, I received a call from a fraternity brother from McGill, Gordon Sharwood,[1] who was consulting for the federal government. He asked me if I would like to take on the challenge of becoming CEO of Space Research Corporation (SRC), a company the government was about to take over as a creditor. SRC was founded by Gerald Bull, a brilliant aeronautical engineer and physicist, and the youngest-ever professor of physics at McGill University. In the early 1960s, he started the High Altitude Research Program (HARP) to develop a gun that would fire up to 31 miles. Originally, the U.S. government and McGill University financed this project. By 1969, the Martlet missiles (named after the McGill symbol) reached a record 57 miles. In 1966, with American and Canadian government funding, a Martlet was fired to a height of 112 miles.

In May 1968, Peter and Edward Bronfman controlled a company called Great West Saddlery through which they bought control of SRC, most of which was owned by Gerry Bull. SRC assembled land on the Quebec/Vermont border and acquired a road crossing at the border. In 1969, Bull bought the company back from the Bronfmans, in the process taking on debt.[2]

At the time I became involved, SRC consisted of three entities: a surveillance division with contracts in Kenya and Iraq; a company undertaking the development and trials of the long-range (STUP) gun; and an explosives company acquired from CIL located in Valleyfield, Quebec, 81 miles west of Montreal.

The group was heavily supported financially by governments, through purchase contracts, loans, and other financial assistance. Operations were out of control, with the company embarking on the construction of a forging facility with insufficient financing. The federal government's plan was to take over the company through a memorandum of understanding (MOU), put a credible board in place, and find a CEO who could develop a business plan and stop the financial hemorrhaging.

I agreed to take this on and was given one week to put together a plan. I went to SRC's headquarters in Montreal as acting president and started the process. My first week I visited the 1,500-acre compound at Highwater, Quebec, at the Vermont border, a scene that was something out of a James Bond movie. Within the compound was a Canada-U.S. border crossing, a range for testing guns by firing into a mountain, a ranch-like house complete with swimming pool and tennis court for the Bull family, and the foundations for the forge on which work had stopped due to lack of funding. A crisis atmosphere enveloped the company, with employees wondering whether the government would bail it out or merely let it go into bankruptcy. Gerry Bull was busy with various ownership matters and customer crises and I saw little of him that week.

The company was losing money on all fronts, with the exception of the explosives plant at Valleyfield, which was marginally profitable. There was a mysterious minority share-holder headquartered in Amsterdam, which was often a source of funds, and a bank in Pennsylvania that provided loans. Management avoided discussing these two institutions, saying that they didn't have sufficient knowledge about them amid inferences that they were connected to the CIA. There were widespread rumours among the employees that the RCMP might be investigating the company, with whispered sugges-tions of illegal shipments of arms to South Africa. An air of mystery and secrecy permeated the organization.

One day there was a buzz about "The Chief" visiting the next day. On inquiring, I discovered the chief was Chief Ajaho of Nigeria. When I asked why the excitement, the response was that the chief was a very important but difficult man, who demanded a 25-percent commission, whereas every other agent received 10 percent. Apparently the chief's brother or brother-in-law was the Nigerian defence minister and SRC either did business on the chief's terms or no business was done. I met the chief the following day, and found him a charming, soft-spoken man, five-foot-six and impeccably dressed. In my private discussions I discovered that he owned a 25-percent interest in a steel plant with Voest Alpine as his partner, and 25 percent of an oil refinery being built by a Japanese partner.

In another incident some months after I left SRC, I read in the newspaper that SRC's two Kenyan agents were killed when their airplane exploded on their flight home from Uganda. Allegedly a barometric bomb had been planted in an animal's head given to the agents by Idi Amin, the agents having been asked to deliver the animal head as a present to someone.

* * *

I was prepared for my first meeting of the new board of directors, at which the MOU was to be ratified giving the government control of the company. However, late on Monday I received an urgent call from Sharwood saying that senior officials were coming to Montreal from Ottawa to have dinner with us that night to discuss a subject that they could not disclose until we met. At dinner, these officials announced that the government was not proceeding the next day. When I asked for a reason, they responded that they were not permitted to discuss it. I then said I would resign, to which they replied, "You can't." I said I had heard rumours about illegal shipments and was not prepared to be left in a position where there might be an RCMP investigation that I would read about in *Maclean's* magazine with my picture in it. They tried to dissuade me, but agreed I was a free agent.

The next morning (May 1, 1979) I met with Gerry Bull and his lawyer, Lambert Toupin. We had a very open discussion about my findings, reviewed my plan, and then I tendered my resignation. Bull and Toupin pleaded with me to stay on as CEO but I said I was not prepared to take the risk. I addressed my resignation to Lambert Toupin and he wrote a postscript on the letter: "Your resignation is accepted with great reluctance.

I would appreciate your agreeing to remain at our disposal on terms to be agreed." Toupin was hoping for a miracle that would keep SRC intact with me as CEO.

Bull was on the verge of tears thinking the game was over, when Toupin said, "I wonder if someone would buy the explosives plant; it's our one profitable entity." After some discussion, I volunteered to put a group together to purchase it. They asked how quickly I could act and I said I needed a few days to construct a proposal and speak to my partners, John Christodoulou and Albert Gnat, but that I would respond early the following week.

I flew to Calgary that night for a Home Oil board meeting and worked out a proposal on the flight. I was very excited by the prospects because the only two other explosives plants on the continent had been built in the Second World War. Replacement costs for Valleyfield were estimated at $500 million, virtually precluding further competition. The federal government had determined that the explosives and munitions businesses were required to protect sovereignty, and one or two sizeable contracts existed with foreign users, including the U.S. military. I persuaded my partners that this was a good opportunity and suggested we buy it with bank debt, conditional on the government's loans being subordinated to our bank position.

A date for negotiations was set for the following week, which would include a visit to the facilities at Valleyfield. Gnat, Christodoulou, the banker, and I were to meet at the Toronto airport to fly to Montreal at 7:00 a.m. I picked up Christodoulou at his home to find him in a lather about a stock he had bought where it transpired that the president of the company had provided misleading information. The stock had collapsed, and legal action was being organized. Christodoulou talked to me incessantly right up to the moment of boarding, at which time we didn't see our travelling companions. Nevertheless, we boarded and John kept me occupied the entire flight with his horror story. When we deplaned, I looked around and said, "John, we're not in Montreal." After some confusion, I realized we were in Ottawa—we had boarded the wrong plane! Fortunately, our colleagues did get to Montreal where they were met for the drive to Valleyfield. John and I rented a car and drove, arriving in the early afternoon.

The explosives facility was interesting, chilling, and sobering. We nicknamed it "Stalag II" because of the general atmosphere. It consisted of about 500 separate huts, most of which were damp and steaming. The number, of course, was for safety: in the event of an explosion, theoretically only one hut versus the whole complex would blow up. We arrived at a deal with SRC, conditional on our financing plan being approved by the federal government.

A week later we met in Ottawa with about 20 representatives of the government from various departments, including defence, supply and services, industry and trade, and their advisers. The government was anxious to have our group take over the explosives facility and negotiations proceeded quickly, up to the point of the government being asked to subordinate its debt to our bank position. This proved to be the only sticking point but, for the government, it became a deal breaker; they had never before agreed to subordinate debt to private borrowings. The three of us caucused and decided to insist on the point. We lost and decided to walk away. Several months later I read in the paper that there had been an explosion at Valleyfield and two people were killed.

I thanked my lucky stars that the three of us weren't the owners of the plant.

* * *

From time to time I read of Gerry Bull, who pleaded guilty in 1980 to exporting at least 30,000 howitzer shell forgings and other materials to South Africa in violation of American law and a UN embargo. He was sentenced to one year in jail with six months suspended. In his biography of Bull, Lowther states:

> Bull never seriously believed they would send him to jail, and the court decision came as a shock. He was convinced he had done no wrong, and he suffered the poison of injustice. As he listened to the sentence he felt, he said later, as if he was drowning.[3]

If one reads any of the biographies of Bull, it is easy to understand why he was so severely stressed during my brief encounter with him. He was a driven man, bitter, disappointed and, above all, angry at the people that fed him—that is, the government of Canada. His brilliance made him impatient, intolerant, and abrasive, and he felt he was above the law. When things turned bad he became desperate and appears to have cut corners by dealing illegally with governments on the blacklists of both Canada and the United States.

Nevertheless, sitting in the boardroom of Martineau Walker in Montreal with his lawyer Lambert Toupin, Albert, and me, Bull was a likeable but pathetic man. He fascinated us with tales of his various accomplishments. During the Vietnam War, for example, U.S. Navy ships armed with

Bull's guns could hover off the coast and fire accurately from a range of 16 miles. Since the guns supplied by the Russians to the Viet Cong only had a range of 12 miles, the Americans could relax and pick their targets, enjoying a 4-mile cushion.

One day Bull received an urgent call from Lieutenant-General Arthur Trudeau (no relation to Prime Minister Pierre Trudeau) of the U.S. military procurement saying the Russians had delivered a new gun with a range of 19 miles and the U.S. Navy was getting pummelled. Bull told us that within 120 days of receiving that call, he delivered a new gun that fired 25 miles with precise accuracy. For this and other accomplishments, he was made a U.S. citizen.

In another story, he asked us if we remembered that Syria had suddenly stopped shelling the Golan Heights one October. The reason was because Bull had delivered his new gun to the Israelis and, for each shell fired on the Golan, the Israelis "took out a building in Damascus." The Syrians got the message. Interestingly, the biographies I've seen seem to imply he began work for Iraq for the first time in 1982, whereas he had the surveillance contract during my time. He was a tragic figure with a death wish.

On March 23, 1990, Bull was assassinated at his Brussels apartment by five shots to his head and neck, fired from about a metre away. The general consensus is that the murder was carried out by Israel's Mossad in response to Bull's development of a "supergun" for Iraq under the name Project Babylon.

* * *

As I was coming to the end of my assignment at Harding Carpets in 1982 (see chapter 9), Tony Gooch (former CFO of Cablesystems) called me from Cablecasting in Toronto, where he was doing financial consulting work for the two principals, David Graham and Jim Meekison.[4] The two entrepreneurs had borrowed heavily from the Toronto-Dominion Bank, which was interested in the cable TV business and where Meekison's friend Robin Korthals was executive vice-president (later president). By the time Gooch called me, they had assembled most of Atlanta (three franchises) and the West San Fernando Valley in Los Angeles, California. Having exhausted the bank financing, Cablecasting borrowed $50 million through Drexel Burnham. Neither David nor Jim were operators by inclination and the businesses in the United States were grossly overstaffed and out of control, when, simultaneously, interest rates began to soar. Gooch had persuaded David and Jim to hire me to run their companies while they dealt with the bank, Drexel, and a variety of ownership and other issues. David was also living virtually full-time in London, England, and would flit in and out of Toronto, Atlanta, and Los Angeles.

I told them I needed two weeks to get my mind around the situation and travelled to Atlanta, where their U.S. headquarters, CableAmerica, was located, and then on to Los Angeles in early July 1982. I met David, who was flying in from London, to give him my findings and recommendations. We both arrived at the Beverly Hills Hotel at about the same time and, as soon as I checked in, I called David's room. He always reserved the last of several bungalows attached to the hotel and suggested I meet him there. The sun was setting as we sat on the porch of the bungalow talking. As it became cooler, probably around 11:00 p.m., 2:00 a.m. in Toronto and 7:00 a.m. in London, we felt wide awake and decided to move into the bungalow and order mineral water and tea.

Since the inside was stuffy and stale, I suggested we open the windows and leave the door open to create a draft of fresh air. Our room service arrived and we talked on, probably for two hours, when I decided to go to my room in the main part of the hotel. David was lying on the bed with a number of papers and organizational charts I had given him and I was standing with my back to the door finishing my recommendations, when suddenly I heard a noise behind me.

I turned to see a large black man, dressed in cowboy boots, jeans, a red chequered shirt, and a straw hat, pointing a revolver at my head from three feet away. He babbled rapidly and unintelligibly as he came toward me, sporadically interjecting, "or I'll blow your head off," the only words I could understand. My initial reaction was that this must be a Halloween prank or something, but as he pressed me, always babbling, I backed away staring at his shaking hand holding the revolver six inches from my forehead. As I quickly realized this was serious, my instincts were now or never. Remembering my high school and college wrestling, with my right hand I grabbed the wrist of my assailant's hand holding the revolver and pushed it away from my head—it fired an inch or two from my head. I threw him to the floor on his back and, holding his wrist against the wall, I used my left arm to press his neck against the wall. I turned my head and yelled to David, "For Christ's sake, come and help me," only to see David lying on the bed, white as the sheets, with his hands up in surrender. When I turned to see what to do next to my momentary captive, I saw another pair of large feet to my left. An accomplice standing guard outside had come to his friend's aid and had aimed a gun at David. I rolled off onto my stomach and was severely pistol-whipped, while they took my $200 in cash (fortunately I'd left my wallet in my coat in my room), my $20 Timex watch, and David's $8,000 Bulgari watch. Since David never carries money, there wasn't any more.

The burglars departed and David picked me up and put me on the bed, which quickly looked like a slaughter pen with the blood from my head wounds. David phoned the hotel and said, "Get an ambulance. A man in my room has just been shot in the head." With this statement, of course, I thought I had been shot. While waiting for the ambulance, all I could think of was Jim Brady, who had been shot with President Reagan the previous year. I asked David to call my lawyer in Toronto, ensure I would have the best brain surgeon possible, and not tell my wife until full details were known.

The paramedics arrived and rushed me off to the UCLA Medical Centre. Dr. Norman Levy was on duty and, after examining my head wound, said, "Mr. Griffiths, I'm going to have to X-ray you; I think there's a bullet in your head." After an anxious wait for the results, I was barely conscious when Dr. Levy came back and said, "You're a lucky man. There's no bullet. I'll sew you up and you can go home." Since the hospital had cut off my shirt and trousers, I returned to the hotel in a hospital gown and paper slippers about 6:00 a.m. Los Angeles time. My head was matted with blood and I stayed in my room all day, suffering periodic dizzy spells, which continued sporadically for about six months. I couldn't retrieve my shoes because the police had sealed off David's room while they conducted their forensic analysis. The bullet went through the picture on the wall.

At the end of the day, David brought me a pair of jeans and a shirt (as I had planned to spend only one night in Los Angeles

I hadn't brought a change of clothes). That evening we watched me being loaded into the ambulance on the 6:00 p.m. news—probably on cable TV.

* * *

I had given David all my recommendations before the muggers arrived, including details of how I planned to budget, flatten the organization, and drastically reduce overhead. There were two critical recommendations that David would not accept: pull the plug on CableAmerica's 200 employees at head office, except for two or three key financial people, and change the method of selling to "bulk" customers like apartment buildings. When David refused to budge on these two fundamental issues, I told him I was not prepared to sign on as the CEO. I agreed instead to become a consultant to the U.S. company and later acted as CEO for Cablecasting, the Canadian operations, while David and Jim thrashed around the United States.

On paper, David and Jim were wiped out, but the bank took the view that they might as well leave the founders in place. I remember one specific conversation with David in Atlanta, where he was down and out, asking me at the point of tears how to apply for a job because he'd always been self-employed and didn't know how to go about it. The end appeared inevitable. Suddenly interest rates began to fall quickly as the recession abated, and larger companies began to buy cable properties again. Prime Cable, introduced by the TD Bank, took over the Atlanta franchises and, later, Standard Broadcasting of Toronto acquired the Los Angeles property. David and Jim came home to Canada with their tails between their legs and little or nothing to show for the U.S. experience.

During this, David asked me to help him in Great Britain, where he had hired Roy Faibish (now dropped by Rogers). My role was to assist with raising money through the merchant banks in London for David to assemble franchises in a formula whereby David would receive a significant carried interest. It was quite bizarre attending meetings with Roy and David at Hill Samuel, James Capel, and Coopers & Lybrand, when in reality, David's interests in North America had virtually collapsed. Nevertheless, it was an interesting project for me and gave me a view of the embryonic cable TV business in Britain.

To finish my story with David, in 1992 Shaw Communications, where I was a director, purchased David's Canadian holdings for $234 million and Tony Gooch negotiated the transaction as a consultant on behalf of Shaw. The lesson? Don't give up: it's never over till it's over.

* * *

During the period 1979 to 1984, I had maintained my association with Connor Clark while working with Harding and then Cablecasting. I also kept my connection with Albert Gnat, who assisted me at Harding, and together we examined a number of investments. One day in 1983, Albert sent me a jumble of papers about a school bus company called Allway, owned by Nick Comsa, who also operated a taxi business. While running the taxis day-to-day, Comsa had assembled about 100 school buses servicing routes in greater Toronto, while also servicing a contract with the Toronto Transit Commission (TTC) to manage the Wheel-Trans service for the disabled. He was entirely a one-man show and, between the complexities of business and personal pressures, had decided to sell out.

When I studied the business, I liked it because it reminded me of CATV: recession resistant, predictable cash flow, and three-year contracts with school boards against which banks would lend. There were two major school bus operators in Canada: Travelways, a subsidiary of the giant Laidlaw, and a strong second, Charterways owned by Scott's Hospitality, a public company. The rest of the industry in most of Canada was composed primarily of small mom-and-pop operations.

Allway was providing such poor service that it was in jeopardy of losing the school board and TTC contracts. We saw an opportunity to buy Allway and assemble smaller local and rural companies on borrowed money. However, as I was commuting to Atlanta and Los Angeles with Cablecasting, I suggested we find a partner who had some background in the vehicle business, including service, repairs, maintenance, leasing, and the like. Through Albert, I had come to know Richard (Rick) McGraw, and recommended him. Rick had worked with National Student Marketing and CBS Records of Canada before going out on his own in the mid-1970s. He owned a major Toronto-based Honda car dealership and a chain of clock stores.

Rick liked the idea and the three of us formed a partnership, giving Rick as the operator more shares than Albert and me, but with equal voting rights. We borrowed the funds from the Bank of Montreal and felt we had made a great deal. Feeling cocky, we then bought G&W Freightways, a small less-than-truckload (LTL) trucking company operating in a very competitive lane between Toronto and Montreal and owned by a volatile and emotional entrepreneur. As soon as we became familiar with Allway and G&W, we realized that both were cans of worms. We had major operating problems, which came close to bringing both companies down before we were able to stabilize them. As we progressed, we succeeded in gaining school bus contracts and gradually built arguably the best-run computer-scheduled operation in Toronto.

Early in 1987, as the stock market was escalating, we were approached by a number of investment dealers suggesting we take our transportation companies public. We created a corporation called Vitran Inc. and sold 28 percent to the public in July 1987 at $7 per share, ascribing a market capitalization of $39 million to the company.

We continued to build the company and matters were progressing well. One day I had lunch with Tony Arrell, who was the chair and CEO of Walwyn, later Midland Walwyn, where I was a director. Tony asked if we would ever consider selling our school bus operations, as he was a director of Scott's Hospitality, which owned our competitor Charterways. We were competing with Charterways and Laidlaw bidding on school board contracts and for acquisitions.

I told Tony I was sure our board would consider an offer providing it reflected the "private values" Laidlaw, Charterways, and Vitran were paying for private companies. These values were arrived at by a rule of thumb formula: the appraised value for real estate, depreciated value of the bus fleets, and a goodwill factor of $16,000 to $18,000 per school bus route. On that basis, Vitran would be valued at about $7 per share compared with the prevailing market price ("public market value") of about $4 per share. Tony understood our parameters and we received a quick response from Charterways.

Negotiations proceeded and the transaction closed on February 5, 1991. An initial payout to shareholders of Vitran of $26.6 million or $4.64 per share was made on March 7, 1991, with another 13 cents per share due to follow on the second anniversary, subject to any adjustments. Based on the purchase price of $27.1 million, the divestiture resulted in a significant return to Vitran of more than 50 times the original investment of $500,000. The remaining transportation businesses of the company had revenues of $100 million and the stock traded at $2.50 after the sale of the division, for a total value of $7.27 for each share. In effect, we sold the school bus division for more than the total market price of the company at the time we commenced discussions.

By 2010, Vitran had revenues of $673 million operating as a predominantly non-union provider of freight surface transportation and related supply chain services throughout Canada and in 29 states in the United States. Shareholders' equity was $99 million.

11

Crisis at Mitel and then British Telecom Calls, 1984–1987

"A thicket within a swamp within a morass."
Unknown

One Sunday in October 1984, as I was packing up the family to return to Toronto from my country home at Creemore near Collingwood, Ontario, Albert Gnat telephoned and said, "We're going to Ottawa on Tuesday." When I asked why, he replied, "We're going on the board of Mitel." I knew nothing about Mitel, except that it had been a "go-go" stock in the late 1970s and had recently been selling off in the stock market, with the share price dropping. I started to ask Albert about the company, but he cut me off saying, "I'll tell you about it on the plane; it's very interesting."

When I met him at the airport, he told me that two independent directors were going to resign in protest against management. As Mitel got into problems, Terry Matthews (a founder and now president and CEO) and his financial staff had been making frequent visits to Toronto to meet with banks, using Lang Michener's offices as a base. Matthews's friend, fellow director, and key legal adviser, Kent Plumley, had a brother Don who was a partner at Lang Michener. In their preparations for meetings with banks, Don Plumley would involve Albert Gnat, who occupied the adjacent office.

As was typical, Albert soon dominated and orchestrated the strategy discussions and became the key adviser on fundraising. When the two directors tabled their resignations, Matthews invited Albert to join the board and asked him to suggest another candidate who had broad business experience and knew the banking community. Albert suggested me and, although I had not yet met any Mitel people, acting on his judgment, I agreed to join the board.

Mitel Corporation was incorporated in Canada in March 1971. It was founded by Dr. Michael Cowpland and Terence Matthews, and commenced operations in Ottawa in 1973. The company's primary activity was the design and supply of telecommunications equipment, in particular private branch exchanges (PBXs) and business telephones.

Initial expansion was rapid, and in 1976, Mitel acquired its own integrated circuit (chip) manufacturing facility in Bromont, Quebec, followed by another plant in Burlington, Vermont, permitting the use of chips of its own design and manufacture in many of its telecommunications products. The company went public in 1979 and quickly became a darling high-tech stock. Sales jumped from $315,000 in 1975 to $22 million in 1979 to $204 million in 1982. Additional public offerings of shares followed in 1980 and 1981, including a U.S. issue. The shares were listed in Toronto, Montreal, New York, and London, and peaked at $48 $\frac{7}{8}$ per share in May 1981, giving a market capitalization of $1.6 billion.

In addition to equity capital, long-term finance was raised from other sources. In 1983, $115 million was raised through two issues of convertible debentures and a further $35 million mortgage note issue was placed by Drexel Burnham in April 1985. The company also received $50 million in government grants in Canada and the UK, and raised $136 million in Canada through the issue of preferred shares and the sale of tax deductions attributable to its research and development (R&D) expenditure under Canadian tax incentive schemes then available. Other commercial banking lines existed from 1982 providing up to $200 million, although these evaporated in late 1984 and early 1985 as operations deteriorated.

Mitel went on a spree with these funds, building factories around the world: Kanata and Renfrew, Ontario; Bouctouche, New Brunswick (which never opened); Ireland; Caldicot, Wales; Deerfield Beach and Boca Raton, Florida; Puerto Rico; Ogdensburg, New York; Colorado; two plants in Hong Kong; and assembly operations in Germany and New Zealand. Competitors around the world, like Plessey and GEC in the UK, Siemens in Europe, and Northern Telecom, AT&T, and ROLM in North America, reacted to Mitel's attack on their markets and the business became intensely competitive.

This early dramatic growth had given management false confidence that it could continue unabated, and Mitel decided to leap from low-end products (switches of under 200 lines) to a large switch, the SX-2000 digital switch capable of handling up to 1,200 lines, first introduced in January 1984.[1] In layman's terms, this was analogous to the company going from selling small personal computers into selling organizational-size mainframes.

This was a crucial transition and laid the groundwork for what was to befall the company after 1984. As I recollect, the original budget for development of the SX-2000 was $35 million, of which the Canadian federal government financed $10 million, and the timeline to achieving positive cash flow was two years. However, the SX-2000 was not just a new product; it was effectively a diversification into a new business, where the costs and management requirements were significantly different and larger than Mitel's traditional low-end business—it required long (expensive) gestation periods to consummate sales, customers demanded a high level of after-sales support, and the product could not be sold effectively through Mitel's existing distribution channels, particularly in the United States and Canada.

Management failed to recognize the financial squeeze that was occurring and the negative consequences were swift and traumatic. The funds raised had gone into bricks and mortar, much of which was underutilized or had never been opened. In 1983, for example, management was forced to close the semiconductor division's plant in Burlington, Vermont, which had been open for only one year.

In addition, the company was being drained of cash on various other fronts, including the development costs of the SX-2000 which had extensive capital requirements and suffered numerous software glitches; expanding admin-istration and salary costs, with 6,200 employees in 1984 (which were pared down to 3,000 by 1993); and ballooning inventories that in 1985 totalled $155 million on sales of $371 million.(By comparison, at March 1993, the end of my last year at Mitel, inventories were $61 million on sales of $423 million.) Finally, gross margins suffered a rapid decline, from a high of 54.4 percent in 1982 to 39.8 percent in May 1985.

While en route to Ottawa for our first board meeting, Albert related the financial condition of the company and the terms under which the existing bank, the Royal Bank of Canada, would continue funding the company. This was October 1984 and the Royal had stated that it would pull its line of credit in January unless a new CEO was hired from outside the company; an equity partner was brought in; and supplementary financial plans were put in place to make the operations cash positive.

Albert assured me, as he had been assured by Matthews and Kent Plumley, that the board was pursuing these conditions and progress was being made.

When we joined the meeting, we learned that an executive search firm had been retained in New York to find a CEO and that a number of potential industrial investors had conducted due diligence on the company. It was widely known that IBM had looked seriously at the company and apparently concluded that the development of the new large switch, the SX-2000, was greatly underfunded and would require significantly more time and funds to complete than Mitel's management had forecast. (After IBM walked away from the Mitel opportunity, it bought another major PBX manufacturer, ROLM Corporation, for $1.6 billion. IBM divested ROLM to Siemens in 1990–93 at an estimated loss of $1 billion.)

Burroughs Corporation, which later became Unisys, was also at the table doing due diligence. The man in charge of the project was Dr. Paul Stern, president of Burroughs, who later became chair and CEO of Northern Telecom (later Nortel), Mitel's arch-competitor in Canada, which was 52 percent owned by BCE (Bell Canada Enterprises). Burroughs was reported to be interested in Mitel in principle, *providing* that it could take control of management. Since Matthews seemed unprepared to turn over management control, there was effectively no one to rescue the company.

After two board meetings, in discussions with some of the non-management directors and Kent Plumley, Albert and I came to realize that management did not share the same sense of urgency as did the rest of the directors concerning the need to satisfy the bank's conditions. Meanwhile, the losses were gushing and cash was evaporating rapidly. Management continued to assure the board that appropriate action was being taken and that the future business outlook was sufficiently positive to bring results back on side. At the same time, there was a considerable lack of communication between management and the bank, and management's view was that a replacement bank could be relatively easily found.

When I realized how bad the situation was, I wrote to Albert on December 27, 1984 (only two months after joining the board), and said in part:

As we became involved, we understood the following were being explored:

- new bank
- Penfund financing
- Drexel financing
- sale of redundant plants
- search for CEO
- search for equity partner

These were to a great extent inter-related to provide both management and financial confidence in the company.

You have been focusing on the mechanics, techniques and technicalities of the financing packages vis-à-vis Penfund, banks, Drexel, etc. without confronting the real problem of management and corporate confidence, internal and external. This confrontation is now inescapably before the board. If we do not deal with this with speed and decisiveness, we risk a debacle on all fronts. My sense is that, individually, the board and management recognize the problem, but have not been able to deal with it collectively.

You and I must fish or cut bait as we have great potential exposure without any real remuneration for the risk. We presently have no ability to exercise control over events unless the board takes action satisfactory to correct our concerns.

Even though I was the new boy on the board, I made up my mind to resign. However, when I mentioned this to two or three other non-management board members, they also said they'd resign. This, of course, would have created a joint responsibility for bringing down the whole house of cards.

The board now was in crisis, and debates ensued as to what to do. Weeks turned into months when, out of the blue, British Telecom (BT) arrived in Canada and announced they were prepared to pay market price, $8 per share, for 51 percent of Mitel for a total of $322 million for treasury shares.

The five people comprising the BT negotiating contingent were led by Derek Vander Weyer, a lifetime Barclays Bank man, deputy chair of BT, and believed to be the anointed successor to the chair, Sir George Jefferson. Vander Weyer announced to the board on Wednesday, "We're here till Friday, and if we don't buy Mitel, we'll go home and buy something else."

We couldn't believe our good luck, but unfortunately the transaction was delayed when the UK Monopolies and Mergers Commission (MMC) announced it wanted to review it. BT was, at the time, a monopoly and there were concerns that other suppliers in the UK, such as Plessey and GEC, might be disadvantaged by BT owning control of an equipment supplier and competitor.

Part of the transaction with BT was that Terry Matthews was to be given a seat on BT's board and have a yet-to-be-defined role as marketing consultant worldwide. The BT contingent went home and, with their support, the board of Mitel formed a committee to search for a new CEO.

* * *

While the search was carried out over the summer, Mitel continued to lose cash at an accelerating rate. The board was in the awkward position of knowing that the company was melting down, while at the same time BT was requesting that no major action be taken that might ameliorate the situation (such as reducing R&D or dropping entire product lines), because BT wanted to maintain all of the technology for the future. Both BT and the board were in agreement that action be taken to *reduce operating losses* (excluding R&D), but management was unable to respond satisfactorily. On July 29, 1985, I wrote Terry Matthews, with a copy to Michael Cowpland, chair of Mitel, suggesting various ways to make board meetings less "confused and undisciplined." Toward the end of the letter I pressed for a contingency plan, on the following terms:

> Now that the BT transaction will be protracted by many months and the odds of completion appear lower than originally thought, it seems to me that a very high priority should be directed to formulating a contingency plan. In one of the meetings leading up to the budget, I volunteered the view that the budget should start with an assumption of making a profit of $40 million pre-tax in fiscal 1986 and work back from there. I did this for three reasons:
>
> 1. I had a low comfort level with the ability to meet current forecasts, which were emanating from field sales (rather than being management driven).
> 2. I take the view as a businessman (investor, banker or otherwise) that a business such as Mitel should make money at this stage in its evolution or it won't survive, especially as an independent competing against giants.
> 3. My experience with turnaround situations is that, if one doesn't start with a predetermined profit objective, it won't happen. The cloth must be cut to fit the ultimate objective.

At a board meeting in late October 1985, with a BT representative present, it was unanimously decided that I should replace Terry Matthews as president and CEO and he would step up to the post of chair, replacing his co-founder, Mike Cowpland. At this stage, BT was confident it would receive approval to complete the purchase of Mitel before Christmas

1985, at which point they could install their own man as CEO. The board, however, still had the problem that BT's purchase might be disallowed, and BT's insistence that no cuts be made in R&D or major product lines, such as the SX-2000, was continuing to suck up cash. Consequently, if for any reason BT did not complete the purchase, the board would be in a very difficult and vulnerable position.

David Golden, chair of Telesat and the elder statesman on the board, suggested that I receive a retainer, some stock options, and be made permanent CEO. (I first met David Golden in May 1975 when we set up CableSat: see chapter 6.) The BT representative opposed this latter stipulation (it was believed by Mitel management that the BT representative coveted the job) and some discussion followed. I broke the log-jam by saying, "We've all got a problem. Why don't I do the job for six months to stop the hemorrhaging and when we get the MMC blessing, BT can put in their own man. If the deal isn't approved, I'll have the problem." Everyone agreed and that's what was done. I decided to pay 20 percent of my compensation to Connor Clark for the six-month period because I felt I would not contribute much to the partnership while I was immersed in the problems of Mitel in Ottawa.

* * *

An aside: Just prior to my appointment I had dinner with Justice Willard Z. (Bud) Estey, my predecessor as CEO of Canadian Cablesystems, now a Justice of the Supreme Court of Canada. I was reluctant to tell Bud of my pending appointment as CEO of Mitel, thinking, "Do I give a judge of the Supreme Court 'selective disclosure' information?" The next day, after my

Mike Coupland and Terry Matthews in the water. (Courtesy of the author.)

appointment was announced, I received a very friendly letter from Bud, saying in part:

> Dear Tony:
>
> You keep a secret very well as you must have been elected president of Mitel the morning after we had dinner. As I mentioned to you more than once, I view the Mitel transaction as a microcosm of our national crisis and I was genuinely relieved to hear the news that you had taken over the management. Of course, I vicariously bask in your success because many long years ago I had something to do with hiring you for a not altogether unrelated executive position. For all these reasons, I am confident that you will pull off the reorganization of Mitel internally and the realignment of ownership externally. I trust you will either move to Ottawa for this purpose or will spend a great deal of time here, in which case we will see you more frequently.

* * *

The investment community and the press reacted positively to my appointment. On October 22, 1985, the *Ottawa Citizen* ran the headline "Mitel latest executive shuffle puts new axe swinger in place." And on October 23, 1985, the *Toronto Star* wrote: "New chief favours team play that analysts say Mitel needs":

> Tony Griffiths, a 55-year-old professional manager, is getting enthusiastic applause from stock market analysts as he takes over as boss at Mitel Corp.

Griffiths, whose appointment as president and chief executive officer of the money-losing Kanata-based company was announced last Friday, says he is a team player.

And that, analysts say, is exactly what Mitel needs.

"My mandate is to return the company to profitability," Griffiths says. "I believe in hiring the right people, setting targets and building a management team."

John Hough, high-tech analyst for Wood Gundy Ltd., says Griffiths was appointed because Mitel needs "a mature, experienced individual who can help the company achieve its potential."

The company is "a Canadian world organization that has learned the technological smarts of working outside Canada," Hough says. "Now it's getting management smarts."

While I didn't know the intricacies of the organization, I had more than an inkling of what had to be done at Mitel, having sat on the board for one year. I also knew I had to act swiftly and take some chances.

Four weeks later, the November 16, 1985, the business section of the *Citizen* captured the flavour of my decisions in the headline "Regions lose power to HQ in major shakeup at Mitel":

It hasn't taken Anthony Griffiths long to clearly establish himself as the man in charge at telecommunications equipment manufacturer Mitel Corp.

In a stunning shake-up announced Friday, Griffiths has restructured the struggling company's worldwide operations, eliminating the existing regionally managed business centres in favour of a so-called functional organization.

As a result of the restructuring about 30 head office positions became redundant and will be phased out, said company spokesman Mary Murphy.

Rather than have each of three business regions responsible for their own marketing, operations and development, the restructuring will allow Griffiths to have direct control over company-wide efforts in these three areas, with Smith, Mayer and Lewis reporting to him.

The restructuring is the latest effort to return Mitel to profitability. Mitel has lost $92 million during the last 10 quarters, and through the first six months of the current fiscal year, equalled its total fiscal 1985 losses for the year ended Feb. 22 of $32.1 million.

* * *

I now found myself in the rats' nest, as one analyst described Mitel. The company was completely decentralized, with each region encouraged to manage all functions autonomously— there were pockets of R&D around the world, for example. In Caldicot, Wales, they were developing a small switch (the SX-50) for the UK market, without providing for technical compatibility with Mitel's other main products, and management in Britain were saying, "We'll show those jerks in Kanata how to design a PBX."

Meanwhile, the purchasing team at BT had decided that they were not going to honour commitments on the SX-2000 because Mitel had repeatedly missed delivery deadlines. Mitel people in the UK were telling me how stupid and incompetent the BT people were, while BT was by far Mitel's largest single customer and, of course, on the threshold of becoming the controlling shareholder. I quickly changed out the top management in Britain, with instructions for the new team to figure out how to satisfy the customer.

Back at headquarters in Kanata, I found myself immersed in what was widely known throughout the company as the product wars. The two major product lines had evolved on different technology platforms: the SX-200 (low end) and SX-2000 (high end). It was generally believed that the company should choose only one of these as the basis for its future operations, since to perpetuate both would complicate selling, manufacturing, and customer support, and require excessive R&D. Meanwhile, the SX-50 was being developed in Britain and, in separate premises in Kanata, the 71-percent-owned subsidiary Trillium was providing key systems (telephones for small offices), and had its own autonomous operations spreading around the world. The semiconductor division saw itself as an arm's length autonomous entity, and its management was concocting a spin-off management buyout, planning to fill their hats with "promoters' shares." To complete the picture, technology to route least-cost long-distance calls and other encryption-type devices was being developed within Mitel, but since the company couldn't afford to bring these products to market, 30 percent of a subsidiary called Datacom had been sold to local businessmen, lawyers, and friends as a tax-driven limited partnership investment.

The R&D group in Kanata was headed by a 32-year-old engineer, Conrad Lewis. Reporting to him were two key managers, Les Kirkland of the SX-200 group and David Levy

leading the SX-2000 team. Kirkland was an affable, dedicated long-time employee, while Levy had been recruited
from Mitel's Canadian rival, Northern Telecom, eight months
previously with the mandate of bringing the stalled SX-2000
development to fruition on an urgent basis. Levy was revered
as a brilliant, hard-nosed engineer, but was also messianic
and abrasive in his approach. This product war was known
throughout the company as a true pissing match. Working on
the same premises, the teams not only shunned each other, they
also bitterly attacked each other's competence and motives.
I spent my first days as president interviewing managers and
listening to this soul-destroying saga. The world of Mitel was
waiting to see how I would resolve the festering mess.

One day Levy came to me and said the SX-2000 was the
technology of the future, necessary for the company's survival,
and further development on the SX-200 products should be
capped. Moreover, he said that Lewis—Levy's boss—was in
over his head and an incompetent manager. Unless I agreed
to support the SX-2000 and change out Lewis, Levy said he
would leave. He did not ask to become head of R&D, although
the rest of the senior management believed that was his aim. I
called Lewis to my office and told him he had a problem with
Levy. He was thunderstruck.

Since Lewis was a good man whom I wanted to keep, I
decided to put him in a product support function and replaced
him with a more mature manager from operations, Bill Craigie.
Craigie assured me he could resolve the internecine war now
that I had moved Lewis. At the same time, he told me that we
owed Levy a substantial bonus because he had met certain milestones established when he was hired. With an endless variety
of ad hoc compensation deals made with specific individuals,

the lack of equitable compensation practices throughout the company was demoralizing to staff. Since Levy's bonus was "contractual," I agreed to pay it and Craigie assured me this would satisfy all of Levy's demands. The next day Craigie sheepishly walked into my office and said, "I can't believe it—Levy submitted his resignation." He left for a job with ITT in Europe. This situation was symptomatic of the state of employee morale.

* * *

I set about assembling as much data as I could find on competitors in the telecom equipment and computer-related businesses. It quickly became apparent what was wrong at Mitel: margins were falling quickly, there were too many plants and too many people, and no critical mass existed in any product line or geographic area. Measuring company expense-to-revenue levels with industry averages, it was apparent that Mitel was out to lunch:

	Mitel	Industry
Marketing	17.1%	12–14%
Administration	13.8%	8–9%
Gross R&D	17.4%	10–11%
Total	48.3%	30–34%

This meant that, on $350 million of revenues for the year ending March 1985, Mitel's expenses were over industry ratios by $50 to $60 million. In addition, 6-percent interest rates were costing the company $21 million per annum.

With the new organization, we established a two-step plan to attain industry averages, improve margins, and radically rationalize manufacturing. We planned to at least break even the first year (fiscal year-end March 31, 1987), and become profitable the following year. In the ensuing months we closed factories in Deerfield Beach, Florida, Puerto Rico, and Renfrew, Ontario, and one of the plants in Hong Kong; put up for sale the never-opened plant at Bouctouche, New Brunswick; closed our warehousing and distribution centre in Slough, near London; and reduced the number of employees from a high of 6,200 to 4,200. This plan was approved by both the board and British Telecom.

In May, I obtained board authorization to make a critical investment in company-wide quality management, which was to produce tremendous benefits for the company in future years. In my opinion, this one decision was responsible for the survival of the company in the difficult times after BT orphaned it in January 1990 by putting its 51-percent interest up for sale. Quality and management processes were egregiously bad throughout the organization. Every week there were long lists of "hot sites"—customers whose switching systems were failing or not functioning, with service and maintenance people flying around the world to fix them. Equipment was coming back for repair and rework. The list of lawsuits for non-performance of equipment and contracts was growing, with one customer suing for $7 million for faulty speaker-phones. Quality management was non-existent.

The manager for Canada at the time, Bill Kiss, recommended we hire Philip Crosby Associates of Florida to train the entire organization in quality management. I identified easily with this need, remembering my army ("do it by numbers") and Consumers Glass experiences of systematizing the company. Even though the company was hemorrhaging cash, I was able to persuade the board to authorize $1.4 million to retain Crosby for this essential training. I believe this was instrumental in BT following the same path on quality management about a year later.

***

On March 11, 1986, BT received approval to complete its purchase of Mitel. I was summoned to London to meet with the minister of trade and industry to whom the MMC reported. We then went to the boardroom at 81 Newgate Street, BT's austere headquarters, where Sir George Jefferson and his board and management were euphoric. Derek Vander Weyer, deputy chair of BT and the new chair of Mitel replacing Terry Matthews, two other BT-designate directors on Mitel's board, and I met privately in Derek's office to draft internal and external announcements. Derek started by saying, "Let's make a list of the synergies." An awkward silence prevailed as the BT people searched for examples. There was mumbling about the resources at BT Research Labs, but also recognition that these were more directed to meeting network applications rather than equipment. Finally I said, gingerly, "Let's face it; there aren't any—other than cash." There was no response and the meeting adjourned with a bare-bones press release.

I then asked Derek, "Where's your new man?" He replied they didn't have anyone and asked me what conditions I would require to stay. I asked for a three-year contract, saying that was the time I needed to get the company back on track: one year to clean up the mess, another to get the company back together, and the third would be profitable. He agreed that this was a reasonable request, but three weeks later in Canada he told me the BT chair, George Jefferson, would not agree because he was retiring in August of that year (1986) and "didn't want to bind his successors." BT would agree to an 18-month contract renewable annually. I felt ambivalent: on one hand I didn't want to give up my role at Connor Clark, while on the other, I had already put so much blood and sweat into Mitel, and was just beginning to see the light on the horizon. I decided to take my chances and stay with Mitel, sold my shares in Connor Clark back to the partnership and took a "leave of absence." Connor Clark maintained an office for me, kept my name in the corporate brochure as a consultant, and encouraged me to return when I'd accomplished my mission.

* * *

By now I knew that I was sitting on another potential bombshell. Terry Matthews was chafing in his new but undefined role as roving ambassador for BT and feeling highly frustrated watching me dismantle the structure that he had created. He was also having a running battle with BT's principal technical guru, Dr. Peter Troughton, and pelted the BT chair, Sir George Jefferson, with written missiles criticising BT—and Troughton in particular.

Meanwhile, Terry had quietly formed a new enterprise, Newbridge Networks Corporation. As I was downsizing Mitel, technical and other people were let go, with fair settlements. Ingeniously, Terry was taking on many of these people and granting them equity participation in Newbridge (instead of paying them a salary), relying on them to live off their severance payments for the initial period of their Newbridge employment.[2]

Terry's secretary and personal assistant, Debbie Conlon, who stayed at Mitel with me, found herself in an increasingly awkward position. Because of her long service, she was privy to the undercurrent at play within the organization and knew the magnitude of Newbridge's ambitions. She struggled with her divided loyalties—on a personal basis to Terry and her responsibilities to the company and me. Very nobly, she wrote Terry and asked him to reconsider his approach and to take her out of the compromising loop.

This all burst like a boil one day when I received an urgent call from a young technical supervisor in Mitel, who reported that Newbridge was entering the high-growth telecommunications business of transmission multiplexers using technology and people from Mitel's organization.

I immediately advised the BT liaison man, Peter Berrie,[3] and the board, which created a committee in Mitel headed by Conrad Lewis (who became an employee of Newbridge six months later) to determine Mitel's position. Lewis recommended that Mitel should immediately assert ownership over the new products and technology. This brought Terry into conflict with BT, who had not made him a director of BT or established a role for him there. On April 17, 1986, I received this note from Peter Berrie:

Two points:

(i) I mentioned your concerns re Terry to David Leakey. We shared the view that the solution was probably an approach by BT to licensing some BT technology to Terry (subject to Mitel agreement) in exchange for BT share of the companies resulting. On Newbridge, he agreed that Terry should submit a proposal to Mitel.

He envisaged this resulting in a proposal from Terry to BT (Sir George), first cleared by Mitel. I offered Terry help in generating such a proposal, either personally or by making (e.g.) Janey Marshall available for financial analysis. He seems not to feel it is needed, but will show me a draft.

(ii) Albert has sent a fairly moderate but very clear letter to Terry, first warning him verbally that it was coming.

The shock waves should reach you shortly!

I was determined to stay out of this emotionally charged issue—I had enough to do sorting out strategy and operations. Albert Gnat, David Golden, David Leakey, and others worked on resolving the matter.

Much correspondence ensued and eventually joint ownership of Newbridge was proffered; apparently at one point Terry himself offered BT a significant minority shareholding of Newbridge through Mitel. However, so much acrimony had crept into the relationship that BT and the board of Mitel decided to break with Terry. Newbridge became a customer of Mitel Semiconductor and Terry continued to hire people away from Mitel and pick up those who were leaving the corporation as Newbridge expanded. Because of the closeness of the small high-tech community in Ottawa, there is an underground relationship between the companies that exists to this day.

* * *

While I was addressing the foregoing issues and hiring some key people from the outside, I realized that every day brought a new crisis and I needed a detached overview of the company to develop a longer-term direction. In the spring of 1986, the board authorized me to hire a consulting firm with extensive telecommunications experience and, after interviewing various prospects, we chose Booz Allen Hamilton (BAH). BAH commenced its assignment early in the summer and, by August, working with management, had developed a framework strategy.

BAH recommended that, in addition to radically scaling down the company and cutting costs out of operations, the company should spin off, sell, or close down the SX-2000, which was placing a cost and overhead layer on the company that it could not afford. The product was now eight years old and still required at minimum an additional $45 million in R&D alone to make it competitive with similar products from AT&T, ROLM, NEC, and Northern Telecom. Worse, Mitel did not possess the distribution or support structure to sell the SX-2000, especially in North America. Taking all these factors into account, together with the company's lack of critical mass both in individual products and geographically, I began to think about finding a merger or distribution partner. More on this later.

* * *

On July 8, 1986, at the Mitel annual general meeting nine months after I became president, the future course of Mitel was changed radically. Derek Vander Weyer, a competent, balanced, experienced professional, retired as a director and chair of Mitel. For health reasons he also left British Telecom in August. David Golden, chair of Telesat Canada, became chair of Mitel and John McMonigall, a recently-hired manager at BT, replaced Vander Weyer on the board of Mitel.

McMonigall was handsome, charming, and socially poised, and apparently had ambitions to build an empire for himself within BT. BT had recently created the International Products Division (IPD), an assortment of miscellaneous, non-core businesses in BT, of which McMonigall was appointed managing director. As such, McMonigall became the point man within BT for Mitel. However, *Mitel was the only BT subsidiary with minority shareholders*, a factor that was to foreshadow future relations between the board of Mitel and BT.

At first the Mitel board members were puzzled by McMonigall, who talked a good game but was very political and seldom followed through on matters. Eventually, Bob Després, a shrewd observer on the Mitel board said, "John should have been a diplomat; he's charming but he shows no commercial sense or experience." Unfortunately, this seemed to be the case.

The chair of IPD, Graeme Odgers, was also a new hire at BT as deputy chair, replacing Vander Weyer. Odgers was personable, highly intelligent, and, like Vander Weyer, refreshingly open and direct, a 44-year-old patrician. In my view, however, he did not have the stature or personality to stand up to the new chair of BT, Iain Vallance, BT's former CEO. By the end of August, everyone within BT who had sponsored or participated in the acquisition of Mitel for BT was gone, including the chair, Sir George Jefferson, and Dr. Peter Troughton, Terry Matthews's nemesis.

On the morning of the Mitel AGM, I had arranged for McMonigall, at his request, to meet with the key executives of Mitel while the board was in session. At lunch, several of my managers came to me and said, "This new guy [McMonigall] doesn't care about making a profit this year; he's talking about longer-term strategy." I realized then that BT was going to be a difficult owner of a public company.

After lunch I collared Vander Weyer and told him what had been reported to me. He said, "Don't worry about John; I'll straighten him out." I responded, "That's no help; you'll be gone next month." Vander Weyer agreed that I had to deal with McMonigall that day, so I invited him to dinner.

Over dinner, McMonigall positioned himself as the link between Mitel and BT, displacing all the others who had previously expressed interest in the role. In the three months since BT had acquired Mitel, there had been a disjointed stream of high-level BT visitors, "tire kickers" as we called them, demanding reviews, information, and follow-up reports. Vander Weyer had contained these quite well.

Then McMonigall talked about "us" as management. This led to a very heated interchange during which I stated categorically that I would not stand for his compromising my role as CEO. I told him unequivocally, "Either you are in management or a board member, but I cannot have someone else sharing my role, issuing priorities, instructions." He accused me of "pulling out the pistol" to which I responded, "There's no pistol—just clarification of what he meant by 'management' in the context used." He then backed off and talked of himself as a "funnel" within BT.

The problem didn't go away, however. Ten days later I received copies of correspondence where Vander Weyer wrote to McMonigall: "I gather that during your visit to Mitel you were challenging the policy. . . . The Mitel Annual Plan and Budget. . .has the endorsement of the Mitel board, chairman and CDCO [BT's internal board]." McMonigall replied, "Thank you for your helpful note of 18 July. Obviously in my first visit to Mitel I was wandering about challenging just about everything (although in a very friendly way of course)."

By now the recommendations of BAH were coming forward, but when McMonigall received them at the Mitel board, he totally disregarded them. BT stated and continually restated that it had big plans based on the SX-2000 technology and would look after the distribution problems, especially in the United States, as part of their overall plan. BT implied that there was a master plan within which Mitel would play an important role. This logic suggested a disregard for the minority shareholders of Mitel.

In November 1986, I received a message that Graeme Odgers, deputy chair of BT and chair of IPD, would visit Mitel on December 4 to make a personal assessment of the company. Management made a presentation and Odgers quickly understood the conundrum: Mitel could not afford to complete the development of the SX-2000 and at the same time make a profit. This led to subsequent extensive negotiations with BT where BT agreed to fund the SX-2000 by direct financial assistance to the extent of $45 million over two years in exchange for future royalties on the product.

At Mandalay Polo Grounds, 1936. (l. to r.): Peg (mother), myself, Dave (father), Paul (brother). (Courtesy of the author.)

My mode of transport to school. Riding Vulcan, 1938. (Courtesy of the author.)

Cavalry drill competition, Company A, 1947. Lt. Bill Deale (with sabre) and myself on the left, holding the lance with guidon. (Courtesy of the author.)

Corps officers: Lt.-Col. Griffiths (Corps Commander) at front, and staff (l. to r.): Capt.- Adj. Spencer; Lt.- Adj. Harden; Lt.- QM. Smith; Sgt.-QM Middleton. My first CEO job at age 18. (Courtesy of the author.)

Receiving "Best All-Around Boy Award" from Headmaster Louie E. (Doc) Lamborn at graduation in June. 1949. "Doc" was a strict disciplinarian and a consummate military equestrian. (Courtesy of the author.)

Williams College freshman wrestling team, 1950. I'm front row, centre. This sport led to my near-death experience with a mugger at the Beverly Hills Hotel in Los Angeles 32 years later. (Courtesy of the author.)

At Consumers Glass, 1960. I have a jar of pickles in my left hand. (Courtesy of the author.)

John H. (Jake) Moore, my boss and nemesis. At board meetings his coterie of Labatt-related directors would rarely challenge him, but I would, to my ultimate peril. (The Canadian Press/Mike Pearce)

The last group photo of the management team of Canadian Cablesystems before the keys were handed to Ted Rogers. Back row (l. to r.): Steve Ferris, Nick Hamilton Piercy, Ted Jarmain, Colin Watson, Graham Savage. Front row (l. to r.): Albert Gnat, myself, David Friesen, Tony Gooch. (Courtesy of the author.)

Gerry Connor (l.) and John Clark (r.) in 1994. These two entrepreneurial invest-ment analysts created Connor Clark & Company, a savvy money-management firm that was sold to the Royal Bank of Canada. I was part of the team for almost 10 years. (Private collection, used with permission.)

Ted Rogers in a control room at the Rogers Telecommunications building in Toronto, July, 1978. (The Canadian Press/*Toronto Star*)

Peter Bronfman as chairman of an annual meeting, March 1990.
(The Canadian Press/Tony Bock/*Toronto Star*)

Gerald Bull with Quebec premier Jean Lesage next to a "supergun."
Bull was assassinated in March 1990, allegedly by the Mossad. (The
Canadian Press)

Brascan chairman Trevor Eyton (l.) and president Jack Cockwell in 1993 when their enterprise had imploded. (Tibor Kolley/ *The Globe & Mail*)

Mike Cowpland (l.) and Terry Matthews—the dynamic techie duo who founded and built Mitel into a world-wide telecom equipment supplier. (Bruno Schlumberger/ *Ottawa Citizen*. Reprinted by permission.)

The Mitel management team in Kanata, 1994, just prior to my arrival. Mike Cowpland (2nd row from back, 4th from right); Terry Matthews (4th row, 2nd from right, with beard); Bill Kiss, aka "Mr. Quality" (top row, 3rd from left); Debbie Conlon, personal assistant 1985-87 (middle 1st row); Janet Finleyson, personal assistant 1991-94 (4th row, 1st on left). (Courtesy of the author.)

Third, to streamline and strengthen our product line while remaining firmly committed to providing our existing customers with an orderly transition to future product families.

Fourth, to institute a major corporate-wide program ensuring our commitment to quality and excellence in our products and in all activities throughout the organization.

In closing let me say that as President and a relative newcomer to Mitel, it is with great satisfaction that I have observed good morale despite some very difficult times in recent years. The loyalty and resilience of people throughout the Company is truly admirable and is greatly appreciated by the Board of Directors. The Company is equally grateful for the continuing support and encouragement of share-holders, distributors, dealers, customers and suppliers. This support gives us confidence and a measure of optimism in our belief

that by working together, we can attain for Mitel a renewed prosperity.

Anthony F. Griffiths
President and Chief Executive Officer

ANTHONY F. GRIFFITHS

Since 1984, Mr. Griffiths has been a member of the Mitel Board of Directors. He holds a B.A. from McGill University and an M.B.A. from the Harvard School of Business Administration. He has gained extensive business experience through his association with Connor, Clark and Company Limited, of Toronto, an investment management firm and member of The Toronto Stock Exchange. Mr. Griffiths has held senior management positions in various manufacturing and investment companies during his 25-year business career.

Board of Directors (below, from left to right): Dr. Michael C.J. Cowpland, Donald Colin Webster, Deryk Vander Weyer, David A. Golden, Christopher Bull, Albert Gnat, Terence H. Matthews, Anthony F. Griffiths and Dr. David Leakey.

Mitel directors, 1986 (l. to r.): Mike Cowpland, Ben Webster, Derek Vander Weyer (the chairman of Mitel), David Golden, Chris Bull, Albert Gnat, Terry Matthews, myself, David Leakey. (Courtesy of the author.)

Chairing a Mitel annual meeting in Ottawa, July 22, 1992. Schroder Ventures had bought the British Telecom 51-percent holding the month before. (Courtesy of the author.)

Early days at Fairfax, c. 1989, at Finks' cottage (l. to r.): Paul Fink, Rob Mills, myself, Prem Watsa, Rui Quintal, Tony Arrell, Bill Andrus, John Varnell. (Courtesy of the author.)

A lighthearted moment with me, Ken Polley, who was CEO of Lindsey Morden, and Prem Watsa, chairman. (Courtesy of the author.)

My favourite picture with Prem Watsa at the Taj Hotel, Bombay, November, 1992. (Courtesy of the author.)

Robert Campeau, at the announcement of his company's takeover of Federated Department Stores. (CP PHOTO/file)

P.I. Huisler, Maryland Glass, myself, and Don
Mingay at a glass industry meeting in 1963. Don
was a great teacher and executive as well as a mentor and lifelong friend. (Courtesy of the author.)

George Mara was the "Elder
Statesman" on the Confederation
Life board. In private he would
agree with me totally on matters,
but in board meetings he could not
draw a line in the sand. We remained
good friends until his death in 2006.
(Courtesy of the author.)

John "Jack" Rhind had a long
career in financial services and
was CEO of Confederation Life
and later chair of the executive
committee. (Courtesy of the
author.)

Pat Burns, CEO of Confederation Life, until it went down in August 1994. (The Canadian Press/John Felstead)

Coffee mogul V.G. Siddhartha, CEO of Cafe Coffee Day, as featured in *Business Today*, May, 2010. (www.indiatodayimages.com. Used with permission.)

After the management review, I met privately with Odgers in my office. He asked me my view of the situation. I told him he personally had no position to defend as he was not at BT when Mitel was acquired, but that, in my view, BT had three choices: leave Mitel as it was, which would be a long, hard struggle and was not acceptable to shareholders; sell the company, though it was doubtful BT would get its investment back; or merge it with a company with complementary strengths. Through Ben Webster[4] (the same person I was associated with at Helix, see chapter 4), a long-time Mitel shareholder and board member, we had had initial discussions with Telex who were vulnerable to takeover and looking for a compatible partner. Telex had an inferior PBX product, but excellent direct distribution—exactly what Mitel needed.

To my knowledge, BT never followed up on these suggestions. It obviously felt it had the resources and clout to go it alone.

I then told Odgers that BT had to either support me as CEO or find their own person, which had been the intention when they purchased Mitel. I explained the problem I had with McMonigall and all the other tire kickers—their interruptions were distracting management, which already had its hands full with a chaotic situation. Since BT had representation on the Mitel board, including McMonigall, other BT management carpetbaggers should be kept at bay.

In January, McMonigall reappeared and demanded a command performance where all employees in Kanata (approximately 1,500) were given a "secret" preview of BT's future plans in telecoms equipment technology. McMonigall behaved as though he was the CEO of Mitel and gave a half-hour futuristic slide show of BT products, including "the Eiger," a future-generation PBX "being developed by BT." The Mitel people left these meetings with at best tongue-in-cheek skepticism. I left with a distinct feeling of déjà vu: I was reminded of Projects X and Y at Curtiss-Wright 28 years earlier.

Early in February, Odgers returned to Ottawa and told David Golden and me that BT had decided to recruit their own CEO, and BT wanted me to stay as chair, replacing David Golden. This agreed, it took till the end of July 1987 before the new man, John Jarvis, a very competent communications specialist from the UK, was hired. This was a most difficult and soul-destroying period for me—trying to hold the company on course while keeping the bureaucrats from BT off the steering wheel. I had now joined the board of IPD and regularly asked for the overall plan promised by BT, which would form the basis for Mitel's future direction. *This plan was never developed.* Odgers left BT some time in 1988 and McMonigall left in late 1989. The "Eiger" never reached the drawing board—at least not at Mitel.

* * *

We accomplished a lot in the year ending March 31, 1987. In fact, if it had not been for a major blunder by our subsidiary Trillium (71-percent owned) buying a troubled distributor, which was written off within months, Mitel would have made a profit. The swing in operating margin from the previous year was $58 million on revenues of $453 million. We took writedowns of $39 million, clearing the decks of past excesses and redundant inventory and plants. With nearly $140 million in cash and no debt, the company was financially very strong, but the pressure on operations needed to be maintained.

In early July 1987, I received discouraging preliminary numbers for the first quarter ending June, and immediately issued instructions to the management to develop plans to downsize the company further. When Jarvis arrived on July 27, I handed him the memo and told him this was his first priority. He ignored my advice and the stage was set for the next painful three and a half years of ownership by BT, when Mitel drifted without clear direction or strategy and its financial resources quickly dissipated.

* * *

In 2000, at the height of the telecom bubble, Terry Matthews sold Newbridge Networks to Alcatel, making himself a multi-billionaire. This was sweet revenge for Terry who had said, "The risk-averse British Telecom effectively ousted him" in 1986. By 2000, I doubt that there was anyone left in the management of BT who would remember that BT had turned down Terry's 1986 offer of 33 percent of Newbridge. In 2001, Matthews was awarded a knighthood. Also in 2001, Mitel sold its PBX division to Terry Matthews along with the Mitel name. The semiconductor division was renamed Zarlink. In 2010, Mitel Networks sold 10.5 million shares in an IPO—full circle! Terry went on to establish himself as one of Canada's pre-eminent high-tech entrepreneurs, establishing over 80 companies.

As soon as BT took over Mitel, Mike Cowpland moved out, leaving me his office. Mike "moved on" both emotionally and in terms of his career. He did remain a sounding board for me, especially related to technical issues, and we frequently played tennis together. He soon formed Corel Corporation, a graphics software company, which he led until August 2000. In 2001, Cowpland went on to buy control of ZIM Corporation, a provider of software products and services for database and mobile markets. Mike has been involved in a variety of start-ups and charitable activities in the Ottawa area.

12

From Provincial Bailout to Financial Collection, 1987

"Relatively few chief executives are either trained
for or selected on the basis of their ability to allocate
capital. They get there through other routes. It's a
different function than functions along the routes to
the CEO's job at most companies."

Warren Buffett, Berkshire Hathaway

As I was disengaging myself from Mitel in the summer of
1987, I went to lunch with Prem Watsa. Prem had come to
Canada in 1972 after studying chemical engineering at the
Indian Institute of Technology in Madras, India. He has a
brother, David, in London, Ontario, who persuaded him to
come to Canada and enter the MBA course at the University
of Western Ontario. On graduating from Western in 1974,
Prem joined the Confederation Life Insurance Company as an
investment analyst. As I had been a director of Confed since
1975, I met Prem on various corporate occasions.

In 1983, Prem and a number of others left Confed and
joined a Toronto-based brokerage boutique. Subsequently they
left to form Hamblin Watsa Investment Counsel, a private
wealth and pension fund management company. In 1985, Prem
and some of his clients bought control of the Markel Insurance
Company of Canada, which was in financial difficulties, by

injecting $9.7 million into the company. Subsequently, Markel's name was changed to Fairfax Financial Holdings Limited, and in 1992, Fairfax acquired Hamblin Watsa.

Prem had contacted me in 1986 when I was president of Mitel to ask me typical stock analyst questions about the company, particularly because Gordon Securities had been touting Mitel as a "turnaround."

At a lunch in the summer of 1987, we conversed on a variety of subjects, and at one point Prem mentioned he had a major investment for his clients in a small high-speed data transmission company based in Saskatoon, Saskatchewan, called Develcon Electronics Limited. Prem said he was unhappy with the investment and wondered if I had any suggestions as to what to do. As I already knew a little about Develcon from my Mitel experience, I immediately told Prem to sell his stock. He said he couldn't because he had too much for the market to absorb: 25 percent of the outstanding stock. When I suggested he look for a merger partner, he replied, "You're good at that; why don't you do it for me?" I responded that I was very busy but would think about it. I explored a couple of logical prospects without success. Then, one Wednesday, I received an "urgent" message from Prem saying, "They can't meet their payroll." I said, "Let it go." Prem argued that the company could be salvaged, while I counselled that it was too small to bother with.

This was in February 1988. One day (a Friday) I made the mistake of taking Albert Gnat along with me to Prem's office, where we continued the debate. I say "mistake," because toward the end of the discussion, Albert sided with Prem saying, "Come on, Tony, you're not doing anything; why don't you go out there?" Rising to the bait, I said, "Okay, but provided they'll see me tomorrow [Saturday]."

Prem arranged for his associate Paul Fink, an ex-Confed man, to fly out with me. Paul had visited the company a week earlier to arrange funds to meet the payroll. Our flight was due to depart Toronto at 8:00 p.m. but, because of an ice storm, departed around 2:00 a.m. After two hours' sleep, Paul and I spent Saturday with the founder (chair) and the president of Develcon working on a survival plan. What we found was a mini-Mitel, with reporting systems so inadequate it was difficult to properly construct a feasible plan. The company had revenues of $17.2 million in 1987, and the current (1988) revenue projections according to management were $17 million, worst case $15 million. We showed them that if revenues were only $15 million they would be broke, but through further downsizing we were able to "force" a break-even scenario with revenues of $13 million.

Discussions in Saskatchewan convinced us that we could obtain provincial government support if we could produce a credible turnaround plan. Before I left Toronto to go to Saskatoon, I had also contacted Jerry Baker, of Baker Harris executive search consultants, and told him that I might need a CEO to put into Develcon quickly. Gerry responded that by chance he had had that assignment two years previously, but the company hadn't acted on his recommendations.

When Paul Fink and I returned to Toronto, we told Prem the chances of salvaging Develcon were remote; time and a lack of cash were working against us. Unless we could persuade the government of Saskatchewan to commit significant financial assistance, the company would be bankrupt in a matter of weeks. Paul set the wheels in motion and got the Saskatchewan Economic Development Corporation (SEDCO), under the direction of Deputy Premier Eric Berntson, working on the project. Finally in June 1988, a financial injection of $8.5 million from SEDCO, matched by $1.5 million from Prem's group, refinanced Develcon. This "bailout" by the province engendered some ridicule in the press.

Unfortunately, while this was going on between March and June, I had been involved in other business and lost track of Develcon. When the financing was completed and the board restructured to include Paul Fink, Prem Watsa, Robbert Hartog, and myself as chair, I was in for a jolt. Revenues had fallen below the $13 million break-even level we had established and finished the year at $9.7 million. Cash was required for trade payables and inventories, and the rapidly falling revenues were causing severe hemorrhaging. The new president and CEO, Rick MacPherson, found himself on the bridge of a sinking ship. We cut staff back radically, which in turn generated major severance payments. Develcon finished the year with a loss of $9.6 million—a novel experience for me, with losses almost equalled by revenues! By now all the directors had waived their fees to conserve cash—we were working for charity to salvage this mess.

On several occasions during the next four years, we contemplated filing for bankruptcy, as no one wanted to commit additional funds to the company. We hired a young accountant, Bill Vancoughnett, who minded the store in Saskatoon, while MacPherson tried to rebuild revenues and distribution. Bill was able to pull a rabbit out of the hat by arranging funds from scientific research tax credits, which provided working capital for a year or so. Paul Fink and I worked feverishly to find buyers, merger candidates, or strategic alliances. Many came to look but all walked away.

One of our attempts resulted in a conditional offer of financing from a New York–based leveraged buyout fund to acquire, through Develcon, 100 percent of Develcon's largest Canadian competitor in the business (Gandalf Technologies), subject to the completion of due diligence. This transaction would have allowed utilization of Develcon's $16-million tax loss, and the rationalization of distribution and manufacturing facilities. We made a proposal to the controlling shareholder of Gandalf, which itself was beginning to experience difficulties. The proposal was at a premium to market price with participation available to the selling group in "Newco." I later learned that this offer was never formally put to the Gandalf board, and since that time, Gandalf experienced serious survival problems, eventually going bankrupt in 1997.

Somehow Develcon struggled on. In 1991 Rick MacPherson left, discouraged and frustrated, and Bill Vancoughnett took over as the new CEO. Before he left, MacPherson had had one beautiful piece of lateral thinking: Develcon's main product was Develnet, which had immense data transmission capability but, because of its size, was restricted to a small market. It was also expensive and aging. MacPherson's idea was to take a small part of this transmission capability and develop a new product line of "bridges." These could be sold in a vast but competitive market at excellent prices to the customer and good margins to Develcon. The development of the bridges was possible because research and development had already been undertaken on the larger product. Vancoughnett was able to build on this opportunity.

Late in 1992, Bill approached the board and SEDCO with a management buyout proposal involving forgiveness of interest and some of the debt. This capital structure provided Develcon with breathing room. When the plan was approved and announced, the stock of Develcon was trading at 20 cents per share; by 1993, it was trading at $1.20 per share. This was a close one, but generally ended happily.

* * *

Shortly after I completed my appraisal of Develcon, I received another call from Prem, "Could I help right away?" With financial help from Confed Life, Prem was negotiating to buy effective control of Walwyn, the stock brokerage firm, which was then a subsidiary of the collapsing Financial Trustco (FT). Prem was having trouble convincing FT's banks that it was better for them to place Walwyn in his hands than to let it melt down. I was able to assist and the transaction was completed. However, this coincided with the onset of the recession, which seriously shrank brokerage volume. At Prem's persuasion I agreed to join the board of Walwyn, together with Prem, Paul Fink, and Jack Rhind, the former chair of Confed Life.

Prem completed Fairfax's investment in Walwyn on the proviso that Tony Arrell, formerly with Wood Gundy, become the new CEO. This was accepted with apparent enthusiasm from all the major principals in Walwyn. With the onset of the recession, the brokerage community was suffering great losses. One firm on the ropes was Midland Doherty. Tony Arrell arranged the merger of Midland and Walwyn in 1988 in order to create an entity with greater critical mass, and the ability to raise capital. Mackenzie Financial entered the scene as a one-third shareholder and financial partner in the combined entity, Midland Walwyn Inc.

Soon after the merger was consummated, factions arose within the management reflecting the various styles of key producers, which led to open political dissent. Arrell did not have the patience to deal with the politics and decided to resign, even though he had the confidence of the majority of the board to continue in his post. Jack Rhind, a director and past chair of Confed Life, was made chair of Midland Walwyn. The dissidents won the day and Robert Schultz, then the CFO, became president and CEO.

The firm needed further financing, though the amount required was the subject of much internal controversy. Watsa, a value investor, was dead set against unnecessary dilution, so an attempt was made to raise further financing within the group to preserve values for the existing shareholders. Time was too short, however, and the attempt failed. Watsa was disillusioned, turned over his interest to Confed Life, and resigned from the board.

Schultz and his management proceeded with a large new issue that, though extremely dilutive, at $2.50 per share was very well received.

* * *

My next major involvement with Prem concerned Magna, the automotive parts supplier founded and controlled, through a class of multiple voting shares, by Frank Stronach. Magna had enjoyed immense success and Prem had invested Fairfax and his Hamblin Watsa clients in the stock. At this point, however, Stronach had decided to enter politics and engage in other non-automotive investments, and took his eye off Magna. His managers had allowed debt and overhead to balloon: the stock came crashing down from a high of $36 in 1987 to the $12 range that Prem had bought in at to a low of $2 in 1990, amid rumours that the banks were going to put the company into bankruptcy.

I suggested we take action as shareholders and, if necessary, refinance the company and change the management. While Prem had maintained an excellent relationship with Frank Stronach, the board of Magna had created a committee of independent directors headed by the former premier of Ontario, Bill Davis, to recruit a new CEO; Prem suggested my name. In June 1990, after a couple of meetings, including an interview with the entire board, the committee offered me the job as CEO with a contract. I said I didn't require a contract and a letter would suffice. The committee chair, Bill Davis, said, "We recommend you have a contract in this case," and sent me one the same day, which fully reflected the terms discussed, and I signed it. Press announcements were prepared and I was ready to take on the appointment at an afternoon board meeting.

However, Frank called me prior to the meeting inviting me to lunch, and produced a revised contract with a job description that more closely resembled a chief financial officer. I was being given a clear message: I would not be calling the shots. Following weekend discussions, where members of the Magna board committee encouraged me to take the job regardless of Frank's alterations to the contract, I decided to pass. Davis said to me repeatedly, "We'll support you." I replied, "Support me now in compliance with the contract." Frank took on the challenge himself and delivered one of the greatest turnarounds in Canadian business. In 1993–94 Magna stock sold for as high as $70 per share, giving the company a market capitalization of $3.4 billion.

* * *

Sometimes you meet yourself coming around corners. When I became involved at Fairfax, I found that the group owned a large position in my old acquaintance Ben Torchinsky's company Agra Industries, and was also involved in a mining joint venture with Agra. Agra was generally over-leveraged and had some investments that required substantial additional capital. Meanwhile, cable television and medical lab properties were selling at peak valuations and Agra had significant holdings in these businesses through subsidiaries Cablenet and Cybermedix. Prem and I determined that the best strategy to enable shareholders of Agra to realize these values and provide Agra needed capital would be to sell the cable TV and medical lab entities. We approached Ben and persuaded him to do this through Walwyn. This transaction was accomplished at the peak of cable and medical lab values and much improved Agra's financial position and shareholder values. A year or so later Fairfax sold its Agra position.

When Prem was in the process of buying into Walwyn, he was very anxious to involve me in that company's rehabilitation, including having me serve as chair. I declined to do this, but agreed to serve as a director and help as an adviser. I was concerned that this new "sell side" involvement could be perceived as a conflict with my position at Connor Clark, which was "buy side," though it would be mainly one of perception rather than fact, as the two were not direct competitors in any way. I was spending an increasing amount of my time on Develcon and other Fairfax-related matters, so I went to my colleagues at Connor Clark and suggested I move on. I made arrangements to move to Fairfax as an "associate" and chair of Fairbridge, an investment banking subsidiary. This ended a very happy 10-year direct association with Connor Clark. I remained a client and friend of that firm for many years until it was sold to RBC in 1999 for $160 million.

* * *

Another opportunity arose in the summer of 1987, when Prem asked me to look into the situation at Financial Collection Agencies (FCA).

Fairfax and associated entities had bought about 27 percent of FCA at $9 to $10 per share. The performance of the company had started to deteriorate and the stock price fell by 80 to 90 percent to the $1.55 range. Occasionally I had asked how things were going at FCA and would get answers such as, "We're not sure"; "They're working on a budget"; and "There's a new president." Prem pressed me to examine the situation immediately, despite my protestations that I was still too busy with Mitel. I decided to take a day to visit the FCA executive offices in Philadelphia and interview the senior management (conveniently FCA was also a Mitel customer and I was able to get a report on Mitel service and performance). I then flew from Philadelphia to Montreal and met the president of FCA for dinner.

It was clear that there was a war going on between the president, headquartered in Canada, and the head of the U.S. operations. This battle had festered for so long that it was consuming the energies of management and was completely divisive throughout the company. Somebody had to go and it would have to be the CEO for permitting the situation to develop. The question became who to put in charge?

On reflection, I concluded that this would be an ideal project for Ted Jarmain, my colleague from Canadian Cablesystems, who was looking for a challenge. After some discussion, Ted agreed FCA represented an interesting opportunity and I introduced him to Prem and Rick Salsberg, both of whom were on the FCA board of directors.

I developed a three-page recommendation on procedure and my plan was implemented. Not long after, Ted took charge as president and CEO and dismissed the head of U.S. operations. Slowly the company recovered and began to prosper again, regaining market share, and morale soared. About a year later I became a director of FCA.

However, the company's progress was not reflected in the share price and some shareholders were becoming impatient. With that in mind, I recommended that we put the company up for sale. We announced this decision at the time the stock was selling at $1.60 to $1.80 per share. We formed a special committee of the board, hired Albert Gnat as legal counsel, retained financial advisers, and invited bids. The expectation among the committee members and advisers was that, if we could realize $3 to $5 per share, all shareholders would be very satisfied (the book value was $2.55). We managed to maintain an aura of competition even though, as the process progressed, there was only one real bidder at the table, the NASDAQ-listed NCO Group Inc.— "a leading provider of accounts receivable management." In other words, a collection agency. When the transaction was completed, the final price was $9.60 per share.

* * *

It is no doubt apparent to the reader that Prem Watsa has played an important role in my life, both as a business partner and a friend. As a long-time assiduous follower of the principles expounded by Benjamin Graham, Napoleon Hill, Warren Buffett, and John Templeton, Prem reflects the characteristics of all of these: loyalty, focus, investment discipline, personal commitment, and altruism. He has the unique ability to profitably deploy capital, while at the same time ensuring the performance of operating entities through the empowerment of management. At Fairfax, the proof is in the pudding: in 2010 Fairfax had four major operating insurance companies, revenues of $6.2 billion, total assets of $31.7 billion, and common shareholder equity of $7.8 billion.

13

Extraordinary Financial Escapades, 1987–1990

"If you lie down with a dog, you will get up with fleas."
A Burmese proverb

In the spring of 1987, as I awaited news from British Telecom regarding the recruitment of my successor as CEO at Mitel, I was approached by my associate Larry Lunn of Connor Clark & Lunn (CC&L) to join the board of Core-Mark. Larry had created CC&L jointly with Connor Clark to manage pension funds. Starting from scratch in 1985, Larry and his partners built CC&L's funds under management to $2.1 billion by 1993, when CC&L became a publicly traded company. (By 2011, CC&L had $40 billion under management.)

As a fund manager, Larry did not want to join the board of Core-Mark because he would become an insider and be constrained from trading its securities freely on behalf of his clients. CC&L represented a substantial part of the ownership of Core-Mark as, by coincidence, did Confederation Life, where I was a director.

Core-Mark International Inc. was a market leader in full-service wholesale distribution of consumer goods, primarily tobacco products (which accounted for approximately 80 per cent of revenues in 1987), as well as confectionary, groceries, health and beauty aids, and fast foods to convenience stores, supermarkets, and liquor and drug stores in North America. This was a highly competitive business where pennies accounted for profit or loss on huge volumes. In 1986 and 1987, the company had growing losses on fairly steady revenues of about $2.3 billion. The principal executive offices had been relocated from Los Angeles to Vancouver because the founder and CEO, David Gillespie, liked living in the Vancouver area, where he owned a two-and-one-half-acre island residence.

In 1987, Core-Mark was in a disastrous financial and strategic mess. This was exacerbated by the fact that David Gillespie was terminally ill, in financial difficulty, and under a personal cloud resulting from some aspects of his private life, which had been well publicized in the press. Because of CC&L's clients' large ownership position, Larry had been allocated three seats on the proposed new board. When Larry asked me if I would represent his interests on the board, I said I would, provided we could agree to the appointment of a lawyer of my choice as another of Larry's representatives to work alongside me. I suggested Albert Gnat, and Larry agreed. Larry had asked another lawyer friend of his from Edmonton, Neil Bowker, to be his third nominee. Larry also asked if I would be willing to assume the presidency of Core-Mark, but I was not free to do so because I was still CEO of Mitel.

By the time of the annual general meeting in June 1987, the ownership balance of Core-Mark had changed radically.

Two groups, First City Capital Markets, owned by the Belzberg family whose CEO was Brent Belzberg, and CapVest Capital, an Australian group whose spokesman was a young lawyer from Melbourne, David S. Teed, had become financially intertwined and acted as if they controlled Core-Mark. The Belzbergs had financially assisted CapVest in taking over David Gillespie's position, which, through multiple voting shares, controlled Core-Mark International.

As the new board of directors assembled for the annual general meeting in Vancouver on June 30, 1987, there was a move to persuade me to take on the CEO role from the acting president, Tony Regensburg, a long-time Core-Mark employee. (An interesting and somewhat distracting habit of Regensburg's was to chew tobacco in board meetings and spit the juice into a plastic cup.) As *The Globe and Mail* commented on June 30, 1987:

> The most visible potential contender for the top job at the moment, meanwhile, is Anthony Griffiths, who is develop-ing a reputation as a turnaround specialist. This is partly thanks to his performance in his current role as president and CEO of Mitel Corp., the bruised former wunderkind of Canadian high technology, based in Kanata, Ont.
>
> Mr. Griffiths will certainly be close to the action at Core-Mark one way or another: like Mr. Regensburg, he is one of four candidates for the company's new board— set for election today—nominated by the institutional shareholders.
>
> He is also a former associate of Connor Clark & Lunn Investment Management Ltd., which spearheaded the institution's successful campaign against the Gillespies.

Although my successor at Mitel had been selected, he was not due to start until the end of July, so I could not be available immediately. In any event, I was also reluctant to devote my career full-time to tobacco, a product I believed was detrimental to health. Albert and I discussed my dilemma at length in his hotel room after the annual meeting, and we concluded together that Core-Mark was "not my bag." Consequently, a search was commenced for a CEO and L. John Clark was hired (no relation to John Clark of Connor Clark), David Teed having been made chair at the annual meeting. Clark had worked for almost 20 years with the Singer Corporation.

Since the company was losing money and had acquired a variety of companies (some in unrelated businesses, such as a telephone interconnect) there was a squeeze on funds, resulting in a certain amount of skittishness by both customers and suppliers, principally the tobacco companies such as RJR Nabisco and Philip Morris. There was an expectation that the two new controlling shareholders would inject equity in some form to provide breathing room and re-establish confidence among the company's constituencies.

After some discussion, First City and CapVest agreed to negotiate an injection of capital in the form of convertible subordinated debentures. There were three independent directors on the board—Bowker, Gnat, and myself—who formed the committee (of which I was chair) to negotiate with Belzberg and Teed.

The appointed day for the meeting was October 21, 1987, at the boardroom of the company's U.S. headquarters, in Hollywood, California. This timing proved difficult, being the Wednesday following the 1987 stock market crash with the company's stock trading at a low of $2.20 and virtually no bids. As the meeting commenced, the air of depression was palpable, and the committee felt tremendously disadvantaged because, under the circumstances, it had no alternatives. The two controlling shareholders had told us there was an urgency to put funds in place because they understood the company's bank, First Chicago, was nervous and applying pressure.

For the committee, it was a long and painful day, at the end of which we agreed to a 12 percent $20 million convertible debenture, resulting in the potential dilution of 9.1 million shares, or more than 50 percent of the shares then outstanding. First City and CapVest purchased these debentures, further solidifying their control over Core-Mark.

That night we all had dinner at David Teed's house in Los Angeles, which he had rented from Gore Vidal, and a major topic of discussion was the hectic trading on stock markets around the world. Teed told me that he and his partners were buying CapVest stock in Australia in an attempt to stem the free fall; because the company was highly leveraged, they were attempting to maintain a certain price level to protect collateral pledged for their borrowings. In any case, the damage was apparently severe enough that, soon after, CapVest was taken over by First Toronto Mining Corporation, a Canadian subsidiary of an Australian group. This company was operated by a couple of mining promoters, who were sitting on $40 million in cash in First Toronto Mining. They, too, would blow their cash in a short period, which again resulted in de-stabilizing the control of Core-Mark.

When First Toronto got into difficulties they told their partners, First City, that they wanted to sell their entire position in Core-Mark. However, since First Toronto was locked into a shareholders' agreement with First City, First Toronto could not sell unilaterally. At the same time, First City didn't want to increase its exposure in Core-Mark by buying out its partner.

John Clark, the new CEO, had retained Salomon Brothers, a New York–based investment banking firm, to search for acquisitions for Core-Mark and now directed the bankers to study the feasibility of Core-Mark itself buying in the convertible debentures from First Toronto and First City.

As a committee we immediately met with Salomon Brothers to outline possible alternatives and determine how best to proceed. This being 1988 and the height of the LBO boom, the bankers were particularly aggressive. They virtually told us how they would restructure the capital of Core-Mark and, when asked about fees, demanded $250,000 upfront, another two tranches of $250,000 staged over the succeeding few weeks for providing valuations and fairness opinion letters, and finally a completion fee of $3 million. We were offended by their cavalier and greedy approach.

The committee caucused and decided as a first step we owed it to the company's commercial bankers, First Chicago, to discuss our problem and determine whether they could assist. The investment bankers told us they would approach First Chicago on our behalf. We declined and made our own arrangements to meet with the bank together with management. The following week, we travelled to Chicago and First Chicago told us they were prepared to finance the company to buy back the debentures entirely on their own. Furthermore, in response to my question, the senior bank representative told me that the bank had been quite comfortable with its position in Core-Mark *before* we had raised the debenture funds.

We then proceeded apace to arrange for Core-Mark to buy back the debentures with financing provided by First Chicago. As a public company, this required valuations and a fairness opinion. I called the New York bankers, who agreed to provide these for a fee of $800,000. The committee thought this ludicrous and authorized me to speak to George Dembroski of RBC Dominion Securities, who had advised the independent committee at the time the debentures were created in 1987. George quickly got back to me with a proposal that RBC Dominion would charge $75,000 to undertake a two-week catch-up study and, if they then recommended proceeding, would charge $125,000 for the fairness opinion. We gave the job to RBC and the New York investment bankers were apoplectic, accusing us of unethical behaviour. Such was the arrogance of Wall Street bankers in 1988. Meanwhile, we saved the shareholders of Core-Mark about $600,000 in fees, together with over $3 million in fees they might have paid had we permitted the investment bankers to "restructure" the company.

The board approved the buyback in late February 1989, and then the fun started. Even though Teed and Regensburg, both directors of the company, had approved the debenture buyback, in March they combined with Michael Foster, the chief financial officer of Core-Mark, to form a group—the Teed Group—to raise money to take control of Core-Mark by bidding on the debentures themselves. The first offer was in excess of $4.75 per common share of Core-Mark for 100 percent of the outstanding issued shares. Later this was reduced to $5.50 per share for 57 percent of the company.

My first inkling of the Teed Group's plan was when I received a call from David Teed while I was on a skiing holiday in Whistler, B.C. Teed said he was advising me as the chair of the independent committee that he had generated "an alternative to the issuer bid." He advised that all senior debt was in place together with mezzanine financing; six people were to put up $30 million in 9.5 percent preferred shares for 45 percent of the company. He said the Belzbergs were aware of the proposal and that he had 30 to 40 percent of the company locked up, including Confederation Life. This latter statement turned out not to be entirely correct, although Confed was concerned about being locked out if the other major shareholders, including the Belzbergs, sold out. Needless to say, this proposal caused a major schism within the management and, in the view of some directors, put Teed, Regensburg, and Foster in positions of conflict. Nevertheless, each was determined to maintain his position with the company and, since the board was divided as to what to do, no action was taken. On May 8, 1989, Core-Mark issued a press release that said:

> The company announced today that its Board of Directors has considered the unsolicited proposed stock exchange bid of 162093 Canada Limited, a company with no assets formed by a small group of former managers, for up to 6,550,000 common shares of the Company at $5.50 per share. The directors are recommending to shareholders that shareholders reject the offer. The directors are of the opinion that in light of the Company's excellent outlook and the recently reported quarterly earnings of 19 cents per common share as compared with 1988 first

quarter earnings of 13 cents per common share (both after Preferred share dividends), the offer price is inadequate, the offer does not reflect the intrinsic value of the Company and is prejudicial to the holders of the Company's Series A Preferred shares.

The Board expressed concern about the uncertain nature of the financing of the bidder and the viability of the plans proposed by the bidder for a second stage transaction, stating in this latter regard that it felt the level of corporate debt on completion of the contemplated transactions would be imprudent.

The Board is opposed in principle to the two-tiered nature of the 162093 Canada Limited offer. If the bidder is able to gain control of the Company through a partial bid, shareholders will not be able to fully participate in the control premium which should be paid for the Company.

The Company has retained RBC Dominion Securities Inc. to provide advice as to the value of the Company and as to the alternatives available to increase value for all shareholders including seeking a fairly-priced offer for all of the Company's shares.

This created the awkward circumstance that, while the company was not officially up for auction, clearly it was now in play. First City was playing a game of wait and see and, as the holder of the controlling block, sending confused messages to the board; it was not prepared to take a position regarding the Teed Group's activities to gain control over the company. Teed, tasting blood, now began to take more aggressive tactics and hired a combative lawyer, John Butler, from Tory, Tory, DesLauriers & Binnington (now Torys), to represent his group. On one occasion Foster, the Core-Mark CFO, met with Confed in the morning endorsing the company's buyback proposal, then reappeared in the afternoon with Teed, which suggested he supported the Teed Group's plan. No wonder there was confusion.

As the company was in play, the board authorized RBC Dominion to generate other bids. Working throughout as legal counsel for the company was Ed Waitzer of Stikeman Elliott.[1]

In late March 1989, Teed sent Butler to see the board. The board told Butler to have his client make a formal offer; on receipt, we would deal with it. To date, Teed's backers had shown no substance, saying they required access to undertake due diligence. Meanwhile, the board was wondering where the Teed Group's backers were getting enough information to respond to the extent they had, being mindful that three officers of the company, including the CFO, were in the bidding group. Some of the board took the view that members of the Teed Group should resign or take a leave of absence while the matter was being resolved because the CFO and Regensburg clearly had dual interests. The chasm between the CEO (Clark) and the chair (Teed) was now divisive, and the board found itself in the position of receiving legal threats from two fellow directors. By early April, David Teed finally resigned as chair and John Clark assumed the position. Foster and Regensburg took paid leaves of absence.

RBC Dominion started to beat the bushes as the company was put up for auction. By the third week in June 1989, there were at least two active bidders: the Teed Group, who had upped their price from $5.50 per share to $6.50, and CMI Acquisition Corporation, formed by a partnership of private investors associated with New York merchant banks. CMI quickly moved to $6.75 per common share, and by July, CMI won the day with the transaction closing sometime in the fall.

In a farewell letter to all Core-Mark directors, John Clark included a personal note. He followed up with a dinner in Toronto that the advisers also attended. John presented us all with a memento, the "Board of Directors Conference Call Register," which succinctly summarized the culmination of the entire series of events from January to July 1989. For fun, he highlighted typical comments of each director, as he remembered them.

In this seven-month period, there had been 55 meetings of the board and various board committees. Our vigilance meant that the value for shareholders increased from $36.1 million, the Teed Group's initial partial bid, to $138.8 million, an increase of $102.7 million. At the end of this saga, I received a somewhat apologetic *mea culpa* letter from David Teed, expressing his surprise that we had received such a high bid for the company, compared to his group's initial offer.

* * *

In January 1990, Bob Després (a fellow board member at Mitel) had persuaded Robert Campeau to appoint me to the board of Campeau Corporation in an attempt to help Campeau out of the considerable mess his company was in.

The story of Robert Campeau is too long to recount here. Briefly, though, he was born into a low-income family in Sudbury in August 1923. He grew up speaking French at home, but spoke English in the bilingual community. After grade 8, at age 14, he quit school and went to work full time as a general labourer at International Nickel. After the Second World War, he went on to become a hugely successful real estate developer.

By 1980, he made a bid to take over Royal Trustco Limited, at the time Canada's largest trust company. This attempt was blocked by the corporate elite. Following a period of personal depression, Campeau resurfaced in 1986 with a bid for Allied Stores in the United States.

"By 1986, Campeau Corp. was a mature company with assets of $1.5 billion Canadian and revenue of more than $200 million."[2] Campeau targeted retailing companies in the United States because he "envisioned a wonderful marriage between retailing and real estate."[3] In late March 1986, Campeau began buying up shares of Allied Stores Corp., based in Manhattan. Among its 24 divisions were retail giants Brooks Brothers, Ann Taylor, Jordan Marsh, and Garfinckel's in Washington, D.C.

In the ensuing takeover battle, Allied found a white knight in the shopping centre magnate Edward DeBartolo. DeBartolo was a powerful man, the largest shopping centre developer and manager in the United States.[4] By the end of the complicated battle, DeBartolo decided to negotiate with Campeau, and the total cost of the Allied Stores acquisition was $3.5 billion. In their book *Campeau: The Building of an Empire*, Michael Babad and Catherine Mulroney write: "In January 1988, he [Campeau] stunned Wall Street with a hostile bid for Federated Department Stores Inc., the fifth-largest retailer in the United States and parent of the famous Bloomingdale's chain with a bid of $6.6 billion."[5] During the battle for Federated, Campeau allied himself with DeBartolo and Paul Reichmann. "After the Federated deal, the Reichmanns held 22 percent of Campeau Corp"[6]; soon after, they increased their holdings to more than 25 percent.

These extraordinary and enormous financial escapades resulted in excessive and unsustainable debt. At the same time, Campeau lost some of his key retailing and financial management and his empire began to unravel.

* * *

My first exposure to Bob Campeau occurred in 1974, when he attempted to acquire Bushnell Communications, where I was a director. At that time, the CRTC rejected his bid, ruling it was not satisfied Campeau was suitable as a corporation to assume the obligations and responsibilities of broadcast undertakings.

When I agreed to join the Campeau Corporation board in January 1990, the company was thrashing around in the aftermath of Chapter 11 in the United States and technically bankrupt in Canada. The banks were keeping the company alive while the board, management, and advisers attempted to minimize the damage with a variety of workout teams and advisers. It was not unusual to attend a directors' meeting with 25 to 30 people present, including bankruptcy experts from New York, lawyers of all descriptions, and multiple financial advisers.

Bob Campeau would chair the meetings and, from time to time, launch into emotional tirades. Much of his venom was directed at the Reichmanns, especially Paul. Campeau's position was that the Reichmanns had agreed to financially assist in the restructuring of Campeau Corporation in September 1989, but had not followed through. Obviously, Paul Reichmann had a different view of the arrangement.

On March 6, 1990, after attending a few board meetings, I went to see Bob Campeau. I expressed my concern about the emotionalism, lack of structure, and lack of progress at the meetings. I told Bob that I found myself like a pawn in a tornado with forces beyond my control, and that it didn't make sense in the current environment for me to remain on the board. I told him I had to resign. This suggestion was not acceptable to him, and he seemed willing to listen to my advice.

I advised Bob that he should form an independent committee of the board comprising Robert Després, Bob Butler, and Harry Macdonnell to consider a restructuring plan that had been tabled. Butler and Macdonnell were independent directors but had the confidence of the Reichmanns. Next, I told him that, because he had lost credibility with his lenders, he had to appoint a credible face to sell the plan to them. Finally, I suggested that he should think seriously about appointing a new CEO for the company, emphasizing that, by selecting someone he found acceptable, he would pre-empt the possibility of having someone he didn't want being forced on him.

Reflecting on my comments, Bob proposed that he should resign as CEO for two years. I responded that he should. On March 20, Bob asked me if I would agree to be CEO. I responded that I would not because I felt that, as his nominee, my independence would be compromised and anticipated that he and I would undoubtedly clash, destroying any chance of my being effective. In addition to my lack of experience in real estate, acting as the liquidator of a company held no appeal for me.

We then turned to a discussion of Harry Macdonnell as a prospective CEO; Harry had been a partner at McCarthy Tétrault for many years. Bob also raised the name of his former right-hand man, Don Carroll, but we eventually settled on Macdonnell, who was acceptable to both the lenders and to the Reichmanns. When this proposal was put to the full board, much pushing and shoving ensued, with Bob putting up various "conditions" under which he would agree to step down. These related to financial matters he had with the National Bank, DeBartolo, and Olympia & York and his requirement that they accept major discounts on their loan positions. None of these could be agreed upon without extended negotiations and, of course, Campeau's threshold for accepting discounts was different from those of the lenders.

In a lull in the conversation, Bob said this was a great opportunity for a new investor. I broke the silence and asked, "What about your old partner and friend Paul Desmarais in Montreal?" I saw a glimmer—a light bulb going on in Bob's head. (More of this story later.)

The manoeuvring continued. Bob agreed to an independent committee, as I had suggested, and insisted I be a member of it. Then Bob agreed Harry would be president and COO. Compensation and other matters were agreed upon in a meeting with Bob Després, Harry Macdonnell, Campeau, and myself. However, at that meeting, Harry also insisted that Campeau resign as chair and CEO, so that he, Macdonnell, would be CEO. At this, Campeau jumped out of his chair and grabbed Macdonnell by the arm and led him out of the room. Harry immediately sent in his letter of resignation as a director.

In the meantime, with the board's permission, I contacted Edward DeBartolo's office in Youngstown, Ohio, and arranged for a meeting of members of the independent committee to determine if we could negotiate a "haircut" on DeBartolo's $480-million loan to Campeau, secured by stock in Allied and Campeau's share in certain shopping malls. Campeau had also pledged 84 percent of the stock in Ralphs supermarket chain, a profitable unit of Federated. On March 27, 1990, the committee flew in a private aircraft to Youngstown and met with DeBartolo, his son, and advisers. Ironically, Harry Macdonnell was part of the delegation, as Campeau had not yet accepted his resignation.

DeBartolo's office was surprisingly unpretentious, filled with banners and paraphernalia of the San Francisco 49ers. Edward DeBartolo looked to be about 80, serious, somewhat humourless, but courteous. Clearly he was unhappy with his relationship with Bob Campeau.

We felt our meeting went well and came back to Toronto with a report to the board and recommendations for further negotiations with DeBartolo—there was a new note of optimism among the board.

On May 8, I had a call from Bob Campeau and met with him at his office. He informed me that he had found an investor, a Canadian, who was prepared to put $500 million into the U.S. operations and lend Bob Campeau $150 million, repayable over the next few years. Campeau would cede control to the investor, whom I presumed to be Paul Desmarais. This was all to be completed by May 30, subject to three conditions:

1. The banks were satisfied. Campeau reported that he had already negotiated a 15 cents on the $1.00 settlement

on his personal loans, with an additional 15 cents payable if the events went according to plan.

2. DeBartolo must be bought out. Bob had been personally negotiating with DeBartolo and was optimistic that this could be achieved.

3. Olympia & York must accept a major discount, as had the bank. On this, Bob reported that O&Y was being very difficult. He said if the new investor put in $500 million and O&Y refused to co-operate, "This will be the second time O&Y has not co-operated," and he would personally sue O&Y and also have the lawyers for Campeau Corporation sue O&Y.

It was evident from these conditions that Bob had been in separate negotiations with DeBartolo, probably on the same day the independent committee flew to Youngstown. Clearly this meant that the board had lost all credibility with DeBartolo.

I asked Bob what would happen if his plan fell through. He replied that we'd be back to where we are, and that O&Y would be sued for obstructing the plan. His intention was to put this solution to the board on May 18. I suggested he should have valuations and fairness opinions with respect to the various interests (and of O&Y in particular) available for the board so that the board would have arm's-length values on which to base their assessment. He thought this an excellent idea and promised to get Tony Fell of Dominion Securities working on this right away.

I commented to Bob that he looked better and more optimistic than I'd ever seen him; I hoped his plan would work. He said he was meeting Conrad Black on Wednesday and was optimistic Black would help with Paul Reichmann, who was also a director of Black's Hollinger Corp.

Meanwhile, the values in the company were eroding rapidly, as real estate values generally continued their relentless slide.

On May 8 and 10, there was an exchange of letters between Paul Reichmann and Bob Campeau, staking out each other's view of responsibilities and commitments to restructuring Campeau Corporation. These were laced with litigious threats.

Throughout July and August, various discussions continued with DeBartolo, O&Y, and the banks, with no progress achieved. On August 10, the board took the decision to terminate Bob Campeau as chair and CEO of the company. The impetus for this decision came from the banks and O&Y. Bob wrote a blistering personal letter to the directors representing the National Bank and O&Y, citing conflicts of interest and other corporate governance matters. While the board finally did what it had to do in replacing Bob as CEO, I too was not happy with the outcome. I spoke to Bob by telephone from my hotel room in Vancouver. He said that while he understood that the banks wanted a new CEO, his nominee would have been George Hitchman (who was a senior banker). Further, he said he had 35 percent of the vote and would block the moves the lenders contemplated. Events had now run past Bob Campeau, however, and, removed from his office by the board, he was powerless.

I went into the hospital on September 4 for a total hip replacement. While recovering, I went to see Bob Campeau at his home and told him I could no longer stand as a director. He accepted my position, but asked me to stay on until he could find my replacement. On October 15, 1990, I wrote my resignation to Robert Després, who was now chair of the board of Campeau Corporation. In my letter, I stated, "Events over the past month or so have made me question seriously whether I have a useful role to play in the future among the major stakeholders of whom I am not one." This resignation was preceded by a private letter I wrote to Després on September 29, explaining my rationale for resigning from the board. In that letter I said in part:

> When I joined the Board, we took a number of initiatives which were correct and, had they been carried out, I think events would have had a beneficial outcome. For example, I think Bob made a mistake in not stepping down as CEO when we recommended it. By insisting upon his "three conditions" he effectively blocked the possibility of transition and, in doing so, lost his office as Chairman and the opportunity to select a CEO who could have been more compatible with him. When I met with Bob at his home on September 20th, I told him this and he replied that he's "happy with the way things are."
>
> Also, I believe my recommendation to establish the Special Committee to negotiate with DeBartolo and O&Y was the right thing to do. I was most disappointed when Bob unilaterally began negotiating with DeBartolo, effectively negating the role of the Committee. Had Bob worked co-operatively with the Committee, in an advisory capacity, I believe we could have made real progress instead of having the divided approach now facing the Board.

In October 1991, Campeau filed a proposed plan of arrangement for the financial restructuring of the company with the Ontario Superior Court of Justice. The plan was conditional on final acceptance of the plans of reorganization of the U.S. subsidiaries.

In early 1992, newly created Federated Department Stores Inc. emerged from the Chapter 11 bankruptcy reorganization process in the United States.

Also, early in 1992, following receipt of creditor and shareholder approval, Campeau received final approval from the Ontario Court of Justice for the company's financial restructuring under Section 181 of the Ontario Business Corporations Act and under the Companies' Creditors Arrangement Act. Effective February 11, 1992, the company's name was changed to Camdev Corporation. In 1993, the shares of Camdev Corporation traded between $2.50 and $6.75 per share ascribing a market valuation of $16 to $43 million.

Campeau meanwhile moved to Austria and became involved in real estate ventures there and in Germany.

14

Mitel: Second Time Around, 1987–1991

> "This is not the end. It is not even the beginning
> of the end. But it is, perhaps, the end of the
> beginning."
> *Winston Churchill*

For three and a half years, from August 1987 to January 1991, British Telecom (BT) assumed the sponsorship of Mitel as the owner of 51 percent of the share capital. Throughout this period the company drifted with no clear direction while the board waited for BT's strategic plan, which was intended to encompass Mitel as a components supplier. BT's upper echelons of staff were continually changing, with the result that Mitel's destiny was subject to variable influences, even though from 1986 through most of 1989, John McMonigall was the Mitel point man as the managing director of IPD (the International Products Division of BT). John Jarvis, the Mitel president selected by BT, appeared to believe that he was reporting to McMonigall, and regularly bypassed the Mitel board. Certainly this is the way McMonigall played it.

Within Mitel, the momentum to reduce costs was lost and overhead started to grow again, while cash decreased from a high of $140 million in 1986 to $90 million by December 1990. Competition in Mitel's markets was severe. As the company drifted and cash dwindled, the non-BT members of the Mitel board became increasingly uncomfortable and, through me as chair, we made our views known to BT. We pressed management for action and BT for finalization of a corporate strategy. On one occasion, just before a Mitel budget planning meeting, I confronted McMonigall about forcing management to reduce costs substantially, a subject we had discussed a number of times and with which he supposedly agreed. McMonigall proposed hiring consultants, which initially I opposed on the basis that the company already had highly paid management to determine strategy. Finally I relented.

This discussion coincided with an article in *Fortune Magazine* that quoted Ross Perot as saying: "If they find a snake in General Motors, they hire a consultant. If we find a snake in EDS, we kill it." When I told McMonigall that he and BT were like General Motors, he assured me he'd get action—but still nothing happened.

In November 1989, David Dey called to tell me that McMonigall had left BT and that he would be the new main contact for Mitel at BT. Dey was also new to BT, having just moved into the post of deputy chair. David was a refreshingly open and direct person who had gained experience at IBM and Plessey. He seemed prepared to recognize issues and implement action.

So when Dey advised me BT intended to carry on as before, I responded, "The directors of Mitel are not prepared to carry on any longer; something must change or we will resign." This led to my meeting with Dey in December

1989 in New York. As I briefed him on the background, he was quick to understand both the degree and severity of the problem. He concluded our meeting by saying BT would no longer orchestrate events at Mitel, and that he and BT would look to the board of Mitel, with me as chair, for results. I said I would communicate this to the board, but he, on behalf of BT, must immediately communicate this to the management of Mitel. David drafted a letter in my presence to effect this important change. As we drove to LaGuardia together, he told me his recommendation to BT would be to groom Mitel for sale over two years, a proposal I allowed made sense.

A month later, in January 1990, I had another call from David Dey, who this time was travelling with Barry Romeril, BT's new CFO. They were on their way to Toronto to see me and I was to get John Jarvis down from Ottawa for a meeting. At the meeting, Dey was clearly embarrassed as he told us that BT had decided to put its 51 percent of Mitel up for sale and, sale or no sale, had no intention of providing any further support to Mitel. Then came the bombshell: BT had entered into an agreement with Northern Telecom, Mitel's giant competitor in Canada, 53-percent owned by BCE (Bell Canada Enterprises), for exclusive distributorship of Nortel's equipment in the UK! We were stunned and immediately sat down to draft joint announcements and, within Mitel, to exercise damage control. BT had publicly orphaned the company.

BT had concluded it should be in network management and services businesses, not in telecommunications equipment manufacturing. During the preceding year, the board of Mitel had pressed BT to either take steps to allow Mitel to be profitable or to buy out the minority shareholders. We knew

BT had examined the alternatives and presumed our pressure had assisted them in arriving at their decision to sell.

Since the Mitel fiscal year ended March 31, we were entering into the planning cycle for the 1991 financial year. Over the next few months, management was pressed to take long-overdue action to reduce costs. The board and Dey were unhappy with progress, but BT did not wish to take drastic action, because with a variety of interested parties conducting due diligence, the company could be sold at any moment. Not only was management distracted by responding to a constant barrage of demands from potential purchasers for information, staff was demoralized. A siege mentality enveloped the organization and people were beginning to worry about their personal positions as the question of survival or, at best, sale to a large multinational began to permeate the company. Management became divisive and increasingly jittery, disoriented, and indecisive. Although not authorized by the board, the CEO had allowed key managers to voluntarily trigger lucrative "retention contracts." Something had to be done.

In early September 1990, I underwent a total hip replacement and, while I was recovering, the board decided to send two directors, Albert Gnat and Robert Després, to BT to demand immediate action or we would all resign. BT agreed that it had to change the management of Mitel, and it became a question of timing and whom to put in place.

The board turned to me. I was barely mobile and felt worn down with exasperation over the events that had occurred since BT bought Mitel. The magnitude of the task was formidable and, with no "big daddy" shareholder, I wondered whether the company was salvageable. Before Christmas I received a conference call from David Golden, chair of the Mitel board's independent committee, and Dr. David Leakey, BT's chief scientist, who had served on the Mitel board since 1986 as a technical adviser. Leakey was a superb individual, a true friend of Mitel, and incredibly constructive and helpful as a director. He continually provided guidance and comfort to the board on research and development projects within Mitel, which led to the introduction of exciting new products later in 1991.

Golden and Leakey proposed that I become CEO with a three-year contract, effective immediately after the new year. I responded that a three-year contract was unnecessary because the company would be sold before then and it would not be proper to encumber the future shareholders with me as CEO. The two Davids then said, "If you're not prepared to take the position, we propose to make Tony Crisalli [the head of manufacturing and the most experienced manager at Mitel] acting CEO and create a committee to run the company with you as chair of the executive committee." I immediately replied, "That's ludicrous. I've never agreed to run a company by committee and won't do so now." I went on, "Why not do it my way, like we did before? I'll do it for one year with an annual renewable contract while we see what happens." They agreed to this; later I came to regret declining their request that I take a three-year contract. Interesting to note: while I took this position, in 1992 when Schroder Ventures bought BT's 51-percent shareholding, it announced, "We run our companies through executive committees."

I insisted that I be paid less salary than the incumbent, because while on the board I had been outspoken that the president and senior management were overcompensated, especially the performance-related portions of their packages. I said I did not want a bonus the first year even if warranted, but would like a significant stock option allotment instead. Later, the figure of one million shares was discussed, but because BT refused to permit dilution of its holding to under 51 percent, I settled for 700,000 options, which were approved at the early January 1991 price of $1.25.

* * *

Over the previous year, I had been pressing management to provide a profitability analysis for the entire company, by product and by country. It was like pulling teeth—management didn't see the need for this nor did it share my sense of urgency. Finally in November 1990, we received an 87-page report, described in the covering memorandum, as the "short version" of the profitability analysis. It was apparent to me that management was drowning in information. I sat in my kitchen one Saturday with this report and reduced it to a one-page summary of profit and loss, capital employed, return on capital employed, headcount, and payroll by major product line by country. My analysis showed a projected loss of $30 million for the year compared to management's break-even budget, on revenues of approximately $430 million, capital employed of over $200 million, and 4,200 employees.

It was quickly evident that, if I could "unscramble the egg" by discontinuing losing products and locations, the company would have sales of $350 to $380 million, pre-tax profits of $25 million, and capital employed of $95 million—not a bad picture. However, to make this all happen, the company would have to shed 700 people, or a payroll reduction of about $35 million, and the severance payments would make a serious dent in the remaining $70 million cash. Of course, other major costs would be incurred in closing plants and sales offices, and moving people around before savings would be realized. All this had to be accomplished without materially reducing R&D, which had to be maintained to ensure the future of the company.

This one-sheet analysis became the foundation of a plan that I initiated when I took over again as president and CEO on January 9, 1991, and remained the basis of the company's direction through to the 1993 financial year, when it finally realized a profit. Unfortunately some targets, such as the reduction of capital employed, could not be met because the real estate markets in the UK and North America became severely depressed—plants should have been closed and redundant real estate divested in the boom of the late 1980s. From January 1991 through to the end of March 1993, total worldwide personnel were reduced by 29 percent, resulting in direct salary costs falling to the order of $60 million.

On the morning of January 9, 1991, I met with the top 20 people at headquarters in Kanata, Ontario, many of whom I knew well from my time as CEO in 1985–87. Using my one-page analysis as a discussion document, I told them what had to be done. I also explained that many in the room would not make it, but that I had no specific plans in that regard and that I needed their help. Finally, I stressed that the game was survival—we had to make decisions and move quickly or we would soon run out of cash. It was more than disheartening to hear many of these senior managers, on studying the analysis, ask, "How come we didn't know this?"

After the meeting, I went to see Tony Crisalli, who had been given six months' notice. He was angry at the waste he had seen in his four years with the company and was anxious to stay on and fight, to which I agreed. The CFO (whom I hired in 1986) had been permitted to trigger his contract, so I hired, on a consulting basis, Jim Ellis, a freelance financial consultant who previously worked for CDC (Canada Development Corporation). Don McIntyre, whom I hired in 1986, was still secretary and legal counsel, and chafing at the bit to get the company back to profitability. By the end of January, the four of us constituted the senior management team, and practically all the previous top management had left, with the exception of those in the semiconductor and dialler divisions. Because the company was still for sale, I designated Crisalli as the operating head of the PBX business, now comprising roughly 85 percent of the operations, while I worried about the other businesses (semiconductor, diallers, public switching) and concentrated on ownership, financing, and strategic issues.

Terry Matthews invited me to lunch down the street at Newbridge Networks. His company had nearly gone under, the stock having dropped to $2.50 from a high of $21. At lunch Terry said, "You're out of your mind—this [Mitel] is going to be a colossal bankruptcy," to which I responded, "Terry, what difference does it make? I'm there as a director anyway; I might as well try to save it."

As far as the senior management team was concerned, what the company had going for it was a strong balance sheet, the best quality ratings in the industry, an incredibly resilient and loyal group of employees, and a committed group of top managers eager to overcome adversity. Mitel's own marketing and public relations group, with the help of an outside agency, came up with the "Elvis ad" (see opposite) that encapsulated the determination the employees felt—we

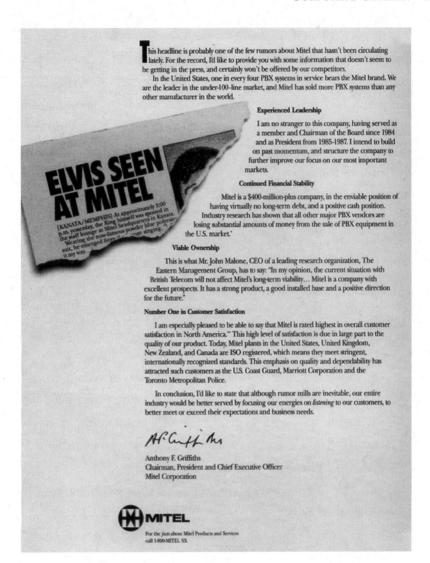

staked out our ground, while our competition fuelled rumours of the company's impending demise.

We engaged in many prolonged discussions with prospective buyers. In most cases, purchasers were only interested in parts of the company and not others. This presented us with a

Hobson's choice: if we agreed to sell segments of the company, the remaining parts would lack the critical mass necessary for survival. As we took the requisite steps to downsize the company in accordance with our plan, cash diminished and confidence amongst customers, distributors, and suppliers eroded. Our competitors were having a field day, telling our customers they shouldn't buy from Mitel as we wouldn't be around for much longer.

In *The Globe and Mail* on July 23, 1991, Lawrence Surtees summarized the general atmosphere in an article headlined:

A second coming for Griffiths
Being Mitel's saviour will prove difficult this time: analysts

Few CEOs are ever called back for an encore performance to restructure a financially troubled company.

But Anthony Griffiths, chairman, president and chief executive officer of Mitel Corp. of Kanata, Ont., has embarked on his second attempt to turn around the former darling of Canada's high-technology industry.

This time, however, most analysts say the 60-year-old businessman faces a tougher challenge due to fierce international competition in Mitel's core business than when he served as president and CEO from 1985 to 1987.

Few, if any, industry watchers expect Mr. Griffiths to unveil a magic cure for Mitel's woes at the company's annual meeting in Ottawa today. But he has established himself in the past as an able corporate doctor.

When Mr. Griffiths was first made president of the telecommunications equipment maker in October, 1985, several months after utility giant British Telecommunication

PLC acquired 51 percent of Mitel and injected $320 million into its coffers, it was weighed down by product delays, mounting competition and the after-effects of over-heated growth.

It had lost money for nearly three years running, a string of losses that did not come to an end until well into 1988, by which time Mr. Griffiths had been bumped up to the chairman's job.

This time, however, Mr. Griffiths must operate without the benefit of a white knight.

British Telecom has been trying in vain for more than 18 months to sell its Mitel shares, which would currently fetch $1.10 each, compared with the $8 share price the utility paid in May, 1985.

The major restructuring announced by Mr. Griffiths in April—the third since 1985—eliminated 400 jobs, or 10 percent, of Mitel's workforce. It will employ 3,500 people when the cuts are completed late this summer.

The restructuring also contributed $83.5-million to the company's $107-million loss for the year ended March 29, 1991.

"Mitel needs to aggressively cut costs just to stand still because of the lack of growth and increased rivalry in its core business," one financial analyst, whose brokerage forbids identifying him, said.

Mr. Griffiths said in April that the changes announced at the time will return the company to profitability. But he declined to either say when or to offer an estimate.

"Breaking even would be a feat," Mark Lawrence, telecommunications analyst at Midland Walwyn Capital Inc. of Toronto, said.

At the same time, on February 7, 1991, *Frank* magazine wrote amusingly: "And now, in these desperate times,
Griffiths is back for an encore. Employees who recall his
previous performance are bracing for the worst, and have
already begun drafting applications to Corel."[1]

In May 1991, I wrote to the premier of Ontario, Bob
Rae, with an appeal: "Consider financial assistance for Mitel
which is suffering from being disowned by BT; 1,200 jobs in
Ontario are at risk." At the same time, we applied to the federal
government's Ministry of Industry, Science and Technology,
for a $5-million grant under the research and development
assistance plan.

To us the logic was simple: by October, we were the
best in the business, but we were dying because of a lack
of confidence in the marketplace in our ability to survive.
As a result of the quality program undertaken in 1986,
Dataquest (an independent industry market research firm)
had ranked Mitel first in six measures in 1990, ahead of
AT&T, Northern Telecom, ROLM, NEC, Fujitsu, and others
(see page opposite). Also, our plants had been rated ISO
9000, the highest quality rating at a time when our competitors did not enjoy this standard. However, no bank would
talk to us, despite our having $50 to $75 million cash on
hand, net of debt. We needed time and backup financing so
that the world would *perceive* we would survive.

While all this was going on, in October 1991 we
announced our new range of products at the international
telecom show in Geneva. The marketing and R&D people had
done an incredible job. In 10 months they had pulled together
and largely completed an entire new concept and set of products for the PBX industry. This showed the communications

world that Mitel had both a winning strategy and a vision for the future. They implemented a fundamental change by unbundling and miniaturizing the traditional PBX, utilizing universal components from the computer industry, and designing modular telephone sets that enabled Lego-like expansion of systems. In doing so, they amalgamated Mitel's existing technologies into a one-product platform, which promised to greatly reduce costs of manufacturing, inventories, and software streams when a complete transition to the new product line was completed.

October 1991 was a pivotal period. While public excitement about the new products was apparent, cash was draining rapidly on the payment of severance packages for nearly 900 people. Internal cash forecasts were frightening and I persuaded the board that we should seek insolvency advice in case cash dried up before the turnaround came. The industry itself was in a depression, with major companies, like TIE International, along with many distributors being put into Chapter 11—including Mitel's largest independent dealer in the United States, RCA. In the summer of 1991, the board approved Mitel's acquisition of RCA on a no-cash transaction, a move that later strengthened Mitel's position in sales and service in the United States.

At the October telecom exhibition in Geneva, I toured the stands of other companies with Tom Mayer, then in charge of Mitel's North American sales and service operations. Tom had left Mitel when BT took over to become president of the PBX division, Intecom, of Wang.[2] I had persuaded him to rejoin Mitel on an annual contractual basis, similar to my own, with the mandate to integrate and reduce costs in the United States and Canada and at RCA. Tom and I walked into the Cable & Wireless booth, which had a live video conferencing hookup with Hong Kong. The polite young Chinese Cable & Wireless salesman asked if we would like our fortunes read by a feng shui fortune teller, whom we could see on a large television screen sitting next to an interpreter at a table in Hong Kong. Tom declined, but I immediately agreed and said hello to the fortune teller. He asked my date of birth (July 19, 1930) and then told me that I was born in the Chinese Year of the Horse.[3] This I knew, and he carried on talking about my lucky colours and lucky numbers, and made some relatively specific observations about my health, longevity, and future, including stressing that I should make certain that my desk faced north or northwest (at the time it faced east). He then invited questions from me. I asked him if Mitel would succeed and would I prosper. To these questions he answered that I was high up in my company and that business generally looked promising. As we ended the interview and I was about to walk away, the feng shui man cautioned once again: "Make certain your desk faces north or northwest." Tom chuckled nervously and skeptically.

When I got back to Kanata, I asked my secretary, Janet Finlayson, to have the maintenance people move my furniture around. The change was not aesthetic because now my back would face the office door. Janet asked, "Would you mind telling me what this is all about?" When I told her she said, "Okay, as long as we don't tell anybody else!" I said, "Why not? If it works, who cares?" Believe what you like, but after October, the company's progress began to improve on all fronts.

* * *

We still hadn't found a buyer or an investor for the company, so we went further afield. We kept enlisting new names and Albert Gnat received some from David Wilson,[4] vice-chair of ScotiaMcLeod, including Schroder Ventures (SV) in the UK. By now we had arranged for an option on the Mitel shares held by BT to be held in trust by the board. We were making progress with the Ontario government, but they were under-standably insistent that any financing they provided should not enrich BT, who had abandoned the company. Also, on Albert's initiative, the board, management, and friends, including Mitel founder Mike Cowpland, assembled $5 to $7 million among themselves to buy back the BT control block, the total cost of which was around $30 to $35 million, meaning the group needed a co-investor or investors with $23 to $28 million. Albert visited Schroder Ventures in London in January 1992, and proposed that SV back the management plus Cowpland group to buy out BT's 51 percent. Schroder somewhat skepti-cally commenced due diligence.

In the meantime, I had identified an ideal merger can-didate, a major multinational competitor, AT&T, which we code-named "MOTHER." In March 1992 I approached AT&T with a plan that persuaded the company that it should have a serious look. Because SV was now actively on the scene, we had to provide SV with a "standstill agreement," which pre-vented AT&T buying without SV approving or purchasing at a higher price than SV might entertain.

Concomitantly, the Ontario government continued its deliberations and due diligence. Internally we code-named this project "EARPHONE," the first part being the reverse spelling of Ontario's premier Bob Rae. EARPHONE was nervous. We had asked for a $40-million low-interest loan on the basis that, with the government backing Mitel, the *perception* of the company would become positive and poten-tially the funds would not be required. As the government watched the cash dissipate, even though its consultants enthusiastically endorsed Mitel's plans, the government became increasingly nervous and settled on $20 million as an acceptable figure, but expressed concern that the company might fail. Eventually the government agreed to extend the $20-million loan, provided we find an investor to put at least $10 million into the company. With the help of the trade minister, Michael Wilson, the federal government also agreed to a $5-million grant on similar conditions. These agreements provided prospective investors with a good safety net for their investments.

With Ontario, the federal government, SV, and AT&T all simultaneously conducting due diligence, internally Mitel was like a three-ring circus. Long hours were put in by the staff, all of whom had been on a pay freeze for more than a year.

SV started distancing itself from Mitel, on the grounds that its lawyers had cautioned them about "disclosure" of the potential purchase. It also said BT was paranoid about disclosure, which both Albert Gnat and I determined to be exaggerated. We told SV, "We do not have a disclosure problem, and when BT has one, only then, will we, so what are you worried about?" SV remained evasive, but continued to conduct due diligence through consultants. SV were clearly nervous and, at one point, asked me if the company would pay $25,000 to fund their studies further. I agreed to this, provided the studies were given to us, whether or not SV proceeded to invest.

Early on in SV's due diligence, its outside technical consultants reported that Mitel's technology would not be competitive in the future. Mitel's R&D people then had to *educate* these consultants on the authenticity of the new series of products, which anticipated the evolution of PBXs to computers. Finally, the consultants saw the light and reversed their negative recommendation to SV.

I decided we should do our own due diligence on Dr. Henry Simon, the head of SV's venture capital group, as well as the company itself. This was not too difficult because SV were investors in Newbridge, where Simon was on the board. With Albert Gnat's assistance and his connections with Terry Matthews and the Newbridge board, we developed a composite reference that immediately made us uncomfortable. I learned Simon was a "micro-managing nitpicker, [who] won't admit he's wrong." One Newbridge director said, "Boards are to guide and help management; stay out of the kitchen. Henry Simon wants to be in the kitchen once a month."

This is what we heard and what we heard is what we got. I was reminded of what F.D. Roosevelt said of General Douglas MacArthur: "Never underestimate a man who over-estimates himself."

We also sought references on Gordon Byrn, the head of Schroders in Canada, and as such, the Canadian face for SV's purchase of Mitel Canada. He was, by his own admission, not an operator. Schroder Canada came into the deal later in the SV due diligence, partly to lend a Canadian presence to the investor group.

British Imperialism Enters the Boardroom, 1992–1993

> "Some men are greedier than others, and they get to thinking they are the power rather than the instrument of power."
>
> *Harry S. Truman*

The first week of June 1992 found me en route to Atlanta to meet with the general manager of Hitachi (USA), some of whose products Mitel distributed through RCA in the United States. From there, I went on to Sanibel Island, Florida, for the annual gathering of the Mitel President's Club to present awards to the outstanding achievers from the previous year's sales successes.

When I arrived at Sanibel there were telephone messages from Schroder Ventures (SV) summoning me to the UK. It appeared that SV was ready to proceed with buying out BT, though I was asked by SV to maintain secrecy and tell no one at BT that I was in the UK. I found this request somewhat ominous.

On Sunday, June 7, 1992, I flew to London from Miami and met Henry Simon and his Canadian partner Gordon Byrn for dinner Monday evening at the Connaught Hotel. While talking about the company and SV's impending investment, two key issues arose that made me uneasy, even though I wanted to accommodate SV's wishes as new controlling shareholders. First, Simon and Byrn were insistent that all Mitel board members be replaced except me, it having already been agreed that Simon and Byrn would immediately replace the two BT nominee directors. I suggested they keep at least two members of the existing board for continuity for a year, but they were adamant that there should be a *clean break with BT.* I explained that the four non-BT directors had fought a horrendously difficult and diligent battle for the minority shareholders during the three and one-half years of BT's regime, but SV was not swayed. Of course, with this, *SV dismissed Albert Gnat*, who had initiated the buyout and had personally invited Simon into our syndicate. When Mitel management subsequently heard of this arrangement, they viewed it as a brazen power grab that gave SV absolute control of the company.

Byrn then produced a list of potential replacement directors, from which we could choose; I later sent him additional names for consideration, which he seemingly ignored. When talk turned to my position, I suggested I stay on for a year, giving them six months to learn about the company and recruit my successor with my assistance; my rolling annual contract as CEO was due to expire January 9, 1993. When they then asked me what kind of person I would select as CEO, a question to which I had already given considerable thought, I replied immediately, "Someone with a marketing background from the computer industry," with which they agreed completely. It was suggested that we retain Spencer Stuart as a search consultant; I knew the firm well and had no objections to this proposal. I was, however, troubled by the precipitous speed of the process for a company that had undergone immense trauma and about which SV knew very little. Their final words on my position were, "We definitely want you to stay as chair," along with gratuitous comments on my considerable talents. It was clear they wanted their own man in, sooner rather than later. And these were the people we had *invited* to back us in the buyout of the BT block.

I flew back to Canada and immediately telephoned my fellow directors and gave them the news. Each one listened in stony silence and thanked me for the update.

Since the fiscal year end was March 31 and the annual meeting was set for July (it was now June), the shareholders' proxy and directors' circular had already been mailed, nominating the existing board, including the two BT nominees.

The transaction with SV and BT closed in Toronto on June 15, 1992, and I flew to Ottawa with Simon and Byrn to make the announcement to the employees in Kanata the following day. Over dinner, I again raised the idea of keeping two existing non-executive directors and suggested extending my term while they got to know the company. Simon responded that I was too old for the job (on the eve of my 62nd birthday).

When the 1,200 Kanata employees were all assembled, I introduced Henry Simon and Gordon Byrn and said, "The survival and success of the company belonged to each and every Mitel employee" and that the staff had succeeded in making the company attractive to these investors. After a pause there were loud cheers and applause.

On Friday, I met with Ontario government officials and firmed up the $20 million financing for the EARPHONE project, which the government had now made contingent upon SV investing $10 million in Mitel.

Byrn said he did not have time before the annual meeting to properly invite new directors to join the board and said he would ask two of his Montreal contacts to become directors "temporarily." The company then sent out a one-page amendment to the directors' circular listing the new names. No sooner was this in the mail than Don McIntyre, Mitel's secretary and general counsel, pointed out that because of various securities and corporate regulations, we did not have enough resident Canadian independent directors to constitute some of the board committees. Therefore, at the annual general meeting on July 21, as chair, I apologized for the last-minute changes and we added a third nominee from Montreal. He too would be "temporary," although by now the management seriously doubted that the new appointees were in fact going to be temporary. This was a novel experience for me, where a new controlling shareholder unilaterally nominates the directors to represent the minority shareholders.

Since March, I had continued discussions with AT&T about a strategic alliance, including the possibility of their buying certain assets of Mitel. Of course, these discussions were conducted with the knowledge and approval of BT and SV. When SV bought BT's position on June 15, I recommended that Simon arrange an early introduction to AT&T. Suddenly I discovered that this meeting had been arranged for July 20 without me. I suggested to Simon that I should be present at the first meeting, as I had initiated the discussions and was intimately familiar with the details of the proposed transaction. Moreover, while SV was quite free to discuss any matters qua shareholders, as CEO, it was essential that I represent the company. Simon's first response was that there were already too many people involved in the meeting, but he later changed his mind and included me.

On July 23, the first meeting of the newly created executive committee was convened. This committee, established by SV to "manage Mitel," comprised Simon (as chair), Byrn, and myself. During most of the day there were three, sometimes four, layers of management present at the committee meeting and Simon conducted what the senior management termed an inquisition—he was indeed "already in the kitchen." His tone and manner were condescending, almost disdainful at times: why are you doing this, why didn't you do that, and so on. For me, this was déjà vu—McMonigall with a Teutonic manner. The more Simon pressed, the more defensive and hesitant the responses became. By the end of the day, there was an atmosphere of depression, as if we'd been "had."

Simon, Byrn, and I then flew to New York for a follow-up meeting with AT&T on Friday, July 24. At dinner on the 23rd at a pricey restaurant no Mitel employee would ever be permitted to visit (I was left to pick up the bill), we reviewed the meetings of earlier that day at Kanata headquarters. Simon expressed disappointment at the lack of spontaneity in the responses to his questions. I finally said, "Henry, let me give it to you straight: First, please never again speak down to Mitel employees. They don't deserve it. Second, please don't issue instructions to my subordinates as long as I'm CEO. You've asked me how BT screwed up the company: by doing exactly what you're doing, overriding management decisions." By now Byrn and Simon had told me, "We run our companies through an executive committee." I told Simon if he wanted to be CEO it was his prerogative as the representative of the controlling shareholders and pulled out my keys in a gesture of offering them to him. He declined, saying he was too busy. I stated my views that, whether he liked my management style or not, he must respect the office of the CEO, and if he wanted something done he should talk to me and we could decide whether it made sense. If it did, I would carry it out. Needless to say, the dinner was unsettling for me and so it must have been for him.

We met the next morning at 8:00 a.m. at Schroders's offices in New York and Simon allowed that I had upset him the previous evening. He had awakened early and already made a list of "actions and requests" for information. Every one of these actions was already under review and the information was readily available. However, before he gave me the final list, he requested we deliver a 20-cent-per-share profit for the year (1993), which was budgeted to break even (following an operating loss of $8.1 million for financial year 1992). Since it was now the end of July, this meant we had eight months to make $17 million to deliver on his request (annualized this would be $25 million). (In February 1993, seven months later, with a new CEO in place, Simon was to approve a budget projecting an operating profit of $16 million for the *entire fiscal year*.)

I looked at him in disbelief. SV had bought into our break-even plan, as had their consultants, the governments, and AT&T in each of their separate due diligence exercises. I replied calmly, "Okay, Henry, tell me which R&D program you want to cut. In the year we've already taken 950 people out of 4,200." (We had not cut R&D to ensure delivery of new products.) Next, he was insistent that Crisalli (COO) and Ellis (CFO) move to Kanata permanently, even though they both maintained apartments near the Mitel offices to which they commuted from their respective homes in Florida and Toronto. (At this point, Crisalli's contract was under review for renewal and he was reluctant to move his wife from Florida; he was 63 and his wife was not well. I had hired Ellis as a part-time consultant and then persuaded him to stay on; his wife had a long-standing career in Toronto.) While Byrn gingerly sided with me on these issues, it was clear that Simon was dissatisfied and was not going to leave it alone; he was like a dog with a bone.

The people from AT&T arrived and, to my amazement, Simon opened the meeting by telling them of our internal discussions concerning management. The meeting with AT&T proceeded until we adjourned for lunch, at which point Byrn caucused with the two representatives from AT&T, then joined Simon and me in the private dining room. Byrn announced that AT&T's chief representative, Bob Egan, had said they would like to resume the meetings after lunch without me present. I repeated what I had said before: this was quite satisfactory as long as they were discussing shareholder-related issues, but I was insistent that any company matters be negotiated in my presence as CEO of the company. (There was reason to believe SV was trying to make a deal with AT&T at the shareholder level.) Later I was informed by Simon and Byrn that AT&T was insistent that the follow-up meeting should be held somewhere other than New York or London, and that AT&T was paranoid about the possibility of being seen with SV people. The next meeting was to be held in Nice, where Henry Simon had an apartment. Since Simon and Byrn were not familiar with any company details, elaborate briefings and the attendance of technical managers were arranged. The meeting was held and led to yet another meeting attended only by Byrn at AT&T's suburban corporate headquarters. Meanwhile, at Mitel we received a bill for first-class airfare to France and a car-rental bill for eight days for the one-day meeting in Nice. These we returned for "correction." It was acknowledged a mistake had been made.

In mid-August I met the top man, and my original contact, for AT&T, Jerre Stead,[1] at an industry meeting in Washington, D.C. He requested that we meet privately later to ensure discussions were proceeding constructively between Mitel and AT&T. I told Jerre that I was puzzled why his representatives had requested I be excluded from discussions. He replied, "That wasn't us. We've been wondering why you haven't been there and strongly believe you should be." Of course this infuriated me, and when I reported this to Simon and Byrn, they maintained that it was AT&T's request to exclude my participation. Someone was not telling the truth. Nothing came of these lengthy discussions and other events arose that changed the course of events.

In private discussions with Simon in July and August, I again asked where he saw me fitting in. In response, he only stared blankly. On one of these occasions I told him I was going to start to "revive my life outside Mitel." He expressed puzzlement and I told him that if they were going to hire a new CEO, I had to think about my future. On August 2, 1992, I followed this up with a letter explaining that a couple of board opportunities were being offered to me, as well as another CEO job, which I realized I could not take while under contract.

About this time, Byrn talked to me privately saying, "It's too bad you got off on the wrong foot with Henry." He then changed the subject, saying, "I have a potential opportunity which you could help me with. It's a very complicated situation;

don't ask me what it is—I can't tell you. I really have a tremendous respect for you; your ability to take complex situations and simplify them." Clearly I was surprised. He reiterated, "I mean it, I really do." I told him I'd be happy to explore the subject with him when he was ready. He asked me how I would describe the role as non-executive chairman when the new CEO was hired. I already felt Simon had usurped that role, but agreed to reflect and get back to Byrn. On September 17, 1992, I wrote him a letter marked "STRICTLY CONFIDENTIAL: Re: Chairman of the Board." The second and third paragraphs of the letter said:

> To establish this role in a meaningful way requires an agreement on the fundamental philosophy of corporate governance. I believe strongly that the key role of the board, in the ultimate, is to hire and fire the CEO. Then management must manage the company under board approved plans and reporting requirements and systems. All directors are equal in their responsibility to the corporation and to all shareholders in law and hopefully in practice. My experience is that this tends (occasionally) not to happen, where there is a family in control, where there is an individual or group who control through multiple voting shares, or where there is a dominant shareholder. The latter was the case at Mitel under BT and under Terry Matthews. Wherever I am a director or chairman, I have fought for proper governance in this respect.
>
> I believe the idea of an executive committee is acceptable in the circumstance such as SV coming in and requiring familiarization and wanting to establish immediate management succession, even though in my view, the timing is

wrong and the stated reason (age) is not logical within the band of one to two years. Soon after a new CEO is installed, I believe the executive committee, at least as a monthly management review committee, as now operating, should be dissolved. If not, then it's essential that the board and CEO should carefully consider the role of chairman of the board vs. chairman of the executive committee.

The letter went on: "I hope you will not read anything negative into these comments, as I intend them in the most constructive way. I need your help in re-establishing the authority and independence of the board."

He said he had not shown the letter to Simon. I responded, "I hoped you wouldn't but I understood the risk that, as his business partner, you might have sent it on to him."

About this time, Gordon Byrn met with me before a board meeting and said he was going to propose a substantial increase in the basic retainer for directors. I explained that all employees in Mitel had effectively been on a company-wide pay freeze for nearly two years and I could not personally vote in favour of such a proposal. Early in September, I went to the UK to meet with prospective distributors, visit key customers, and attend a two-day Mitel executive committee meeting, first at the factory in Caldicot, Wales, and then in Slough at the Mitel distribution office. On arrival, I met privately with Henry Simon to discuss a number of issues, including a proposal to issue stock options to directors. When I asked Henry why we were contemplating granting options to temporary directors, he replied tersely, "Ask Gordon Byrn."

At this meeting, Henry expressed surprise that I had accepted a new board position at the Ondaatje Corporation.

I reminded him of our conversation on the subject of my future and the letter that followed. Furthermore, I assumed that as chair of the executive committee he was keeping his fellow directors abreast of our discussions, but apparently one director had called in surprise upon hearing of my new appointment. Byrn would raise this matter again on Friday at Slough.

Henry Simon had invited David Dey, my former counterpart at BT, and me for lunch at Schroders's private dining room in London. To my regret, Dey had left BT over a policy dispute sometime in 1990 and was now operating as an independent consultant. After dessert Simon excused himself, leaving Dey and me to linger over coffee. Dey asked me, "How are you getting on with these people?" I hesitated, then said: "I know you well, David, and therefore will tell you openly. We approached Henry to have Schroders back a group of management, Mike Cowpland, and the board to buy BT's block, and he left us out." Without blinking, Dey blurted out, "Why that's unethical!" I then explained that Henry was calling the shots over my shoulder, which was what BT had done before Dey came along. He responded, "Henry doesn't have the background or experience for a company like Mitel; I don't think it will work." By now, our investor group realized we had been double-crossed—cut out of our own transaction.

The next day at the executive committee meeting at Caldicot, Simon asked a wide range of questions, while Byrn appeared to doze through most of the meeting, admitting later to severe jet lag. The two left early to travel back to London, missing the employee get-together planned over dinner, arranged partly to introduce them. The following morning the meeting reconvened at Slough and I asked for an hour's private discussion before we parted to catch our airplanes for home.

Management was excused from the meeting, leaving Simon, Byrn, and myself. Henry began by huffing and puffing, his body swaying from side to side, "I can't understand how you run a company by writing memos. Yesterday you didn't ask any questions." He ranted on as I contained my growing anger. I responded to Simon's criticisms, pointing out that, while his marathon two-day monthly meetings may be useful to bring SV into the picture, from management's viewpoint, they were time-consuming. Not only did we spend two days of key managers' time presenting information but also senior management reviewed these presentations for two days prior to the executive committee meetings, or four days a month or forty-eight days a year. I said, "Of course I didn't ask questions yesterday; as CEO I knew what was going on and had already reviewed most of the material being presented." I pointed out in frustration that not one question asked by Simon or Byrn in this two-day session provided any added value.

I also pointed out the two instances in the past in which Mitel had been rescued from bankruptcy under my leadership, and on both occasions most observers believed it had been too late for the company. I then acknowledged that his style of management was different from my own: he was a stickler for detail and wanted to be part of management decisions. I told him I believed in empowering people at all levels of the organization, which it was clear he did not accept. I again offered to turn the CEO job over to him. I told him that my modus operandi had worked time and again for me, not just at Mitel, but also in other industries: I developed a plan, chose the people to implement it and devolved responsibility and decision-making throughout the organization, and monitored progress through a management committee, which met weekly followed by regular meetings with individual business units. This dissertation generated a look of disbelief on Simon's face. Byrn understood and briefly came to my defence. I asked if they had not checked me out during their due diligence and suggested they contact a few key people in London, Montreal, and Toronto who knew about my past performance. They responded that they had checked me out and asked if I'd checked on them. I said I had, but refrained from giving the report I'd assembled on Simon—it would not have improved the atmosphere!

I reiterated my bewilderment about their actions to date: ignoring my advice about keeping one or two of the previous directors, and not leaving me in place as CEO for another six months while they got a better understanding of the company. Henry repeated that I was 62—but so was he. I stood up and drew a line across the whiteboard stressing that I would be 62 for nine more months: what was the rush? Byrn then asked what I wanted them to do with my contract, which was due to expire January 9, and on which they had to give notice or renew by October 9. I replied that it was their decision, but we could not go on without agreement on how to manage the company.

Among the senior management committee, we had initially speculated that SV had entered the picture with a secret agenda, and it certainly seemed that way, despite SV and their consultants endorsing the company plan to the letter. One morning I arrived at the weekly 7:30 a.m. management meeting and my three colleagues said, "We've concluded there is no secret agenda; these people are just inept at running a company." I agreed they were inept, but their timing on buying out BT was perfect.

On several previous occasions Simon had expressed anxiety about "his $40-million investment." SV had been in for three months, the recession was still in full force, and the restructuring benefits were yet to come. The company was barely meeting targets and the pressures were still great. I pointed out that so far he and Byrn personally had zero money at risk. At risk were their reputations for investing $40 million of SV client funds; if the company failed they would not lose a nickel and, if it succeeded, they would benefit handsomely. I told him I was worried about the shareholders of Mitel—all shareholders—not just those represented by Schroders's $40 million. I then said I could not understand why, in their position as investors, they had not encouraged management to invest when they came in and, more specifically, why the assembled group of management and friends, including Cowpland, had been excluded from the transaction. I emphasized that Albert and I had been prepared to risk $1 million each of our personal funds. To this, Henry replied blandly that there seemed to be a liberal stock-option plan in place. Simon stumbled on this. In fact, the options to which he was referring were those granted to management when the new regime took over in January 1991 and had nothing to do with the buyout of BT organized by Albert with the board and management. Simon didn't seem to (want to) recognize that we had been prepared to put up cash for our participation, and seemed uncomfortable when I asked why he didn't invest cash himself. Either he was risk averse or had no cash—or both, a classic case of using "other people's money." I pressed him on the point that he was approached by Albert on our behalf as investors. Why did Schroders exclude us? He replied, "Albert approached me with that scheme. Why didn't he put it in writing—he's a lawyer." What could I say? I was speechless. Simon seemed befuddled. Thinking about it later, I concluded that Henry Simon was not used to such a blunt confrontation that presented an unanswerable dilemma for him.

We continued our heated discussion. Byrn interjected, "We'd like to work with you," to which I agreed to, but said we had to agree philosophically as to how to operate. At one point Byrn expressed "shock" that I had taken on a board appointment without their approval. I reminded Simon of our discussions on my situation. It seemed that Simon had not communicated this to Byrn. Byrn asked how I would fulfill my contract, to which I replied, I would do so completely. I had told my new board I could not become involved until after my contract with Mitel had expired.

We launched back to operating matters—these two men were clearly nervous Nellies. I explained that everything had been disclosed to them and their consultants; there was a safety net already in place with $20 million from the Ontario government and another $5 million from the federal government. I gave them this analogy: A train pulled out of a station in January 1991 headed in a specific direction at 150 miles an hour. A year and a half later they got on the train, having understood where it was going. The worst thing they could do was to tamper with the direction because it was on course and progressing. I told them, "You bought at the right time; we've given you a package with a pink ribbon neatly wrapped around it." Seeing his nervousness, at one point I asked Henry, "Would you like me to come and speak to your partners?" I thought he was going to have a stroke.

Also about this time, I ran into Simon at the Ottawa airport after we had left Mitel headquarters in Kanata separately to catch our planes. He asked me about each of the new directors, one by one: who they were, what they did, what their reputations were. I knew very little myself and ended my comments by saying, "You'll have to ask Gordon. They're his friends." This incident was yet another disappointment on the issue of corporate governance. At that time, all of these non-SV directors were still declared to be "temporary." It seemed clear that to Simon, the board was only a necessary appendage, and its composition was not particularly relevant. This was his deal and he intended to run it his way.

At a board meeting on October 5, it was agreed that my contract as president would not be renewed. By the third week in November we were interviewing candidates for CEO, none of whom were marketing people from the computer industry. Also, we were beginning to plan a major equity financing around SV's new $10-million investment, which was required to obtain the $20-million loan from Ontario (EARPHONE).

On December 9, at a board meeting in Montreal we hired a new CEO to start January 9, 1993, when my contract expired. At a recess, Gordon Byrn asked to talk with me privately, and told me there had been a meeting of the board of directors over dinner at his house the previous evening. He said the directors had decided that Byrn would become temporary chair in January and I could stay on the board if I wanted to. Byrn also said he would negotiate a consulting contract with me to work on projects as required, if I were willing. Right or wrong, I perceived this to be an indirect question to ascertain what I would want to "go away."

After he finished, I responded that in light of events to date I was not surprised. However, I was getting the message, for whatever reason, that "the board" had decided I was no longer acceptable to be the chair of a company that I had been chair of for five and a half years, three and a half of which had been under BT, who had enormous strategic and philosophical differences with me and the rest of the board, but had always fully supported me as chair. I had continued as chair as well as CEO since January 1991.

I acknowledged the prerogative of the board to change the chair at an appropriate time. However, in view of this development I said I would decline to stay on the board and, if needed, would be happy to provide consulting advice if called upon; I did not need or want a contract.

* * *

When I reflected on these events over the weekend, I realized that I was becoming implicated in a most flagrant example of unacceptable corporate governance. Suddenly I was confronted with the incredible situation where the company had three new "temporary" directors and was going to appoint a "temporary" chair without any stated explanation, internal or external, for the change, on the eve of a major equity financing. The cavalier attitude and disregard for the board and shareholders at large rankled me. As one member of the management committee, Don McIntyre, put it: Schroders has 50 percent of the vote, but behave as if they own 100 percent of the company.

By mid-week the board had dispersed for Christmas holidays: Byrn and two others to the Caribbean and Florida, Simon to the UK and later California, and myself to Bermuda. From Bermuda I faxed Simon and Byrn and said that the board had the power to replace me as chair, but I would insist it be implemented at a properly constituted board meeting. The bogus meeting at Byrn's home had not been properly constituted: there had been no notice or agenda, and neither I, the chair and CEO, nor Crisalli, the COO and a director, had been notified. The rest of management was opposed to the timing of the change, fearing it would abort the equity issue. I suggested a board meeting be held January 9, 1993, and attached a proposed agenda, which included the resignation of a director (me), the election of a new director (the new CEO), and the election of a chair.

Byrn sent me and Simon a handwritten fax dated December 24, 1992, which insisted there had been a meeting on December 8 at his house, and whether I agreed or not, he had been elected chair. Byrn ended this memo with: "In summary, Tony, the board made their decision. I tried to decline suggesting others, but they felt I should accept the role at least on a temporary basis. On that temporary basis I acquiesced." The situation was now getting ridiculous, awkward, and unpleasant.

I consulted Jon Levin, of Fasken Martineau, the outside legal counsel to Mitel's special committee, which had been dissolved on the change of ownership. I concluded my next fax to Byrn and Simon on December 27 with:

We [the management] are concerned what you are orchestrating is guaranteed to create uncertainty in the marketplace and may well jeopardize the proposed underwriting and have a negative effect on the share price. We do not perceive the marketplace will perceive in any way what you are planning as an orderly transition.

I returned to Toronto on January 4, 1993, and contacted the two investment dealers who were preparing for the equity issue, ScotiaMcLeod and Midland Walwyn. I asked each, without editorial, "What would your reaction be if I resigned from Mitel at the end of the week?," which was the termination date of my contract. Wolf Raymer of Midland Walwyn immediately replied, "There would be no deal." David Wilson of Scotia said, "Uncertainty would be the main message. You are a known entity in the business community with an excellent reputation—how would Mitel explain this?" Both advised they would expect a delay of at least three and probably six months to the financing.

Even though I quoted Raymer and Wilson, Byrn called them to confirm their statements. I understand that didn't satisfy him; he then called their bosses, Bob Schultz and Austin Taylor, only to be given the same message. A board meeting was called for Thursday in Montreal. I suggested another director chair the meeting because of the controversial subject of the meeting conflicting me. Byrn was still in the Caribbean and Simon now in California. The meeting was inconclusive, but I received a fax from Byrn conceding that he had been wrong regarding the meeting at his house. His handwritten fax dated January 7, 1992 (it was now 1993), was headed," My Previous Memo" and said: "Tony, your comment is correct. Paul Vien and the other outside directors refreshed my memory vis-à-vis the chairmanship discussions. It was a discussion of the board members not a board meeting nor a vote and any previous fax to you was in error." The meeting reconvened the next morning by telephone. I got up early and made a list of 13 points following the question, "How we got to where we are?", recounting events back to the December 9 meeting when Byrn wanted to replace me as chair. I concluded by saying, "We can continue arguing or we can rise above all this and raise the financing." Byrn immediately started spoiling for a fight, but Simon interrupted and said, "Let's get on with raising the money." The meeting ended by my agreeing to remain as chair until the annual meeting in July, at which time I said I would not stand for election to the board. On March 16, 1993, I went to the Midland Walwyn office to pick up a cheque for $51 million on completion of the share issue. Suddenly Mitel was cash rich again and the stock price firmed up.

In January, in accordance with the business plan for the financial year 1993, the new president approved reducing R&D by 200 people. In the two years since I had become CEO again in January 1991, we had restructured and reduced staff by nearly 1,200 people, nearly 30 percent, and the company worked better.

* * *

After nearly nine years, my time with the company ended at the annual meeting in July. Following the meeting the new president, John Millard, and chair, Gordon Byrn, were happily greeting the press as they remained at the podium with Henry Simon. As I was leaving, Alistair Sinclair, the Ernst & Young partner in charge of the Mitel audit for the past nine years, came over to say goodbye. Looking over at the podium he said, "You know, none of those people would be there if it wasn't for you." I replied, "Thanks. I know. Maybe they'll call me back in three years."

Having hit a low of 70 cents in December 1991, in late summer of 1993 the stock moved to $6 to $7. At the annual meeting on July 20, a shareholder asked SV when and how they would sell shares, to which the reply was, "We're in for five to seven years." Not long after the annual meeting SV sold 10 million of its 50 million shares at $6.20, effectively recouping its total investment after only one year. Not bad. In the report for the first quarter ending June 1993, the company's public relations announcement talked about the turnaround orchestrated by SV. As Winston Churchill said about history: "When you're dead, the little people will pee on your grave."

About six months after the 1993 annual meeting, one of the senior managers of Mitel came to see me. Commenting on SV, which had now sold 22 million of its shares, he said, "You know, these guys are carpetbaggers; that's really what they are." They certainly were opportunists.

Predictably, when the Mitel stock was trading at about $8 per share, the British press carried an article that was highly critical of BT when the publication of its financial reports showed a loss of $300 million on their Mitel investment. BT should have listened to David Dey and groomed the company for sale. BT had invested $367 million six years earlier. (This included the special funding for the SX-2000.)

On June 10, 1994, *The Globe and Mail* carried a story by Lawrence Surtees entitled "Mitel reaps rewards from revamp" saying: "Mitel's turnaround, orchestrated by chairman Anthony Griffiths, has resulted in the company posting six consecutive profitable quarters, a string of gains that has yet to ignite its share price."

* * *

Later I discovered my problems with Schroder Ventures were not over. After I left Mitel in 1993, I was approached by OMERS (Ontario Municipal Employees Retirement System) to be nominated as a director and chair of Canadian Marconi, controlled by The General Electric Company (GEC) in London. Lord Weinstock chaired GEC for many years, during which time Canadian Marconi was viewed as a cash-rich, underperforming dinosaur, with no entrepreneurial thrust whatever. Apparently all actions were orchestrated by GEC, giving the Canadian board the appearance of window dressing. As a result, 35 percent (or 69 percent of the minority shareholders including OMERS) formed a group called the Canadian Marconi Shareholders Association (CMSA), whose mission was to replace the Canadian directors.

I learned that my nomination was rejected by W.I.M. Turner, the chair of Canadian Marconi—the same Bill Turner who tried to recruit me from Consumers Glass.

Turner was at the same time a *director of Schroders in London and chairman of Schroder Canada*, where Gordon Byrn was CEO and a major shareholder and chair of Mitel. I obtained access to extensive correspondence surrounding the battle with the dissident shareholders, wherein I learned that Turner said to the CMSA, "I don't think it would be effective having Griffiths on the board. When *we* [Schroders; emphasis mine] got Mitel it was a mess. Mitel was much better after he [Griffiths] left. Griffiths is not the right kind of guy—he's a turnaround guy." The reader should note that the word "we," regarding Mitel, indicates that Turner identified himself with the management of Schroder Canada. By 1996, GEC had been taken over by a group led by Lord Simpson, the name GEC was changed to Marconi, and Lord Weinstock was replaced. Turner and the Canadian board were also replaced. Then, as the BBC News World Edition for

September 7, 2001, reported, "Lord Simpson's sacking from the post of chief executive of Marconi follows one of the most catastrophic declines in UK corporate history."

In November 1998, I sent Steve Jarislowsky the Mitel chapters and followed up with a personal visit. At the time, Steve was on the board of Canadian Marconi and its nominating committee. After this I received a rather empathetic letter from him saying (in part):

> Strikes me you must be a masochist to put up with all that 'c..p'. Your experience with the Brits is very familiar to me. There are the good guys, the bullies, the 'by the budget' boys, and a few other types. Many I have enjoyed a great deal. One always speaks of Britain as a cradle of democracy, but my experience is that they can be highly 'teutonic', except with more flair but less thoroughness or discipline.
>
> Why you would take such a job floors me. Hopefully, you now have more sense to stay in the green pastures of investment. Possibly you looked for a 'real' challenge.

When I reflect on all of the above, I am reminded of Kipling's lines, "If you can wait and not be tired by waiting, / Or being lied about, don't deal in lies."

* * *

To conclude the Schroders connection with Mitel: in 2001, Zarlink, the successor name of Mitel Semiconductor, was created with Henry Simon assuming the chairmanship until 2009, when he retired. Simon's only real criticism later of my tenure at Mitel Semiconductor was not moving faster on the semiconductor division. Let's see how the business unit performed under Simon's watch, which commenced in July 1992 when he became a director of Mitel and ended 17 years later in 2009. Simon became chair of the board of Mitel on July 21, 1994.

Zarlink became a public company in 2001. In the chairman's letter to shareholders for the fiscal year 2007, Simon brazenly stated, "Three years ago this was a *company in turmoil.* Today, Zarlink is a profitable company with positive cash flow." Whatever the turmoil in 2004, it clearly occurred on Simon's watch—no mention of *mea culpa.* One wonders what might have accounted for this glitch. The stock would be an embarrassment to anyone: at the sale of the switching business to Terry Matthews, Zarlink was trading at $14 per share; at the end of 2009, it had fallen to 25 cents. To correct the "turmoil," the board of Zarlink brought Kirk Mandy back as CEO in 2005; he had served as CEO of Mitel from 1998 to 2004. (This made me think that David Dey's comment about Henry Simon's lack of experience in the Schroders dining room was quite prescient (see page 243).

As further indignity, in July 2008, a dissident shareholder group launched a proxy action for *positive change* against the board of directors and management. The campaign targeted the replacement of the CEO, Mandy, and the chair, Simon, as well as three other board members. Apparently, the outcome of this proposal resulted in a very close vote in favour of the existing management. Nevertheless, I understand it was a humiliating experience for Simon and Mandy.

Finally, in September 2011, Zarlink succumbed to an unsolicited bid from California-based Microsemi Corporation at $3.98 for 100 percent of the company. Mandy stepped down as CEO of Zarlink in February 2011.[2]

16

A New-World Colonial: The Ondaatje Corporation, 1992–1995

"There is nothing either good or bad but thinking makes it so."

Shakespeare, Hamlet

My friends and the business community thought I had lost my mind and, within months, events proved them right. On February 18, 1995, the *Financial Post* ran the following article:

Griffiths takes over Ondaatje

Ubiquitous corporate fixer Anthony Griffiths has been appointed president and chief executive officer of merchant banker Ondaatje Corp.

Griffiths, who has been on the firm's board for two years, picks up the CEO title from company founder Christopher Ondaatje, who will stay on as chairman. The previous president, Patrick Moriarty, resigned mysteriously last November after only three months on the job.

In a terse press release, the company said Friday that Griffiths "understands and is committed to the business plan approved by the board."

Griffiths could not be reached for comment Friday.

What happened? Well, that's a long story . . .

* * *

I first met Christopher Ondaatje in the 1950s in Montreal, where I was working at Canadian Resins & Chemicals (see chapter 2) and he was selling advertising space. We were both displaced British colonials, he by family circumstance from Ceylon and I as a Second World War refugee from Burma. He played tennis and learned to ski, as did I. While we didn't see a great deal of one another, by background and circumstance we were kindred spirits.

I moved to Toronto with Consumers Glass in 1960, and Ondaatje moved there later working with Maclean Hunter in publishing. We played tennis and saw each other since our families were growing up in the same general community. In 1968, Chris and Chuck Loewen jointly bought a property near mine at Mansfield on the Boyne River north of Toronto. (I sold my property in 1970 and bought another 20 miles farther north at Creemore.) In 1970, Chris and Chuck, together with Fred McCutcheon, founded Loewen Ondaatje McCutcheon (LOM), the investment brokerage house.

When I joined Jonlab Investments as CEO in 1971 and later (in 1973) became CEO of Canadian Cablesystems, I would occasionally see Chris and Chuck socially and over business opportunities, but nothing of substance came of these

discussions. LOM became a very successful institutional boutique. In 1967, Chris started a publishing company, Pagurian
Corporation, and his first major success was a brief biographi-
cal history entitled *Prime Ministers of Canada*. I thought this a
unique idea and bought 100 copies to give to my customers
at Consumers Glass and, at the same time, to support Chris.

* * *

Sometime in 1988, the guard changed at LOM and the partners recruited Bob Atkinson as president. Apparently there
had been a dispute as to who would be responsible for the
firm's capital, a role Ondaatje had traditionally assumed.
Eventually this issue bitterly divided the shop, with Ondaatje
demanding that either he manage the firm's money or someone buy him out. Atkinson and associates did so at $12 per
share and Ondaatje left, with somewhat bruised feelings all
around. Ondaatje had already moved to the UK (in 1984)
and now went off to write books, go on safaris, spend time
at his homes in Bermuda, Chester, Nova Scotia, and Devon,
England, and, in 1990, visited Ceylon (now Sri Lanka), the
country of his birth.

The early 1990s heralded a euphoric investment climate
in the emerging markets throughout southeast Asia: China,
Malaysia, Indonesia, India, and Sri Lanka. At the same time,
LOM was falling apart. A number of bad deals had been made;
a merger with Vancouver's Canarim was a cultural misfit;
and with the world economy and stock markets in recession,
LOM's capital was becoming seriously impaired.

Finally in 1992, Chris Ondaatje returned to LOM, purchasing treasury shares at approximately $1.75. He closed

down the expensive offices, extricating LOM from a horrendous lease at the downtown Toronto Scotia Tower, left Garrett Herman in charge of day-to-day operations (but not the capital!), and then methodically sold the operating entities of LOM to its employees. The name of the top LOM public company was changed to "The Ondaatje Corporation" (TOC). Subsequently, Ondaatje raised $38 million to take TOC into emerging markets, first targeting Sri Lanka and then India. That's where I came in.

In the summer of 1992, I was sitting at my desk at Mitel when Ondaatje telephoned to ask me to join The Ondaatje Corp. board. I knew he was raising money to expand TOC, but knew little else about the company's operations. I was preparing to go back to Toronto because my contract as CEO of Mitel would expire in January, but I was hesitant about agreeing to join Ondaatje's board. While he was known as a mercurial, charismatic investor, he also had the reputation of being a one-man show, and had a legacy of broken business partnerships and discarded employees. As I played for time on the telephone, he cut me off saying he had to have my answer because the prospectus was being mailed on Monday. Bearing in mind our long history, it was still with some trepidation that I agreed to join the board. Hendrik (Henk) Hooft, a mutual acquaintance, joined at the same time; Hooft and I were the only independent, non-management, and non-family directors of TOC.

The first year was somewhat uneventful; money was raised, opportunities were reviewed, and emerging markets took off. In October 1993, TOC purchased Forbes & Walker (F&W), paying approximately $8.4 million for 100 percent of the Sri Lankan company, a 113-year-old profitable trading company based in Colombo. F&W fit Ondaatje's business and romantic fantasies to a tee—it was a classic southeast Asian trading house with great colonial roots and a wonderful name, all reminiscent of his icon, The East India Company, but on a smaller scale. F&W operated like a partnership—the European partners had long gone and now the Sinhalese partners were split into factions and in need of capital.

Shortly after closing this transaction, the company raised $48 million through a private placement of special warrants that ultimately resulted in the issue of 15 million common shares at the price of $3.20 per common share.

An intense reorganization and re-focusing of Forbes & Walker Limited resulted in the establishment of a new company in Sri Lanka, Forbes Ceylon Limited (Forbes Ceylon). That company was capitalized with approximately $66 million, $33 million of which was invested by the consolidated group of The Ondaatje Corporation. The balance was invested by international institutional investors and the investing public in Sri Lanka. At the time of this financing, Forbes Ceylon Limited was the single largest primary financing ever accomplished through the facilities of the Colombo Stock Exchange.

* * *

In mid-November 1994, Chris asked Henk and me to join him for lunch at TOC headquarters. The purpose of the lunch was to share with us, as the independent directors of TOC, his concerns about management (or lack thereof) in TOC. Ondaatje had been busy: TOC had purchased a building in London on St. James Street; hired an expert on India, Ravi Singh, to prospect for opportunities and raise financing for expansion in India; and opened a New York office. The overhead was soaring.

There were two key people in management at Toronto headquarters: Jim McGlone, a 40-ish burly, jovial, competent financial man who, when he thought necessary, would work all night. McGlone had come from Vancouver and was at LOM when Ondaatje came back to rescue the firm. McGlone was also intertwined with Ondaatje and his family holding company, South East Asia Plantation Corporation Limited (SEAP). McGlone had hired Paul Davis, at 32 a partner at a prominent Toronto law firm. Davis had worked on a variety of TOC transactions and was invaluable in maintaining balance in events to come.

Two other people had been hired from the audit firm, KPMG, to be resident in Colombo, overseeing the capital and operations in Sri Lanka. Max Webb and Sheila Ferguson, a married couple, were in daily contact with TOC people in London and Toronto. Max worked on special projects, while Sheila vetted tea plantation loans and ensured that proper accounting and timely reporting were practised at Forbes & Walker and Forbes Ceylon.

At our November lunch at TOC, Ondaatje was visibly distressed and frustrated. He was worried about the untidy and confusing administration in Sri Lanka; the euphoria of the buyout had worn off, and what was left was a loose partnership with no leadership or clear direction. Systems were antiquated and quarterly reports to TOC were tardy and unreliable, no budgeting or plans existed, and public relations were negative. A couple of F&W partners who had left under bitter circumstances were stirring the rumour mill. Ondaatje pleaded, "I need your advice."

Hooft and I were clear that we had to hire a professional CEO and let him run the company, reporting to the board. There was no argument, but Ondaatje said he didn't know how to go about it and was cautious because of two earlier bad experiences. We agreed to hire a search firm and at Hooft's suggestion, settled on Egon Zehnder Associates,[1] a leading international organization based in Europe. I said we should draw up an organization chart and define responsibilities for the CEO position, as both of these would undoubtedly be the first requirements of the search firm. We involved McGlone and Davis and soon had these matters agreed upon. To give Ondaatje comfort about "control of capital," I suggested creating an investment committee of the board, which he would chair, with Hooft, myself, and the CEO as members. I then agreed to contact Zehnder to get the recruiting process underway.

Since the future operations would be primarily in southeast Asia, the Zehnder people in Toronto recommended that Ondaatje meet their managing partner in London, who was responsible for Asian recruiting assignments. Since there was no leadership in F&W and no one calling the shots in Toronto, the bees were starting to whirl around in increasingly dysfunctional circles. Morale was dropping, suggestions were not dealt with, and frustration was settling in. Again, now in the presence of McGlone and Davis, Ondaatje asked for "advice" from Hooft and me, and suggested one of us should become CEO. We both realized that neither of us could work for Ondaatje because he was too unstructured and unpredictable, and insisted that we hire a professional CEO or return the money to the shareholders. This was an honest, at times blunt, discussion, and Ondaatje offered no argument. However, we were at a stalemate, and Hooft and I were becoming concerned about our situation as directors. We could not persuade Chris to meet with Zehnder. Hooft would say, "How do we get him to visit the dentist?"

By now TOC and its management vacuum intrigued me. With a pool of liquid capital of $90 million and opportunities abounding, it was a situation where my operating experience could add value. Also, the prospect of working in London and southeast Asia was very appealing to me. I finally told Ondaatje that I was willing to help, but only on a consulting basis. We entered into a three-month consulting contract until the end of March 1995. As acting president of TOC, I would determine the organizational structure and management requirements of the company, travel to Sri Lanka, where I would choose a leader at F&W, institute formal budgeting and planning, and evaluate various pending investment proposals. In addition, I would visit India where a major investment opportunity, identified by KPMG with Ravi Singh and evaluated by TOC management, had been awaiting Ondaatje's attention for many months. Ondaatje would meet me in Colombo after I had had a chance to do my review for a week or ten days. TOC signed the consulting agreement with me on December 13, 1994.

On January 19, 1995, I left for the UK on my way to Sri Lanka where I met a wonderful group of people at F&W.[2] They were crying out for direction from TOC. With the help of the senior directors and Sheila Ferguson and Max Webb, we commenced a budgeting and management reorganization process. I toured tea plantations with Chrisantha Perera, one of Forbes's senior partners. The tea country was exquisitely beautiful and my hosts most hospitable. I quickly felt a rapport building with the organization.

Before I left Toronto for Sri Lanka, I had asked that Sheila visit Bangalore to meet with V. G. Siddhartha, the 34-year-old proprietor of the ABC Company (Amalgamated Bean Coffee), a coffee grower, processor, and broker, the enterprise in which TOC was contemplating investing. While TOC management and the local (Bangalore) mergers and acquisitions specialist for KPMG had been conducting preliminary due diligence on ABC, we had not yet received a complete financial analysis. When I arrived in Colombo on Sunday, January 22, waiting for me at the Galle Face Hotel was an excellent management and financial report from Sheila, with a strong recommendation that I go to India immediately to see the operations for myself.

Because I hadn't obtained a visa for India in advance, we spent most of Monday pulling strings at the Indian Embassy in Colombo, finally getting the visa about 4:00 p.m. If I hadn't already had an expired Indian visa in my Canadian passport dated 1992, that process could have taken three weeks. I left on the evening flight to Madras (Chennai) and on to Bangalore the following day.

I met extensively with Siddhartha and his senior management team. In addition to ABC, Siddhartha owned Sivan Securities (later renamed Way2Wealth), a stockbroker and investment dealer, significant real estate, and a considerable portfolio of Indian "small cap" securities, on which there was substantial appreciation. I was immediately impressed with Siddhartha: he was bright, aggressive, energetic, successful, and wise beyond his 34 years. For generations his family had been coffee growers, and approximately 15 percent of the coffee beans ABC processed came from his family estates. During the socialist regimes of Nehru and the Gandhis, India had set up a monopolistic coffee marketing board, through which all brokers had to sell their crops. Since India was allied with the Eastern Bloc, the Soviet Union was the main consumer of coffee from India and, consequently Indian coffee was not known in the West. When the new regime under Narasimha Rao privatized coffee marketing, Siddhartha formed ABC. In the 1994 season, the company had processed beans worth $15 million and was planning to increase that to $30 to 35 million in 1995.

The transaction proposed by KPMG in India was for TOC (through Forbes Ceylon, a 50-percent-owned public company) to inject $15 million into ABC for a 50-percent share of the company, and Siddhartha to top up the $9 million of book value in ABC to an equal amount of $15 million. Free cash (over and above working capital requirements) would be maintained in a separate subsidiary, to be released only with *joint authorization* from TOC and Siddhartha. In order to secure the transaction, a $5-million loan would be provided by Forbes Ceylon, which, on closing, would be converted into a portion of the investment. In two years' time, Siddhartha was confident that 25 per cent of ABC could be taken public in India at a value of between $70 and $90 million, resulting in TOC and Siddhartha each retaining 37.5 per cent of a publicly traded stock. Siddhartha, with ABC, was to become both the nucleus and launching pad for TOC's future investments in India.

Given the events that ensued, it is important to note that Siddhartha did not seek out TOC as an investor; he was satisfactorily financed by banks for his seasonal requirements, albeit at high interest rates. It was KPMG who developed the acquisition idea in response to their Canadian partners' advice that TOC was interested in finding an investment vehicle in India.

* * *

When I met Ondaatje, who had arrived early Friday, January 27, in Colombo, one of the first things he said to me was, "I've only been here two hours and I've received two death threats. What do you think I should do?" I instinctively responded, "This is your country, not mine. It depends on how serious you think these threats are. If they're real, I'd get the hell out—who needs it." While he assured me the calls were real and that one of his local family members had verified the seriousness of them, he chose not to leave. I had found that his confabulations sometimes did not jibe with reality, so was not overly concerned. I spent the rest of the week immersed in meetings (some of which Ondaatje attended), touring the various businesses, and trying to put things in place to get the companies operating properly, so that Sheila Ferguson, Jim McGlone, and Paul Davis could follow up. In my mind, I wasn't returning to Sri Lanka. But by mid-week, when Ajit Jayaratne (the chair of F&W) and Chrisantha Perera asked at the end of management meetings who would be in charge when I left, Ondaatje would respond, "Don't worry, he's going to be here, and he's going to be involved." I told Chris he was putting us both in a very awkward situation.

   At the end of the week, before I left for the airport to fly home, I had dinner with Chris. It was a very pleasant, sometimes amusing evening as we recounted the events of the week. Ondaatje reiterated that both he and his wife Valda wanted him out of managing TOC and that I was the right person to take over.

At the end of the dinner, Ondaatje said, "Don't try to decide now. When you're back in Canada at home, everything will be clear. You will want to do this [meaning take on the role of full-time CEO]." He was staying in Sri Lanka a couple of weeks, touring a game preserve, and planning a three-week trip to India to meet Siddhartha, see ABC, and tour coffee and tea estates and a game park.

* * *

On Sunday night, February 5, I called Ondaatje in Colombo from Toronto, and told him I did not want to be CEO. He was clearly disappointed. However, I offered to continue as a consultant and, as a director, would assist in any way possible, including directly monitoring Sri Lanka and India.

Monday morning I felt badly about the call to Ondaatje. It had been disjointed because the lines were full of static and we'd been cut off two or three times, and Ondaatje seemed depressed. I decided to fax him a letter, which read (in part):

> Dear Chris,
>
>   It's twenty-four hours since I telephoned you at the Galle Face. I think it is important for me to express my views for clarity and give you my thinking about TOC. My only reason for declining your offer to be CEO is one of strong intuition. I see you presently in the classic dilemma expressed in Jefferson's essay on "head and heart." Logically you want to divest yourself

of all executive responsibilities, but emotionally you are not ready to do so yet. I understand this and have great empathy knowing of your feelings of obligation to your shareholders, your personal aspirations, and enormous energy.

The opportunity you put to me was exciting in every way, but the critical element for any CEO would be the relationship with you, the founder and major shareholder. Consequently, it is a most difficult situation and decision for me. I think it is important to clarify your mind going forward and, to help you, both Henk and I have suggested consulting with Egon Zehnder. Even if you do not retain Zehnder, I think you would find it helpful regarding roles and structure.

Fundamentally, in corporate governance jargon, you must be ready to effectively become "non-executive" Chairman and Chairman of an Investment Committee of the Board. Otherwise the roles and responsibilities of a CEO and Chairman will not be clear. Take your time in deciding about the CEO. You have all the support from me and others.

I then made some specific observations about the Sri Lankan business, suggesting that by either disposing of or joint venturing the food businesses, Forbes & Walker could focus on the tea brokerage. I felt I had developed a solid rapport with the team there, and would be happy to hold their hands through this, as well as pursue Chris's hope to obtain a banking licence. I also strongly recommended that Chris pursue the opportunity with Siddhartha and ABC in India, and that he should meet Siddhartha to make up his mind. I offered to assume responsibility for India—I thought the venture could absorb a lot of TOC time, with which I could help.

On receiving my missive, Ondaatje immediately faxed a copy to Paul Davis, general counsel of TOC, and asked him to draft a contract that I would sign. Davis and McGlone (and the Sri Lankans) were all hoping I would become CEO and get the company moving—and, after much angst, I finally agreed to take it on. On February 18, my appointment as president and CEO of TOC was announced.

My first request to the CFO Jim McGlone was to give me an estimate of one year's income from all sources in TOC (mainly Forbes and T-Bills) and expenses. This was a shock: expenses were soaring and income was stagnant—we were on the road to major losses.

During the week of February 13, I had several conversations with Chris. On each occasion he reiterated his pleasure at my taking on the role of CEO and that he was content to be non-executive chair and director, saying, "I've crossed that bridge, it's your company." There was discussion about my giving up some of my existing directorships, and I soon resigned from a couple and advised others that I intended to do so or reduce the number of committees on which I served. I warned Chris that my management style was to be a delegator, quite different from his, which meant that he, like many entrepreneurs, couldn't let go.

In Toronto, Davis was finalizing the terms of reference for the investment committee that Ondaatje and the board had agreed would take responsibility for overseeing capital allocation. More on this later.

* * *

Now that I'd signed on as CEO, we agreed I should go back to Colombo and pull together the budget, appoint Chrisantha managing director, and review a variety of opportunities. Then I planned to visit Siddhartha to review his business plan, including allocating the proposed joint venture's capital. Davis and McGlone had been to India and, with the assistance of lawyers and accountants in India and Canada, virtually completed the due diligence on ABC. Everything looked positive.

Then on February 28, ten days into my tenure as CEO, I received a memo from Ondaatje:

> You are the right person at the right time, and I am really glad that you have accepted the responsibilities of the CEO.
>
> However, I am very uncomfortable about the far-reaching consequences of my agreement to have an investment committee. I thought it was a simple agreement and had no idea that I was abdicating my commitment to shareholders to be responsible for the capital of the company . . . I disagree with Paul's interpretation of the "Quorum" of the investment committee, and am literally terrified of any delegation of the responsibility of the capital to anyone by the committee or anyone else. These are dangerous times and no one knows better than I about the ultimate responsibility to the shareholders for the preservation of capital. I've been there before with this very same company . . .
>
> I will support you totally as I have with India. I also agree with you that we should be extremely cautious about <u>any</u> investment in Sri Lanka. It may be an accident waiting to happen!

By now I was intuitively uncomfortable, but hoping for the best.

On March 3, 1995, we announced our agreement with Siddhartha to invest in ABC and expected that the transaction would close shortly. (Unfortunately for TOC this was not to be.) I asked my wife, Penny, to join me on my trip back to Sri Lanka and India. As I was readying to leave on March 23, the entire investment world was buzzing about TOC: rumour was that the company was available for sale. This was the end of my first full month as CEO.

In Sri Lanka, I finished up what I had started in early February: finalized the budget, appointed Chrisantha managing director, and set down criteria for new investments. As I contemplated my trip to Bangalore in early April, I was troubled about TOC's relations with Siddhartha. He had agreed to joint venture ABC, presuming Ondaatje and the existing management would continue in place. He liked and trusted those he had met. Now, if TOC was up for sale, and the company was merged or taken over and control changed, Siddhartha could find himself joint ventured with potentially incompatible partners.

Ondaatje had made it known to me and others that he was prepared to sell his 37-percent position in TOC down to 20 percent. I developed a plan by which Siddhartha would gain control of TOC by rolling his 50 percent of ABC plus other assets into TOC and, alone or with partners, buy half or all of Ondaatje's stock, depending on Ondaatje's wishes. TOC would effectively become an Indian-sponsored fund with extensive overseas investors. The more I thought about this, the more enthusiastic I became about the idea—but how to enlist Ondaatje's support?

When we arrived in Bangalore, I went to Siddhartha's office where he was finishing up a management committee meeting with his six or seven key managers. He introduced me to the gathering and I decided to put my proposition to the group. Siddhartha chuckled, and thought I wasn't totally serious, but the research manager of Sivan Securities quickly picked up on the concept and liked it. Over the next week, as Penny and I travelled with Siddhartha through the coffee estates in Chikmagalur, Hassan, and elsewhere, Siddhartha would revisit my proposal. By the time we got back to Bangalore, his enthusiasm for the proposal was apparent, and he even confessed that he'd called some investors (friends in Bombay), who were prepared to put up $20 million to buy some of Ondaatje's stock in TOC.

From Bangalore I called Ondaatje, who thought this a great idea, but cautioned, "Hurry up, because I've had two bids for my stock over market." This sent a chill up my spine: I had suspected this might happen. But I was also excited as I felt I'd solved several issues at once: Siddhartha would be happy and control of TOC would be assured in good hands; TOC would be an exciting investment vehicle in India; and Ondaatje would have achieved his stated objective of selling half his shareholding.

On April 11, I sent Chris a long fax from Bangalore, outlining the transaction, how it would be accomplished, why it made sense for TOC shareholders, and explaining it would provide a springboard for expansion in India, something Chris and Ravi Singh had promised shareholders. Up to this point, I had not told Siddhartha of my communications with Ondaatje because I did not want to disappoint Siddhartha if Ondaatje were to pour cold water over the proposal. Later that evening, I heard from Ondaatje by fax:

> Dear Tony,
>
> Thanks for your fax. Good advice. I'll go along with your recommendation and make 20% available <u>for cash</u> at a fair price if it is good for shareholders. I think you are right. However, you must act quickly as I have a bid for <u>all</u> today a little above market.

When Siddhartha picked Penny and me up that morning to take us to the airport to fly to Madras, en route to London, I told him, I had a surprise for him—and then told him of Ondaatje's fax. Siddhartha pulled the car over to the side of the road as we neared the airport. We talked for half an hour about what each side had to do to accomplish the transaction. Both of us were excited.

Penny and I flew to Madras (Chennai), where we had an eight-hour wait for our flight to London. We went to the Trident Hotel near the airport, from where I sent a fax to Ondaatje in Toronto, outlining the proposed transaction in greater detail, and attaching a term sheet. Among the terms was a 60-day "standstill" agreement that would allow each party to do their due diligence, clear regulatory hurdles, etc. I told Ondaatje I was glad he liked the plan and that I would proceed only if he was happy. I ended the fax telling Chris I would call him from London on our arrival, on Thursday, April 13, 1995.

The British Airways flight from Madras arrived at Heathrow at 5:00 a.m. We checked into the hotel, freshened up, and then Penny and I walked, in the cool clear sunshine, across Green

Park to 62 St. James Street. I called Ondaatje in Toronto and the gist of the conversation was that he had decided that the "standstill agreement would have to be announced." I disagreed based on legal opinions in similar transactions. Ondaatje also insisted that the transaction be undertaken in two separate steps: first, he would sell roughly half of his 37-percent block of shares to Siddhartha, and then the board would meet to consider the VGS plan, as it was now called. I pointed out that Siddhartha would not proceed unless Ondaatje's block was part of the whole transaction—why would Siddhartha want to buy 20 percent of TOC and risk being locked up as a minority shareholder?

After the lengthy and at times exasperating conversation, Penny and I strolled back across Green Park to the hotel. I made up my mind to take the ABC transaction off the table; I wasn't going to upset Siddhartha. I telephoned Siddhartha and told him it was over. This was the end of my second month on the job.

On Good Friday, April 14, in a long phone call with McGlone, he reported that the previous day, Ondaatje had been discussing selling his shares to a group in Toronto. He also said that Garrett Herman (CEO of Loewen Ondaatje McCutcheon) had reported that key TOC shareholders believed the company was in trouble and did not know what to do.

On April 17 and 18, McGlone and Davis called me in London several times, telling me that Ondaatje had settled down, or had not; that he was expecting a confrontation with me, or was satisfied that I was agreeable to his sale of his shares; that I was trying to take over the company, or he was happy with me in my position. His volatility made it impossible to please him on any front.

I flew back to Toronto on Wednesday, April 19, and when I walked into my home about 6:00 p.m., there was a message waiting from Davis asking me to attend a dinner at 7:00 p.m. with representatives of the Guinness Peat Group (GPG), who wanted to buy Chris's block at 15 percent over market price, through a company called PICO. During all his discussions about selling his block, Ondaatje kept saying to shareholders he would only sell "if management [Tony Griffiths] would endorse the deal." This created paralysis: there was no deal possible until Ondaatje agreed to sell his 35-percent block, and the company could not divulge confidential information to a prospective buyer if it was not party to a transaction. Moreover, management could not "endorse" GPG or others who were buying Ondaatje out, as management had no knowledge of the acquirer's plans for the company.

When I walked into the office on Thursday morning, April 20, Ondaatje welcomed me with smiles and warm questions as to whether we had had a good trip. He then said he thought the deal with Siddhartha was best for TOC and the shareholders; we should move ahead on it. I responded, "It's off the table—it's dead." Ondaatje protested that we should proceed!

On Monday, April 24, Ondaatje walked into my office and handed me a handwritten memo:

Tony,

   Just to confirm what I just said to you:

   If you think the "Siddhartha" deal is a good deal for the company and the shareholders—I will do it. *Don't* be ashamed or emotional about what you have recommended.

If it is good for TOC shareholders (including me) and you are behind it—we should proceed, *quickly.*

Chris

I found him too unpredictable to have confidence in what he said. I suggested to Penny that we go to Bermuda for a week while Ondaatje evaluated the offers to buy him out. I had a phone and fax in my den if anyone wanted to communicate with me. TOC stock was now down to $1.80 to $1.85 per share, at a time when the cash in the company amounted to $1.85 per share and the estimated breakup value of the company was $2.20 to $2.25 per share. Shareholders were obviously upset and jumping ship.

Thinking things through in Bermuda, I decided that I had to resign. I made it known through John Stransman[3] and Henk Hooft (who always said we would leave TOC arm-in-arm) that I was prepared to leave TOC on three conditions, *in sequence*:

1. McGlone and Davis must be provided with "retention contracts."
2. My contract had to be paid out and I would return my stock options for cancellation.
3. The press release had to say explicitly that I chose or elected to leave TOC because of differences over strategy and management process. It could not say or imply that I had been let go or fired.

Early the following week (back in Toronto), Ondaatje agreed to review my conditions, which consumed some weeks. Finally, with conditions agreed, the press release went out on Wednesday, June 14. The next day, four months after I had become CEO, *The Globe and Mail* ran this:

Ondaatje chief quits

A terse company release said Mr. Griffiths resigned because of differences in opinion about the Toronto-based investment banking company's direction and management process.

* * *

When I took my leave of TOC, I maintained contact with Siddhartha, periodically sending him news clippings related to coffee and India in general.

As soon as we reconnected, Siddhartha told me what had happened to him when TOC walked away from the ABC transaction in 1995. Siddhartha received a request to go to Colombo to meet the new principals of TOC following Chris's sale of his shareholding to GPG. Apparently the meeting was short, and Siddhartha was asked to pay a $5-million loan or face a lawsuit. This amount had been advanced pending the closing of the equity deal. With that, Siddhartha got up and replied, "If you sue me, I'll sue you," refusing to deal with the TOC people, whom he thought rude. Some months later, when a Sri Lankan investment group bought F&W, Siddhartha immediately arranged to repay the loan.

In 2008, Siddhartha invited Penny and me to visit Bangalore. He and his wife Viky were most gracious hosts. We toured Kerala for three days, spent three nights at their home, and visited many of his facilities. Café Coffee Day was now a household name throughout India (akin to Starbucks in North America), and he had:

- 10,000 acres of coffee plantations

- 918 cafés in 139 cities across India, plus one in Vienna and two in Karachi
- 14,000 vending machines.

His progress had been astounding and I was disappointed not to have been involved in this exciting enterprise. Siddhartha was euphoric—telling everyone that the best luck he ever had was not selling 50 percent of his company to TOC in 1995 for a small fraction of its present value.

The May 16, 2010, issue of *Business Today* carried a cover story of Siddhartha entitled "Coffee billionaire" with the subheading, "A fast expanding coffee-to-infrastructure-to-financial services sprawl already ranks V.G. Siddhartha among India's 50 richest people. And, this is just the beginning."

Quite a story!

* * *

Having sold all of his holdings in the Ondaatje Corporation at a premium to market, Christopher went on to exalted heights, acquiring a knighthood on the way. He is a serial philanthropist, donating to museums and education. He is an accomplished writer and photographer, with many books as his legacy, and an occasional magazine commentator. It is with a sense of sadness that I feel that my brief episode as CEO caused him to end our long relationship.

17

Catalyst for Change: The Saga of Confederation Life, 1989–1994

"Every now and again, you watch a disaster unfold and seem powerless to stop it."
Joshua Steiner, chief of staff at the U.S. Department of the Treasury, about the Whitewater hearings

In 1975, I was invited by the then-chair, J.K. Macdonald, to become a director of Confederation Life Insurance Company (Lifeco), a great Canadian financial institution. Confederation Life was a mutual life insurance company that operated in Canada, the United States, and the UK. The company was over 100 years old, and that long history seemed to dictate an atmosphere of formality to board meetings that was completely unlike the boards of other industrial enterprises on which I had served. I looked forward to the privilege of being associated with such a well-managed, well-regarded company. Unfortunately, I was to be a member of the board that saw the company's demise.

I enjoyed board meetings because of the wide variety of interests represented by my peers, who, over the many years I served, included chairs of banks, industrial corporations, and other members of the financial community, many of whom are household names. I also came to know members of the management team, resulting in long-term friendships and business associations. Confed was a training ground for investment analysts, many of who became frustrated with the bureaucracy of a mutual life company and branched out on their own. One of these entrepreneurial groups formed a company that was led by Tony Hamblin, Prem Watsa, Roger Lace, Brian Bradstreet, and others, which evolved into Fairfax Financial Holdings Limited (see chapter 12).

Board meetings were orchestrated by the chair, president, and an inner group of executive committee members. In 1976, the board decided to recruit a president from outside the company, John (Jack) Rhind, who also happened to be my next-door neighbour. For many years, the life insurance business seemed to grow exponentially, year on year, and by 1993 Confed grew to $19.2 billion in assets and annual premiums totalled some $3.1 billion.

In 1982, Rhind recommended Pat Burns as his successor and growth continued into the late 1980s without interruption. At the time of Burns's appointment, the life insurance industry in North America was becoming increasingly competitive and pending deregulation in Canada was threatening even more competition from the powerful chartered banks. Burns decided to diversify the company into other financial services, including leasing, trust services, and eventually derivatives. In May 1990, Rhind also handed over the title of chair to Burns, while he moved to the position of chair of the executive committee.

However, as the corporation diversified, for me, the underlying question was how a mutual company could fund its expansion into these activities. By their nature, mutual companies are owned by policyholders, so sourcing capital externally is not an option. As a result of some work I had done with Fairfax in 1988, I had become aware of the mechanics of the demutualization of one or two U.S. mutual life companies, resulting in their having access to private capital markets. Thinking that this would be a course of action that Confed should seriously consider, I began canvassing some of the Confed management. I learned from Bill Douglas, senior vice-president and Burns's principal strategist, and others that Pat Burns "would never agree" to the demutualization of Confed and, if necessary, capital could be raised through subsidiaries Leaseco and Trustco.

I then decided to canvass the board and found a few colleagues on my side, including the elder statesman George Mara, Sir Anthony Jolliffe, Conrad Black, David McCamus, and one or two others. Knowing of Burns's resistance on the issue, Mara decided to try to interest Jack Rhind, as chair of the executive committee. However, Burns remained adamantly opposed, and the company's relentless growth continued, amid many, mostly superficial, discussions about raising capital. At the time, there appeared to be no urgency: with the numbers continually positive, the board acquiesced to Burns's course of action.[1]

On September 20, 1989, senior officials from the Office of the Superintendent of Financial Institutions (OSFI) attended a Confed board meeting, an unusual request from a regulator. The spokesman for OSFI was Michael Mackenzie, superintendent of financial institutions, who expressed serious concerns about the extent of reserves supporting the company's activities, particularly those outside the core life insurance business. Mackenzie referred to the continual decline in the capital of life insurers as a result of the decline in profit margins, saying the business was not self-financing. Double counting of subsidiaries' reserves, alone and together with the parent company's figures, meant that reserve figures were overstated. While OSFI was generally satisfied with management, who were exploring means of addressing these capital requirements, they noted that these anomalies in reporting were not in line with industry standards among Confed's competitors.

Then Donald Macpherson, the deputy superintendent of deposit-taking institutions, reported on OSFI's views of Confederation Trust Company (Trustco). This report was more ominous, highlighting the fact that the company was overexposed in two markets, Toronto and Vancouver, and any severe downturn in the real estate market would spark problems. He also cautioned that the company had to introduce controls respecting the quality of their new loans, their loan documentation and underwriting, as well as officers' authorized limits, which were higher than those for other companies of a similar size. He said that if the pace of growth of the company continued, more capital would be needed in the short term and commented that plans for a branch operation would be costly.

Mackenzie then said that Confederation Trust was the most rapidly growing trust company in Canada and the company could expect to see a fair amount of attention from the Canada Deposit Insurance Corporation (CDIC), especially because the company was so heavily reliant on brokers and agents, with the concern that Trustco was delegating control of profit to people who were compensated by volume.

Management was excused from the meeting, leaving the non-executive directors to engage in a private discussion with the OSFI representatives. I again took the occasion to raise the possibility of demutualization, for which there was no interest.

After the OSFI representatives left, Burns rejoined the meeting and a discussion ensued in which Burns effectively dismissed the OSFI concerns, saying that management was aware of most of the issues raised and was dealing with them. I remember thinking to myself, "We've been given a message and management is not hearing it." I decided to take notice.

This board meeting was notable for another reason— management informed the board of the decision to build a new Canadian head office in Toronto at Jarvis Street and Mount Pleasant Road. The extent of commitments taken on by the company took many board members, including myself, by surprise. The board seemed to acquiesce, however, and asked for a formal report and a resolution authorizing the capital expenditure for consideration at the next meeting. When the building opened officially in 1990, the total cost to build was $90 million. As we took the inaugural tour, I remarked to Tony Jolliffe that this was "Burns's Drydock" as Canary Wharf was Reichmann's, a Taj Mahal to Burns's ego.

The September 1989 meeting was a pivotal one for me. Until then, I had assumed that the executive committee had been monitoring management. Instead, I concluded that this committee was *enabling* management to expand as it wished.

* * *

The company continued growing throughout 1990 and 1991. In late November 1990, I was in Vancouver and called George Mara, a call I had been deferring for some time. I told him I was increasingly concerned about the management of the company and asked what role the executive committee was taking. He allowed that he had concerns as well, and would speak with the chair, Jack Rhind.

At board meetings of Confed Life, suggestions had been made that there should be two or three non-management directors of the Lifeco attending Trustco board meetings and sometime in the spring of 1991, Pat Burns asked me if I would serve as a director of Confederation Trust. I told Burns I could do so, but would have to step down from the audit committee of Confed and would join only if the Trustco was functioning smoothly—being mired in Mitel at the time, I could not devote myself to a troubled situation. Burns agreed, and it took several months to qualify me for the Trustco board because of the voluminous paperwork required by various regulatory bodies.

I attended my first meeting of the Trustco on December 16, 1991, and was appalled to find that the main topic on the agenda was crafting a response to the Ontario regulator, who had served the company with a very critical report, citing its rapid, seemingly-chaotic growth without adequate controls. I found myself, joined by David McCamus, giving a lecture to the board about directors' and officers' responsibility. I appealed to the management to deal straight up with the regulator and put everything on the table, but management seemed only to defend actions already taken without addressing how to correct the situation.

As soon as I reached my office, I called Burns and told him I was upset. I asked if he remembered the two conditions under which I agreed to serve as a director of Trustco. He repeated the stipulations to me precisely and I replied that I was immediately faxing my resignation from the Trustco board. He said he understood my reasons and could not disagree.

* * *

Back at the October 16, 1991, Lifeco board meeting, two years after OSFI's initial visit, Burns reported on the latest OSFI report, which said that the capital adequacy position was not sufficiently robust to support sustained rapid growth in the range of the 20-percent annual rate that had been achieved over the previous four years. OSFI recommended that we strengthen controls over the investment function of the company and its subsidiaries; Burns had decentralized this function and it was difficult to assess the global investment picture. We later discovered, for example, that the mortgage portfolio had expanded from $1.2 billion in 1982 to $8.5 billion in 1993. The company had 71 percent of its assets, more than any other life company, invested in real estate—directly or through mortgages, both commercial and condominiums.

OSFI also identified serious concerns with Trustco regarding arrears in general, and a concentration of exposure to condominium promoters such as the Reemark Group, which, as a borrower, had a number of elements of unsound underwriting.

The general thrust of Burns's response was that there were a few problems but everything was under control. He agreed that there were significant exposures with certain major real estate projects, but that management had initiated action to respond to each of the OSFI recommendations, in particular suspending commercial lending within the Trustco group until all OSFI concerns were addressed in a satisfactory manner.

However, I was becoming very concerned that management had no idea how bad things were, concerns that were shared by David McCamus, chair of the audit committee and a member of the executive committee, and Sir Anthony Jolliffe. As a result of my probing, a joint meeting of the executive and audit committees was arranged, for December 9, 1991. I had suggested to McCamus that we establish a special independent committee of the board to look into the issues raised by OSFI. Having recently retired as CEO of Xerox, McCamus had the time to devote to the project and he agreed to my suggestion that he serve as chair on the proviso that he received the unanimous support of his peers. Privately, Mara agreed with my recommendations, but in meetings he was unwilling to draw a line in the sand.

Mara, on whom I relied for support, was not able to attend the December 9 meeting due to illness. When I expressed my concerns and recommended the establishment of a special committee, I was met with unanimous opposition from Jack Rhind, George Albino (ex-chair and CEO of Rio Algom), John Allen (retired chair and CEO of Stelco), and, of course, Pat Burns. They responded that McCamus and I were "over-reacting," and said, "We have good management and we have an executive committee." In great frustration, at the end of the meeting I turned to Burns and said to him directly, "Pat, you are chairman, president, and CEO. Do you think this company is in trouble?" He stumbled a bit, but effectively said there were problems that were manageable. I then said, "You're wrong. You wait and see." I left the meeting feeling as if I were a skunk at a garden party and flew back to Ottawa.

This joint meeting of the committees led to a full board meeting in mid-December, where I put forth the following memorandum:

> The situation in the Life and Trust operations is of utmost concern to the board. At this date, the scope and ramifications of the potential problems have not been quantified to the satisfaction of the board and this was reinforced at

a meeting on December 9 with the executive and audit committee members. It is critical that the board take action immediately to understand the situation and take corrective action.

Members of the board have a high level of discomfort in what management have reported. The regulators appear to believe that the problems are more severe and perhaps deeper than management have expressed. There is no evidence of precise management accountability: who is responsible, what corrective actions, what management changes.

The board must take immediate steps to satisfy itself, independently, as to the severity and depth of the problems. It is recommended that the board retain outside advice to make an assessment and audit the situation. A qualified individual has been identified and is available on reasonable notice. The scope of the assessment should include:

- Strategy of investments
- Assessment of present situation
- Situation analysis—present and future of Confed Trust
- Situation analysis—present and future of Confed Leasing
- Assessment of management and controls
- Future directions
- Action plan

Simultaneously with the above, the board must establish a new structure for corporate governance including the appointment of an outside chairman and an active executive committee, as well as reviewing the roles and

composition of all committees and reviewing management
controls and the succession plan. Time is of the essence.

The meeting turned into a shambles, with Albino saying
there was already an executive committee in place, and Mara
attempting to compromise by re-staffing the committee. At
one point, McCamus threw up his hands in frustration and left
the room and I had to coax him back. We failed to achieve a
resolution of the committee composition and Albino recommended we meet again as a board on January 16, 1992, to
determine the makeup of all board committees.

Then Jack Rhind presented the compensation report on
behalf of the executive committee, which set out recommendations for raises, including a large one for Bill Douglas,
the "strategist" on whom Burns had been relying. I quickly
calculated that some of the proposed raises were in the 8 to
11 percent range. I went on record as opposing the raises.
I pointed out that with North America well into a recession
and from my experience with other companies, the maximum
justifiable increase was 3 percent; at that point, Mitel had
already been on a one-year wage and salary freeze, which was
going to continue throughout 1992.

There was a growing sense of concern—and lack of
unity—amongst the directors. While I was proposing a new
committee headed by McCamus, word came back to me that
Tony Jolliffe and I were part of a "conspiracy" on the board.
In exasperation I called Jack Rhind in his capacity as chair of
the executive committee and said, "We've already had this
discussion on December 9 and I presented a plan. Since no
new plan has surfaced, let's get on with my recommendations." I assured Rhind that there was no plot, and that all my

recommendations had been made in public and were supported by McCamus and Mara. I also expressed my belief that Burns should stay in place until McCamus could complete his study.

That same morning I talked with McCamus, who warned me that the auditors had made "shocking findings" at Trustco. The next day I took my family, together with my brother and his family who were visiting from Australia, to my country home at Creemore for part of the Christmas holiday. When I unpacked my briefcase I found the Coopers & Lybrand report on Confederation Trust. I was soon horrified at what I was reading, and called Mark Edwards in his capacity as general counsel. I recommended we hire outside legal advice "to determine what actions should be taken, if any, with regard to the activities in the Trustco." We had apparently rewarded Trustco senior management on building assets, not profits. They had done their jobs well, but simultaneously had sacrificed loan quality, and when their poor management became evident, three people quietly departed the company, sharing $10 million in incentive payments.

In the meantime, I had also been studying the *1991 Management Report from OSFI* dated October 25, 1991. I wrote to Pat Burns on December 29, 1991, with three pages of detailed questions, concluding with:

The more correspondence I read, the more confused I become concerning:

- The financial impacts to the Lifeco—what is the ultimate exposure as we see it today? Reasonable case and worst case? Unfortunately, I cannot find a concise framework for this.

- The inter-relationships in management. Where was the accountability for the various investment actions and where is it now?

It is essential that we achieve an understanding of what has transpired—at this writing I don't have one. The questions I am raising are all related to OSFI observations and therefore your staff should have answers readily available. It seems to me this background is important as a framework from which to understand your action plan, when you table it.

I received my reply the next day by fax and was invited to lunch on December 31 with Burns, Edwards, and Mike Regester, then executive vice-president of Confederation Life. Over sandwiches we reviewed all the issues and again I suggested that McCamus form a team to help deal with the board's concerns. To my surprise, Burns seemed to welcome this, admitting that he (Burns) was "a good manager for growth but not a turnaround man." I told him I did not care about the past, but wanted to ensure we took steps to survive in the worst case, and that Burns should table a plan for early January that took into account the worst possible exposure for the company.

* * *

Prior to the January 16 board meeting, I had a call from Pat Burns asking if I would agree to serve as chair of the audit committee. I deliberated—my head said resign from the board, while my emotions said stay and fight. I finally decided that chairing the audit committee would give me the authority to do what had to be done. Meanwhile, I lost my strongest, ablest ally when McCamus announced he was resigning from Confed to join the board of Trilon (which included London Life, companies controlled by Edper).

At the organization meeting of the board following the annual general meeting on February 21, 1992, I was duly elected chair of the audit committee. Within a day or two, I received a telephone call from Michael Mackenzie of OSFI requesting a meeting on February 27. Mackenzie said he had serious concerns about both Trustco and Lifeco, and that Trustco was the worst-managed trust company in Ontario. He went on to say that Lifeco had serious problems as well, about which Mackenzie had tried to warn Burns in 1989, including a failure to understand new businesses and products. He concluded by recommending that I meet with his friend Adam Zimmerman who had recently joined the main board, to solicit his help.

I chased down Adam Zimmerman, and we met in Ottawa on March 17. I had prepared extensive notes on the history of events, and concluded by asking for Zimmerman's support, citing the recommendation of his friend Michael Mackenzie. Like Mackenzie, Zimmerman's early career was at Clarkson Gordon (E&Y's predecessor). While Zimmerman had already joined the board, it was clear he had little inkling of the events I described. He was also an old friend and neighbour of Jack Rhind. I told him my recommendation, shared by McCamus, Jolliffe, and Mara, was to recruit a new CEO as soon as possible. The question was how to get the board to act, because there was no sense of urgency.

Michael Mackenzie attended the April 22, 1992, board meeting and, in camera without management, stated that he believed the board had "been a bit sleepy" since the time he had sent his letter the previous fall. He advised that "directors must address the basic responsibility of management." Nan-b Beaubien, a recent addition to the board, who resigned soon after this meeting, asked Mackenzie, "Is this the right management to lead us out of this?" observing that "people who build empires can rarely change." The regulator replied that he was not optimistic, and suggested that the company needed new management.

The morning of April 24, I received a call from Rhind. He had come to the conclusion that we had to start the search for a CEO and was going to convene a meeting of the executive committee as soon as possible to strike a search committee comprising myself, Zimmerman as chair, Mara, and Allen, with Burns as an ex-officio member.

On May 14, I had another conversation with Mackenzie. He commented that the "problem was very serious and went much deeper than the CEO." By now it had surfaced that Bill Douglas had a special arrangement whereby he held shares in Leaseco. This arrangement had been approved by Burns but was not disclosed to the board or its committees. To rectify this, the company had arranged for Douglas to be bought out of the deal at a substantial profit. When Mackenzie told me of this, his only comment was, "TILT!" Mackenzie said he was concerned that the company's profit forecasts were unrealistic, which raised issues about the solvency of the company, and that we could be hit by a credit downgrading. Our conversation turned to merger, with Mackenzie suggesting Canada Life, Sun Life, and several others. When I reported this to Adam Zimmerman, he responded that he thought Mackenzie was overreacting and that our current focus should be on finding a CEO.

For some time I had been pressing to hire an external consulting group to assist us in developing an ongoing strategy for the company, but Burns and Rhind had resisted. At one meeting, Rhind said that he thought the situation was "too confidential" to involve an outside consultant. I pointed out that he was naive if he didn't think the problems of Confed were the talk of the town, particularly among the wide population of Confed alumni.

I ran into Michael Mackenzie at the Toronto Island Airport on May 28, 1992, and he advised that the regulator, out of its concern over the top management, was considering issuing a compliance order to change the CEO. I told him that we had started a search, but he said that whatever we were doing, it wasn't fast enough!

* * *

In mid-June, Zimmerman recommended that he, Rhind, Burns, and Regester meet with Mackenzie and tell him what they were planning to do. I found this troublesome, because it made me wonder whether they were questioning my reports of the regulator's concerns—but said nothing. Following their meeting, I received a call on June 15 from Mackenzie, who reported that he had told Rhind, "the sooner things get resolved the better," meaning that they had to get rid of Burns. Mackenzie said Rhind left unhappy, but commented that he didn't think he left any doubt in Jack's mind as to what was needed.

On June 23, I received a long rambling call from Jack Rhind. For the first time he indicated some appreciation for my role, commenting on my "strong and wise voice" and asked my views on Zimmerman becoming chair. Rhind had told Burns that he should step down as chair, and Burns was naturally concerned about his position when the new CEO was appointed. Rhind's suggestion was that Burns would be vice-chair, which I said I could not support.

At the June 23 audit committee meeting, the news was worse. The Trustco exposure to condominiums was larger than thought and OSFI was requesting an additional $25-million infusion of capital into Trustco. Bill Douglas said management planned to use $17 million of Lifeco funds to shore up the balance sheet of the Trustco, which would offset a possible "public panic." Burns was now worried that the rating agencies would downgrade Confed.

I pressed yet again for "survival alternatives"—to have in place *actionable* plans before we lost control of the process. Looming was a potential $1.2-billion liquidity problem, triggered by an adverse credit rating and/or serious further deterioration in real estate values. The company could face having $500 to $600 million of its credit cut off in the event of a downrating. Even the external auditors were saying, "options don't look as feasible as at first glance," indicating nervousness on their part.

Since there still seemed to be a wide disparity of views within the audit committee, I decided to canvass the committee and asked each member to tell me, on a scale of 0 to 10, with 10 being worst case, what level of concern each felt with respect to liquidity and capital adequacy. Rosenfelder, the corporate actuary, said 8 to 9; Regester, executive vice-president, 8 to 9; Douglas, 9 to 10; Burns, 8; and myself, 10. At least this finally put on the table the seriousness of the situation.

When management was excused so that non-executive members could meet privately, I recommended again that the company retain Ernst & Young's M&A group to assist in designing a survival plan. This proposal was finally accepted for recommendation to the board.

Over the summer, Ernst & Young's M&A group, under the direction of Fraser Mason, commenced its study. I was unhappy with the pace of the group's investigations and, even worse, its reporting relationship through management and the executive committee. Also, during this period, the search committee, of which I was a member, finally set about recruiting a new CEO. Overall, a genuine sense of urgency was still lacking, although board members and management were becoming increasingly nervous.

On September 17, 1992, I spoke again with Michael Mackenzie. I recorded the conversation carefully and sent it to the audit committee with copies to the board, the audit partner, and the head of Ernst & Young's M&A group. The memorandum read in part:

> Every day Burns is on the premises is bad and the company was getting very close to the capital level where the regulator would require that the company stop payment of dividends. He said a new team is needed quickly. And in the longer term, the company must merge. He suggested that we talk to other mutuals, as it's in their interest that Confed not go further down. I asked who we should talk to, and he said the MET, SUN, MANU, CANADA and N.AM. His final comments were that the company's analysis is good, but is short on solutions.

In response, I received an irate call from Jack Rhind on September 21, who had Pat Burns with him. He was incensed at the contents of the memo, especially Mackenzie's statement that, "Every day Pat Burns is on the premises is bad." I told him I wasn't editorializing, rather reporting factual statements made by the regulator that we should know about. Rhind said, "What would your reaction be if there was a headline in *The Globe and Mail* tomorrow saying that Pat Burns had resigned for health reasons!" I replied, "I don't know why Burns would do that." Jack went on in an aggressive manner but I stood my ground and remained calm. Earlier in the day I had sent a memo to Rhind, copied to Zimmerman and Fraser Mason of Ernst & Young, pleading that we should get on with finding a merger partner.

Time marched on and the recession was relentless. Real estate values deteriorated every day. Our search committee was closing in on hiring a new president and, finally, we were determined to have a non-executive chair: Burns was not to remain on the board. In October 1992, Confed hired Paul Cantor as president and CEO; Cantor had left the Canadian Imperial Bank of Commerce when his rival was tapped for the CEO position. A lawyer by training, Cantor had spent time in the federal Department of Finance before joining the bank.

During the interview process I gave Cantor the facts about the situation at Confed and cautioned him that, from my experience in troubled companies, the company was undoubtedly in much worse condition than anyone knew. I urged him, if he took the job, to immediately explore merger with another life company.

In mid-February, I made a point of meeting with him to discuss his initial impressions. He told me he was comfortable with the situation and was persuaded it could be turned around. I told him he was making a mistake and that, even as a precaution, he should identify one or two candidates for merger; I had already sent him copies of my extensive correspondence with the board and the regulator. I suggested, for a small additional fee, he get Ernst & Young to complete its study on strategic alternatives and identify prospects for merger. He insisted the company could survive on its own. I finally said that we could not take a risk with safeguarding the policyholders and, if we left it too late, the directors and he would not have done their duty. My final words were, "I hope you're right. You could be the best manager in the world, but it won't do the trick because you're sitting on a melting ice cube." Later it occurred to me that Paul came into a situation where his peers were comfortable that the company was not in danger, so why would he listen to my maverick views?

I went back to my office and wrote him a note, attaching an article by J.D. Davidson from the *Wall Street Journal*, dated February 11, 1993, headed, "The depression of the 1990s—it's already here." In part it read: "Too many people have become complacent about deflation. From Toledo to Tokyo, few believe that the inevitable consequences of deflation are inevitable. But watch out. Debt has grown too large to be sustained out of a cash flow. As soon as the balance sheet is depleted, a deeper crisis of asset liquidation will catch the world by surprise."

By May 1993, panic set in. The rating agencies decided to downgrade Confed and the internal financial picture deteriorated. The ice cube was indeed melting. Concern among the board and management transformed into fear, reflected by irritability at meetings. Merger was now the main topic on the agenda and, early on, Rhind suggested Great-West Life Assurance Corporation (GWL), one of the few remaining Canadian stockholder-owned life insurance companies, controlled by Power Corporation. Cantor wanted to hire financial advisers, but I pressed for more immediate action saying that financial advisers would take weeks to catch up and we knew the insurance business and what had to be done. By approaching the most likely merger prospects directly, we would maintain control of the process. I repeated that the ice cube was melting fast. Management saw it otherwise and J.P. Morgan and Wood Gundy were retained.

Our financial advisers combed the world for a merger prospect and toward the end of 1993, serious negotiations were commenced with the only real candidate: Great-West Life. Astutely, GWL would only negotiate on an exclusive "lock-up" basis with enormous penalties in the event Confed got a better offer elsewhere. GWL then commenced protracted discussions, which allowed them the luxury of doing the transaction on terms most favourable to themselves—a form of Chinese water torture for Confed.

In late August 1994, the world of Confed crumbled. On July 31, Confed had failed to meet the deadline for closing the "alliance" with GWL, and on August 4, had announced that it was seeking to raise $600 million from a syndicate of six Canadian life insurance companies. Lengthy all-day and all-night meetings ensued with other life companies such as Sun Life, Manulife, Mutual, Canada Life, and GWL, as well as the various regulators and the federal Department of Finance. By August 11, these attempts to construct an industry- and government-backed safety net failed and the board of directors signed a resolution turning Confederation Life and its subsidiaries over to the regulators and resigned.

On August 18, Peter Cook wrote an editorial in *The Globe and Mail* entitled, "Why can't we regulate better?" In the second paragraph he posed the following questions:

- Why wasn't management smarter?
- Why weren't regulators quicker to spot what was going on and insist investments be diversified?
- And why weren't whistles blown sooner?

I think my account of events answers these questions: the regulators *were* alert and doing their job; and I, together with David McCamus, Tony Jolliffe, and to some extent, George Mara, were blowing the whistle. It all reminds me of Barbara Tuchman's epilogue in *The March of Folly*:

> The refusal to draw inference from negative signs, which under the rubric 'wooden-headedness' has played so large a part in these pages, was recognized in the most pessimistic work of modern times, George Orwell's *1984*, as what the author called 'Crimestop'. 'Crimestop means the faculty of stopping short, at the threshold of any dangerous thought. It includes the power of not grasping analogies, of failing to perceive logical errors, of misunderstanding the simplest arguments . . . and of being bored and repelled by any train of thought which is capable of leading in a heretical direction. Crimestop, in short, means protective stupidity'.

As soon as the regulator moved to take over Confed and put it into insolvency in August 1994, I decided to hire a personal legal adviser and pay for this out of my own pocket. This was new territory for me and I wanted to make sure I had proper advice. I selected Don Plumley of Lang Michener and never regretted doing so nor begrudged the expense. When I met with Don, I delivered a cardboard carton of documents from my own papers, including a 35-page chronological summary of my actions in attempting to forestall the debacle.

As time passed, a variety of legal suits, including class actions, were launched against Confed's directors and officers. Perhaps the most significant of these was by the Michigan Insurance Commissioner, purporting to act on behalf of the U.S.

policyholders of Confed. As I remember, the separately incorporated treasury management arm of Confed (Confederation Treasury Services Ltd.—CTSL) had transferred assets generated from Confed's U.S. activities to Canada to enlarge the capital pool. To comply with the Michigan regulator's requirement that Confed maintain assets in a trust account physically located in the United States with a value sufficient to meet Confed's U.S. liabilities, Confed periodically substituted notes issued by CTSL for the U.S. mortgages, bonds, and similar assets acquired to match their U.S. insurance liabilities. Apparently the Michigan regulator was informed of this practice and did not object, never dreaming that the whole house of Confed might ever collapse. When the Canadian regulator took over the company, Michigan immediately moved to repatriate the U.S. policyholders' funds. The Canadian regulator blocked this, with the result that the Michigan regulator now had egg all over his face. The lawsuit from Michigan accused the management and board of fraud, looting, etc. No question: the Michigan regulator had a seriously embarrassing problem of his own.

When discoveries commenced around the summer of 1996, I suddenly twigged to the fact that Conrad Black was no longer listed as a defendant. At my first morning of deposition, I asked Jeff Bramlett, the lead defence lawyer for the officers and directors of Confed, why Black's name had been removed from the list. At a break in the proceedings, Bramlett asked the lawyers for the prosecution for an explanation. Bramlett quickly returned with their response: Black was let off the hook because he "didn't attend Confed board meetings." My recollection was that Black attended many more meetings than he missed! When the shit hit the fan, he did stop attending and the meetings became much more frequent, complicated, and time-consuming. As both ridiculous and amusing as this was, some of his fellow directors were miffed that he was able to pull off this Houdini act. I had been counting on him along with Jolliffe and a few others to bolster our defence.

Throughout the discovery process, when the prosecutors were feeding back to me my memos to the board, asking me to expand on my thoughts and actions, I had a growing irritation that this was unfair. I had been the catalyst at the board pressing for change to prevent an accident waiting to happen. Now I was captured in a wonderful legal principle called "joint and several." If I were to write a book on the Confed fiasco I would choose "Joint and Several" as the title. A real lesson learned. I continue to believe that directors who fight for constructive change in situations such as this should be considered for exoneration, something that is contemplated now in "whistleblower" policies.

Confed's directors and officers got lucky because real estate prices recovered. As the value of Confed's real estate assets rose over time, Confed's Canadian and U.S. regulators transferred blocs of policies (with assets of matching duration) to other insurers in an orderly liquidation. Policyholders received the coverage they paid for with minimal disruption. Secured debt holders were paid in full. Some unsecured debt holders took a modest haircut, but many vultures who bought up unsecured debt at pennies on the dollar fared very well indeed. The Michigan Insurance Commissioner paid The Palmieri Company, the outside turnaround firm who handled resolution of Confed's U.S. business and managed the U.S. litigation against directors and officers, a $15-million bonus for presiding over the inevitable. Confed's directors and officers liability insurers, who spent less than $15 million on the defence of

U.S. and Canadian litigation over an eight-year period, assumed for years that their $35-million policy limits would have to be paid out in full to the Michigan regulator to extract me, my board colleagues, and Confed officers from the perils of U.S. litigation. Ultimately, these insurers kept more than $20 million in their pockets because, with the exception of one New Jersey class action that eventually settled for a mid-six-figure payment, all U.S. litigation was resolved without payment of a dime to the various parties who sued the directors and officers.

Latterly, there were also some pleasant expressions of appreciation for my conduct, even though certain individuals did not endorse my actions at the time. In particular, soon after the deposition phase, Adam Zimmerman invited me to lunch and basically said he was now sorry he had not listened to me. I also had lunch with David McCamus, who had jumped to the Trilon board, leaving the Confed board in the middle of the fracas. David said that, in hindsight, he should have stayed at Confed and helped me fight. Even though David left well before the liquidator took over, he was enjoined in the lawsuits.

When all was over and we were cleared, I understood the meaning of the term "joint and several." Even though I led a small faction of the board clearly trying to prevent a fiasco, I was still jointly fully liable.

I also felt badly for Paul Cantor, who arrived at Confed at the peak of the financial tsunami that devastated the financial sector. While it was gutsy to take on the CEO job, it was probably already too late for anyone to save the sinking ship. Following the receivership, Paul showed great resilience and went on to have an illustrious career as managing partner of Russell Reynolds Canada, senior adviser at Bennett Jones LLP, and chair of the board of governors at York University.

In Closing: What To Do When Faced with a Company in Trouble

"It is essential to keep a sense of humour."
Tony Griffiths

I have *The Globe and Mail* to thank for a spate of speaking engagements that arose as a result of an article it published on July 10, 1997, which read in part:

> One of Canada's busiest salvage specialists is Anthony Griffiths, who made his mark during two separate stints at telecommunications equipment maker, Mitel Corp. of Kanata, Ont.
>
> Mr. Griffiths, now an adviser at Toronto-based Fairfax Financial Holdings Ltd., has been at the helm of several near-sinking ships. Most recently, he was acting president of Peerless Carpet Corp. of Montreal, before stepping down in March when a permanent replacement was found.
>
> The 66-year-old strategist does not particularly like the term turnaround. He sees his role as a catalyst for

positive change—"offering leadership and refocusing the company on the things it does well, where it makes money or can make money."

Of all his jobs, Mr. Griffiths says Mitel's second work-out, much of it through the recession in the early nineties, was the most rewarding.

"This is a company that had been shopped around the world [by 51-per-cent owner BT PLC] and nobody seemed to want it," says Mitel's former chairman. "We had to keep the revenue alive while our competitors were waiting to eat us alive. We considerably downsized and streamlined the organization, but the one thing we didn't cut was R&D because if we did we would have killed the company."

Professor [Donald] Thain [of the Richard Ivey School of Business] says turnaround artists are typically savvy dealmakers, attuned to internal politics and able to make tough decisions quickly. The best of them know how to cut overhead, shed redundant workers, and sell off unprofitable pieces.

But, he says the real skill comes in when they start to rebuild. Sometimes the surgeon cuts too much, and the patient will bleed to death. The great people know how to do the build job.

Undertaking these speaking engagements (for, among others, the Ontario Securities Commission and the Ontario Teachers' Pension Plan board) caused me to reflect more deliberately on how I did what I did throughout my career in a way that I had not when I was in the thick of things.

My varied career seems to intrigue people, as many of the companies where I became CEO were on the brink of receivership or, where not immediately in financial peril, drifting without a strategy. The subject of "fixing up troubled companies" engenders an element of mystery as to how one goes about it. For me, it became what I did (and still do) for a living, and while it is not easy to deal with such difficult situations, through repetition I have become comfortable in the role.

If there is an overriding theme to this book, it is one of exercising leadership and taking action to transform a negative or complex situation through proactive management and the development, implementation, and subsequent monitoring of a strategy.

I find that the challenge of these companies energizes me. This is followed by a quick sense of accomplishment and fulfillment when one sees a company back on its feet, with a solid direction and reinvigorated employees. While this is often accompanied by significant financial reward, this is not the primary attraction.

So, how do you turn a company around?

By the time you arrive at a company on the brink of financial ruin, the picture usually contains some or all of the following elements: It is usually very late (too late) to fire the CEO; the damage has been done and the wrong people are at the helm. Cash is gone or running out. The competition is having a field day—why buy the company's product when no one will be around to service it? Cash resources are needed for staying power and credibility; they are also needed for cost reduction and severance payments. Debt requires restructuring at a time when lenders are skittish. Good people are leaving, demoralized by the situation around them.

Your first priority is to assemble a new team. More often than not, there will be three or four dedicated, decisive people who will come forward. It is very unlikely that the incumbent CEO and some members of the senior management can be salvaged. In re-staffing, you pay off the employment contracts of those who are leaving and treat them fairly and with dignity. They would have been the problem, or at least part of the past, which has brought the company to where it is and the culture must change radically. There are always good people in the ranks waiting and hoping for change. They understand how dire the situation is and they want action. It is critical to assess quickly those who are willing to work and fight for change. Equally important is to get rid of the fence-sitters promptly.

The second priority is to determine which parts of the business are making or losing money. Be prepared: it is inevitable that when you see the internal figures, the company is in worse shape than seen from the outside. Unfortunately, this is true even if you have been sitting on the board as a director. You have been hearing what management wants you to know . . . or they do not know enough to alert you to underlying problems.

Over time I have developed a methodology—a template—that works for me. This is what I used in my second term as CEO of Mitel and comprises a one-page outline that serves as a *strategic dashboard for profitability*. It consists of a simple matrix of financial facts and ratios showing, first by major product lines and then geographically: Order Backlog, Revenues, Gross Margin, Percentage Gross Margin, Earnings Before Interest and Taxes (EBIT), Net Income, Capital Employed, Return On Capital Employed, Capital Expenditure, Headcount, Revenue/Employee, and EBIT/Employee.

I have applied this matrix many times over the years and it has never let me down. It quickly brings to the surface the profitable entities (divisions or units) in a company and highlights the losers. It measures the past three to five years for each entity, and then projects the businesses three to five years into the future. It provides a concise income statement to the pre-tax profit level for each business, as well as return on capital invested and capex required going forward with the resulting pre-tax return on capital. This is usually the eye-opener. Finally it shows the number of employees in each business and the resulting productivity per employee. This matrix illustrates a snapshot of the businesses in relation to one another and in total. If nothing else, it serves as a "back-of-the-envelope" dynamics of the enterprise from which to determine where to reshape the company.

Predictably, most management of troubled companies is reluctant to provide this information. They are *process oriented* versus *results oriented*, and usually resistant to examining return on capital, which is a real indicator of their performance, especially when compared to industry benchmarks. In the majority of cases, they simply do not see the need for it—it's one more exercise (pain in the ass) they don't wish to bother with. However—and this is the tragedy—all companies have the basic data to construct the template readily available in existing accounts. Over the last few years, I have been approached by five or six companies to serve as either a director or an adviser. In each case I have proposed the framework to gather this information and have not received a response. Consequently, I have declined to get involved.

Assuming one can obtain the relevant data, a plan of action must be developed. In many cases management will not act fast enough or go deep enough. My rule of thumb is to do what has to be done to regain profitability *once*. To try to accomplish this incrementally leads to disaster. It means that layoffs, downsizing, and the selling off of assets will be revisited two or three times, creating uncertainty and continual demoralization.

The company may have to sell a good division or brand to survive. Generally management doesn't want to make such a drastic move, but not doing so in a timely manner may reduce options and jeopardize the ability to survive. In recent years, many companies have been criticized for not doing this when they had the opportunity: General Motors, Nortel, and CanWest Communications, among others.

Developing the matrix will produce a strategy—a clear focus for the future. The task then becomes *setting priorities*:

What has to be done?
Who will do it?
Set milestones. Set deadlines.
Make people accountable.
Make decisions! A poor decision is usually better than no
    decision or indecision.
Encourage people to "think outside of the box."
Monitor rigorously.
Instill a sense of urgency.
Emphasize SURVIVAL.

Strategy is the *easy* part—worth maybe as little as 5 per cent of the recovery process. Implementation and execution with discipline are the hard tasks.

The turnaround plan must establish financial targets. What profit can (should) this company make in its business? How do we get there? What should the profile of the company look like when the plan is completed? One of the keys in assessing this is to benchmark against the competition. *Work back from the targeted result.* Ensure that the plan meets the required objectives of Return on Capital Employed and Return on Equity to make the company attractive to investors.

The third priority—once the plan is in place and management has signed on—is to communicate the plan throughout the organization. It never fails—employees have known there's a problem and are *looking for leadership.* If the company is in serious difficulty, adversity can, ironically, be a morale enhancer. The psychology of "a band of brothers" rescuing a ship in hard times will assist in lifting morale.

People have to change. Be honest—up front. Give everyone the choice—we can save 80 percent of the jobs and save the company or we can end up with nothing. Provide updates—every quarter—hold town meetings and, for distant locations, video conferences. Explain where we've been—where we're going. Show the way—the vision. If they see fairness and action, people will adapt—if they see the framework for progress. Good people will come forward.

It is critical that the leader shows confidence and commitment to the plan's objectives. He or she has to create a sense of urgency, but be unflappable in all situations. And finally, it is essential to keep a sense of humour.

Common to underperforming companies is a lack of discipline combined with weak leadership. A good, simple example is when I attended as CEO my first meeting of the Mitel semiconductor division in 1985. The meeting was scheduled to start at 7:00 a.m. By 7:15 managers were still strolling in. The general manager drifted in about 7:20. I then announced,

"Next time we call a meeting at 7:00 a.m. everyone must be on time or they will be excluded from joining." Discipline and leadership result in good execution.

* * *

I'm also often asked how regulators can spot a company going bad in time to save shareholders. I would say that they should watch for:

- Companies that consistently hype their reports or companies that attract contentious PR.
- Companies where shareholder relationships are not clear—particularly where family or ownership squabbles appear—and companies that attract shareholder activists.
- Situations where the CEO appears to have an overly inflated ego.
- Companies that are marginally financed or highly leveraged, or that exhibit volatile performance.
- Companies that tend to be less than observant of the regulatory requirements.

Shareholder activists have become common. This is a good thing where it is responsible and warranted but is dysfunctional where the activists or raiders are attempting to force short-term actions to the detriment of long-term shareholders, for example, through greenmail (a premium paid to a raider to get them to terminate a takeover attempt).

Many volumes are being written about corporate governance. Generally this is healthy and most companies take governance seriously. Professionals (accountants and lawyers) are striving to raise the quality of governance and the body of knowledge is growing and improving. Unfortunately, this subject also attracts many "do-gooders," usually self-proclaimed governance practitioners, academics, and other consultants who have never actually been involved in operating a business. Regulators should avoid overkill—crooks and cheaters will always exist. Instead, regulators should err on the side of practical versus costly overzealousness that will stifle enterprise. Penalties for fraud and criminality exist and are just and fitting for the guilty.

Despite this concentration on the importance of governance, in my experience, the *single* largest problem is getting boards to face CEOs who are underperforming. This is particularly difficult because humans avoid confrontation; we are reluctant to act and step out with the unknown—opting to "stay with the devil we know"—and we are trapped by personal relationships and friendships. The most disciplined and fair method to address this issue is for the board to maintain consistent performance appraisals of the CEO.

Since 2002, regulatory requirements such as Sarbanes-Oxley have created new concerns for managers. Generally this type of regulatory intervention has been perceived as overkill and disproportionately costly for businesses. There is little evidence that it has prevented fraud or reduced any aspects of corporate ethical abuse. The resulting compliance creates high risk in certifying financial statements and creates delicate or sensitive disclosure issues beyond common sense.

Some general observations I would make are that regulators should be careful not to put directors into financial jeopardy. The directors are not there to manage; rather, they advise, coach, and supervise. The concept of joint and several liability for directors should be revisited, since it lumps together the competent with the incompetent. With respect to conflict, I would suggest that it is generally bad practice for a company's legal adviser or investment banker to act as a director. That way the legal counsel is always available to the board for advice; to be on the board as well as counsel can conflict, where the individual has to decide whether he or she is acting as a director or as an independent legal adviser.

The strategy above summarizes the principles and methodologies that work for me: they are simple, clear, and effective.

In concluding, I am reminded of an article by psychologist Perry W. Buffington, Ph.D., sent to me by a lifelong Bahamian friend Basil Kelly. Buffington describes a personality style he calls "Type C—for chaos changers, or expert problem solvers." For these individuals:

> Neither liking chaos, nor living for it, is the real issue. It's taming the chaotic situation, solving the problem, accepting the accolades, and then successfully moving on to another threatening situation that guarantees the real thrill. These people are expert problem solvers who have found a niche in rapidly changing times . . . what most people don't realize is that the personality style is not magical. Type C abilities, like any others, can be learned . . . These individuals are fearless in their pursuit of new ideas and have confidence in their work. They thrive on uncertainty and enjoy the realm of the unknown.[1]

Appendix: Board Membership

(* denotes non-public company)

C = Chair/Vice Chair
LD = Lead Dirctor
P = President/Interim/Acting

A.M.J. Campbell Van Lines*
AbitibiBowater Inc.
Absolute return Fund*
Alliance Atlantis Communications (LD)
All-Way Transportation* (C)
Benz Gold (Studer Mines; Golconda Resources)
Binscarth PVC Ventures
Biochem Medical Laboratories
Blue Ant Media Inc.* (C)

Bowater Incorporated
Brazilian Resources (C)
Bronco Oil & Gas
Burgundy Asset Management* (C)
Burgundy International* (C)
Bushnell Communications
Cablecasting (C)
Calian Technologies (LD)
Campeau Corporation
Canadian Cablesystems (C) (P)
Canadian Tire Corporation
Carpita Corporation
Cassidy*
Commonwealth Insurance Company*
Confederation Life Insurance
Confederation Trust
Connor Clark*
Consumers Packaging Inc. (Consumers Glass)
Contronics
Coremark
Counsel Corporation
Crum & Forster Holdings Corp.
Cunningham Lindsey (Lindsey Morden)
Develcon Electronics (C)
Dynex Power
Edmonton Oilers*
Fairbridge Inc.*
Fairfax Financial Holdings Limited (LD)
Fairfax Realty Inc.*
Federated Insurance Company of Canada*
Financial Collection Agencies

G&W Freight* (C)

Gateway Casino Income Fund

Gedex Inc.*

General American Technologies

Global Election Systems

Gruen Watch

Gruen Watch Canada* (C)

Harding Carpets (C) (P)

Helix Investments*

Home Oil Company Limited

Hub International

Jaguar Mining

Jonlab Investments* (P)

Jutras Die Casting* (C)

Leitch Technologies (C)

Lombard Insurance Company*

Markel Insurance Company of Canada*

Meridian Technologies (C)

Midland Walwyn

Midnorthern Appliance Industries*

Midnorthern Leasing*

Mitel Corporation (C) (P)

Northbridge Financial Corporation

Novadaq Technologies (C)

Odyssey Re Holdings Corp.

Paribas Participation

Peerless Carpet Corporation (C) (P)

Peoples' Jewelers*

Perkins Paper Products*

PreMD Inc. (IMI)

QLT Inc. (Quadra Logic)

Quartet Services
Rous & Mann Brigdens
Russel Metals (C)
Shaw Communications (Shaw Cable)
ShawCor (Shaw Industries)
Slater Steel Inc. (C) (P)
Specialty Food Income Trust
Teklogix International Inc.
The Brick Group Income Fund
The Ondaatje Corporation (P)
Trillium Telephone Systems
Trojan Technologies
Vector Inc.
Ventra Auto Parts (P)
Vitran Corporation (C)
Whistler Brewing*
Zenith National Insurance

October 2011

Endnotes

Chapter 1

1   Adrian Havill, *The Last Mogul*, (New York: St. Martin's Press, 1992).
2   Ibid., p. 70.

Chapter 3

1   In 1993, Jack Geller became vice-chair of the Ontario Securities Commission.

Chapter 4

1   In 1969, I stuck my nose into politics. In consultations on tax reform, the newly-elected Trudeau regime, under Finance Minister Edgar Benson, invited presentations from the private sector to respond to the White Paper on Tax Reform. This was a radical document with frightening punitive aspects relative to U.S. and European tax practices. For example, one recommendation was to tax, on an annual basis, unrealized capital gains. I joined a volunteer group in Toronto, comprised mostly people in finance and investments, to put together constructive alternatives to some of the more radical

proposals. We hired, at our expense, competent financial advisers to assist in framing recommendations to make Canada competitive in taxation, with particular emphasis directed to our giant neighbour to the south. As someone working in industry, I was chosen, together with other participants in the investment business, to present our paper to Benson, Minister without Portfolio Barney Danson, and Finance Department officials, including Deputy Minister Robert Bryce.

This was a most disillusioning event for me and my colleagues. The arrogance and cynicism displayed by these officials was despicable. They were on a course that we had no hope of modifying. For example, we proposed income tax rates and stock options for managers of Canadian businesses, which would be competitive with U.S. and UK practices. At one point Bryce said to me, "Why don't I get stock options? Why doesn't the head of the engineering department at Carleton University get stock options?" I had to bite my tongue, wanting to suggest that if he and the dean wanted stock options, they should seek employment in the private sector.

2   Subsequently, Placer Dome was taken over by Barrick and Rob Franklin became lead director of Barrick.

Chapter 5

1   Bryan Burrough, *Barbarians at the Gate*, (New York: Harper & Row, 1990).

2   The original Laura Secord was Canada's first effective undercover agent, operating during the War of 1812.

3   For more commentary on the Sukunka project and other Brascan investments during this period, see Patricia Best and Ann Shortell, *The Brass Ring*, (Toronto: Random House, 1988), p. 38, where they say: "Then Moore launched a diversification plan for Brascan in Brazil and Canada that laid the groundwork for a holding company that, by and large, exists today. Often, however, his grand plan failed magnificently. In 1970, Moore sank $40 million into Elf Oil and Gas, and soon after he had to write off $10 million of it. In 1972 he spent almost $10 million on an investment in

the Sukunka coal fields in British Columbia, and subsequently wrote the whole thing off. Explorations in the Philippines, United States, and Canada failed to result in any commercial production. Meanwhile, Brascan's rate of return in Canada and Brazil steadily plummeted."

4   Peter C. Newman, *The Canadian Establishment: Volume Two: The Acquisitors*, (Toronto: McClelland & Stewart, 1981), p. 293.

5   *The Brass Ring*, p. 39.

Chapter 6

1   Terry Pocock was a local London, Ontario, IT services expert.

2   For Rogers's account of this incident, see his book *Relentless: True Story of the Man Behind Rogers Communications*, (Toronto: HarperCollins, 2008), p. 96: "Bassett suddenly saw value in my operation. First, he called in his lawyers and told them he had to find a way to get this cable thing from me and into Baton Broadcasting, where I was still on the board of directors and a minority owner. It would be too harsh to say he wanted to steal my fledgling cable company, but he sure wanted to get his hands on it any way he could. . . . Bassett then called and told me he wanted me to hand over at no cost these cable television licenses to Baton, as per the agreement. I told him to 'go fly a kite.'

"I offered him half the cable company if Baton put in two-thirds of the money . . .

"'Done,' he said."

This was August 1967. Clearly this was not an entirely happy partnership, foreshadowing further acrimony in the Rogers/Bassett/Goodman relationship. On pp. 102–103, Rogers continues: "On July 10, 1969 . . . our company changed completely when the CRTC ruled it would renew Rogers Cable licenses 'only if Baton sold its stake and get out of the cable TV business.'

"In 1970, six months after the CRTC decision, Bassett gave me my first 'three month deadline' to come up with the cash, to pay for the cable company.

"This happened over and over throughout 1970 and into 1971."

And on p. 128: "We were now several years past that fateful CRTC decision *that forced the Eatons and Bassetts out of Rogers Cable.*" (Italics are mine.)

3   In June 2009, I had lunch with Arnie Cader and Lori Waisberg, two of Eddie Goodman's junior law partners at the time. I asked why Eddie had been so incensed when Rogers purchased that block of Cablesystems stock in 1974. Without hesitation, both said, "Because Rogers used the CRTC decision to do an end run around Bassett." According to Waisberg, Jonlab made a series of block purchases on the floor of the TSE orchestrated by Wisener & Partners, taking Jonlab to 26 per cent.

4   In 1984, Golden was a director of Mitel when I joined the board and became my chair in 1986.

5   *The Brass Ring*, p. 39.

6   Caroline Van Hasselt, *High Wire Act: Ted Rogers and the Empire that Debt Built,* (Toronto: John Wiley & Sons, 2008), p. 161.

7   *Forbes*, August 16, 1993, p. 92.

8   Korthals and I were fraternity brothers in Zeta Psi and had known each other since 1951.

9   *High Wire Act*, p. 116.

Chapter 7

1   In September 1989, Robert Wright became chair of the Ontario Securities Commission.

2   *High Wire Act*, p. 118.

3   For a detailed account of the Noranda takeover, see Peter Newman, *The Acquisitors*, pp. 317–318. For Zimmerman's version of these events, see his book *Who's In Charge Here, Anyway?* (Toronto: Stoddart Publishing, 1997).

4   Later on I was very touched by a refreshing silver lining. After Ted Rogers took control of Cablesystems, John Tory Sr. and Gordon Gray of Royal LePage, both directors of Rogers, recommended me to the board of Home Oil. Apparently they admired and respected the fact that I held together the management and board of Cablesystems during the stressful takeover battle with Rogers.

5   In his book *Relentless*, Rogers devotes a page and a half to this caper. See pp. 32–33.
6   Later Foster set up an investment boutique, Capital Canada, which he still manages today.
7   *High Wire Act*, p. 124.
8   *High Wire Act*, p. 125.
9   *High Wire Act*, p. 95. Phil Lind was born August 20, 1943, into a well-to-do family. Lind admired Rogers for years and maintained contact with him during college years. He joined Rogers in 1969 and became intimately involved in Rogers's radio and cable TV programming—evolving into Rogers's regulatory and overall government relations executive. I would describe Lind as Rogers's *consigliere*.
10 *High Wire Act*, p. 122.
11 *The Acquisitors*, p. 303.
12 Ibid., p. 305.

Chapter 8

1   Sheikh Yamani, at the time, was an international figure as Saudi Arabia's oil minister from 1962 to 1986 and the spokesman for OPEC.

Chapter 9

1   Ralph Barford is a Harvard Business School graduate who built a company called General Steel Wares (GSW), later GSW Limited, into a very successful enterprise.
2   In December 2001, Eric divested Sprott Securities to the employees and moved on to form Sprott Asset Management.

Chapter 10

1   Gordon Sharwood passed away in April 2010.
2   For a detailed account of this transaction, see William Lowther, *Arms and the Man: Dr. Gerald Bull, Iraq and the Supergun* (Toronto: Doubleday, 1991).
3   Ibid., p. 128.
4   Cablecasting was incorporated in May 1969. On April 16, 1973, Cablecasting Limited's Class A shares were listed on the Montreal

Stock Exchange and, at the time, the company was the fourth-largest listed in the cable industry in Canada, ranking behind Premier Cablevision, Canadian Cablesystems, and Maclean Hunter Cable TV.

Chapter 11

1 Mitel's product line of small switches comprised the SX-100 (capable of handling 80 extension lines), the SX-20 (48 extension lines), and the SX-10 (32 extension lines). The largest switch to date was the SX-200 Superswitch (capable of handling 150 extension lines), which had been introduced in 1978. Additionally, Mitel was in small-business telephones, "Key Systems," through a 71-per-cent–owned subsidiary, Trillium Telephone.

2 Mike Cowpland was also hiring Mitel staff at Corel, but after severing his ties at Mitel. The most important of these was the brilliant Patrick Beirne, who became Corel's chief design engineer.

3 Peter Berrie was sent to Mitel by BT as an observer from the time of the announcement of BT's purchase of Mitel until MMC approval was received in March 1986. I then hired Peter as vice-president, international. While at times acerbic, Peter was a good diplomat—very even-handed. He was a tremendous help to me both because of his knowledge of the industry and his ability to guide me through the thorny bureaucracy of BT.

4 Webster had bought 10 percent of Mitel for $100,000 through Helix Investments in 1976. See Ross Laver, *Random Excess*, (Toronto: Viking, 1998), p. 52.

Chapter 13

1 In November 1993, Waitzer became chair of the Ontario Securities Commission, replacing Robert Wright.

2 Michael Babad and Catherine Mulroney, *Campeau: The Building of an Empire,* (Toronto: Doubleday, 1989), p. 217.

3 Ibid., p. 218.

4 Ibid., p. 222.

5 Ibid., fly leaf.

6 Ibid., p. 278.

Chapter 14

1 *Frank*, February 7, 1991, p. 15.

2 Wang later went into Chapter 11 and Intecom was sold to the French company Matra.

3 People born in the Year of the Horse have an exuberance and a love of life that is probably without parallel; they hate to be tied to one place and are at their very best when allowed to follow their own, somewhat erratic, course. The Horse can solve most mental puzzles in a flash and does not find it at all difficult to perform several totally different tasks at the same time. Human horses are resourceful, willing, funny, nervy, and kind. Change and variety are especially important in the lives of these individuals, who probably have a lower boredom threshold than just about any other animal in the Chinese Zoo. Conformity is not something that the average Horse person is particularly interested in and there is always a radical and different streak. (from Tung Jen, *Tung Jen's Chinese Astrology*, Slough, England: Foulsham, 1994)

4 David Wilson became chair of the Ontario Securities Commission in 2005.

Chapter 15

1 In 2009, Jerre Stead was one of six independent directors recognized by the Outstanding Directors Exchange (ODX) and their peers as leaders who have gone above and beyond the call of duty, demonstrating judgment, courage, and integrity while acting in the interests of shareholders.

2 I finished editing this section the weekend of February 17, 2011. On February 28, I received an e-mail from Kirk Mandy advising me that Simon had passed away on February 24, 2011.

Chapter 16

1 Coincidentally, Egon Zehnder was a classmate of mine at Harvard Business School.

2 In London, I stayed overnight at the No. 11 London Cadogan Gardens hotel, where the next day I met Chris Ondaatje and his wife Valda

for breakfast in a private room. To my surprise, Valda stood up for me in a debate with Chris about spending money immediately to solve an IT problem. When Chris left the room to pay the bill, I indicated to Valda my concerns about working with Chris. She immediately responded that it would be okay, saying, "He completely trusts you."

3   TOC's outside legal counsel.

Chapter 17

1   For reasons unknown to me, Burns underwent a transformation by about 1991, and suddenly became a proponent of "demutualization." However, by then, other events overtook the agenda at Confed.

Chapter 18

1   Perry W. Buffington, "No Problem!", *Sky Magazine*, June, 1989, pp. 33–38.

Index

Italicized numerals indicate endnotes.

Federated Insurance Company of Canada, 316

Feldman, Zane, 71, 72

Fell, Tony, 211

Ferguson, Sheila, 262, 264, 265, 267

Fiat S.p.A, 119

Finance, Dept. of, 298, 300

Financial Collection Agencies (FCA), 192–94, 316

Financial Post, 70, 114, 257–58

Financial Trustco (FT), 188

Fink, Paul, 185, 186, 188

Finlayson, Janet, 229

First Chicago, 199–201

First City Capital Markets, 197, 198, 199–200, 203

First Toronto Mining Corporation, 199–200

First World War, 1, 7

Fisch, Gerald G., 20, 21–22

Flatt, Bruce, 108

Food and Agriculture Organization (FAO), 4

Forbes & Walker Limited (F&W), 260–70, 278

Forbes Ceylon Limited, 261

Forestry Service (Burma), 2

Fortune Magazine, 17, 216

Foster, Bob, 98, 204, *323*

Foster, Michael, 201, 202

Foyston, Don, 116

Frank magazine, 226

Frankin, Rob, 45–46

Franklin National Bank, 84

Franklin, Cecil, 40–44, 45

Franklin, Rob, *320*

Fujitsu, 226

G

G&T Investments Inc., 46

G&W Freightways, 50–51, 60, 317

Gaasanbeek, Matthew, 64

Gallotti, Antonio, 49

Gambino family, 84

Gandalf Technologies, 187

Garber, Bram, 129, 135

Garfinckel's (store), 206

Garrett, Geoffrey, 9, 34

Gaston, Don, 78, 79, 81, 84

Gateway Casino Income Fund, 317

Gedex Inc., 317

Geller, Jack, 28, 32

General American Technologies, 317

General Electric Company (GEC), 160, 254

General Impact Extrusions (GIE), 35, 37–40, 41

General Steel Wares (GSW), 52, *323*

Gilchrist, Peter, 135

Gillespie, David, 196

Glass Containers Ltd. (GCL), 34

Glass Containers Manufacturers Institute, 29

Glenshaw. *See* G&G Investments

Global Election Systems, 317

Globe and Mail, 41, 77, 114, 125–26, 197, 224–25, 253, 277–78, 297, 300–1, 305–6

Gnat, Albert, 40, 43, 63, 64, 72, 93, 103, 104, 109, 110, 111, 112–13, 115, 117–18, 131, 141–43, 146–47, 149, 150, 153, 154, 157, 158, 174, 184, 193, 196, 198, 218, 229, 231, 234

Golan Heights, 144

Golden, David, 75, 162, 174, 180, 218–19, *322*

Gooch, Tony, 102, 144–45, 149

Goodman, Eddie, 57–58, 63, 64, 69–70, 78, *322*

Goodman, McIntosh, 63–64

Gordon Capital, 87

Gordon Securities, 88, 184

Gowling Henderson (firm), 73

Graf Spee (ship), 3

Graham, Benjamin, 194

Graham, David, 58, 99, 145–49

Graham, John, 87

Granite Club (Toronto), 118

Grant, Peter, 123

Gray, Gordon, *322*

Great Depression, 11

Great West Saddlery, 137–38